The Zen Teachings of Jesus

The Zen
Teachings
of Jesus

Kenneth S. Leong

CROSSROAD • NEW YORK

1995

The Crossroad Publishing Company
370 Lexington Avenue, New York, NY 10017

Copyright © 1995 by Kenneth S. Leong

Printed in the United States of America

Library of Congress Cataloging-in-Publication Data

Leong, Kenneth S.
  The Zen teachings of Jesus / Kenneth S. Leong.
    p. cm.
  ISBN: 0-8245-1481-5 (pbk.)
  1. Jesus Christ—Teachings. 2. Jesus Christ—Person and offices.
3. Jesus Christ—Buddhist interpretations. 4. Christianity and
other religions—Zen Buddhism. 5. Zen Buddhism—Relations—
Christianity. I. Title.
BS2415.L45 1995
232.9'54—dc20   95-9839
                                                 CIP

Contents

Finding Zen in our own backyard • Zen is transcultural and transreligious • The lost dimensions of Jesus' spirituality – joy, humor, and poetry • The pitfalls of being "serious" • Seriousness as a sign of the ego • Humor as a way to truth • Jesus as poet • The sober Jesus versus the smiling Buddha • The "irreverent" tradition of Zen • The kingdom is NOW! • The wonder of ordinary magic • True spirituality is art • The curse of Bible inerrancy • Love versus moralism • The sensuous anointing • Initiating the beginner's mind

Can Zen be defined? • "Holy outrageousness" • Zen does not mean sitting meditation • The eccentricities of Zen • Zen as mental culture • A mini-history of Zen • Zen as the bridge between the spiritual and the mundane • Zen and the Chinese mind • Zen as a spirituality without the trappings of religion • Zen as the poetization of life • Zen and Taoism • Hui Neng, the sixth patriarch • Zen has no formula • The notion of discipline in Zen • Zen can only be shown • The Sermon of the Flower versus the Sermon on the Mount • Presence as the basis of spirituality • Zen, art, and ordinary magic • Recovering the zest for life • Zen and the "Aha!" experience • *Wu-wei* is not doing nothing • The playful way to excellence • The use of uselessness • Zen and the fine arts

Zen, motherhood, and apple pie • The *yin* and the *yang:* creative
tension • The artful gentleness of Butcher Pao • Spiritual judo:
understanding the power of weakness • True freedom as a
reflection of gentleness • The "magic of thinking small" •
Learning simplicity from the Cosmo-girl • Paradoxity as the
heart of Zen • The Zen world of poetic craziness • Zen lessons
from the flops of artificial intelligence • The value of fuzziness •
Left-brain versus right-brain thinking • Zen experience can't be
verbalized • Zen and soul • Zen as inward quest

The mystery of time • Clock time versus psychological time •
What is it like to be an angel? • The Tao cannot be sought •
Eternity as the disappearance of time • The kingdom and peak
experiences • "The kingdom of God is not coming with signs
to be observed" • Entry into the thoughtless zone • The pitfalls
of hope • What is happiness?

Fuzziness as opportunity • Enlightenment as creative visualization
• Reverse bodhisattvas • Real alchemy • Being "born anew"
• "Nirvana is not the result of anything" • The koan of the
Son of Man • Lessons from the Fiery Serpent • The mystery of
Sisyphus's smile • Hell as the path to heaven • The First Noble
Truth revisited • Seeing is the only truth • "This is it!" • The
paradoxes of life

The topsy-turvy world of Zen • Who is Jesus? • The Son of
God as archetype • The death koan of Jesus • The Tale of the
Unfortunate Traveler • Choicelessness as freedom • The Stranger
revisited • Death as healer • The culture of *wabi-sabi* • The
beauty of inverse laws • Living dangerously • The poignant
bitter-sweetness of life • Finding nirvana in samsara

Acknowledgments

I would like to express my gratitude to all my teachers, particularly J. Krishnamurti, who has greatly inspired me in his unique maverick way. I wish also to express special thanks to William Burrows for his kind advice and referral, which made the publication of this work possible, to Jack Williams for being such an invaluable help throughout the writing and many revisions of this book, to Lee Paton for painstakingly going through the manuscript and offering many thoughtful and superb comments, and to David Cheung and Simon Tang for their continuous encouragement and support.

Other individuals who have contributed to this work in one way or another are Thubten Chodron, Eric Kampmann, Milton Kwok, Lou Mattutini, Heng-yueh Li, and all my friends, colleagues, and students at Wainwright House, New York Open Center, and the World Young Men's Buddhist Association. I also wish to thank the many Christian friends with whom I am in constant dialogue. Their curiosity, intelligent questions, and willingness to share their experiences have enormously enriched this book.

I am grateful to everyone at Crossroad for their enthusiasm and confidence in this work and for their continual support.

Last, but not least, I wish to express special thanks to my wife, Vivian. Her generosity, understanding, and support have been instrumental for the successful completion of this book and are much appreciated.

Reading the Gospels, Zen Style

In the world you have tribulation; but be of good cheer.
                                    –JOHN 16:33

I left Jesus to search for the Tao when I was sixteen. Now I am forty, and I realize that I could have found the Tao in Jesus.

This book is partially a reflection of my journey. It may look like a round trip, but it is not. Without the trip, I do not think that I could have come to any real understanding of Jesus. The point that I would like to make here is that Zen is not a foreign import. Zen is *everyday spirituality.* And we have always had it in our own backyard! It is just that most of us haven't noticed what is right in front of our eyes. Zen is a transcultural and transreligious phenomenon. No matter where you are, you can always find it. For Zen is in you.

Jesus is perhaps the most famous figure in human history. The Christian Bible is a perennial bestseller, and Christianity is still the most popular religion in the Western world. But even two thousand years after his death, Jesus of Nazareth remains as enigmatic as ever.

Who is Jesus? What does he really stand for? What did he teach? There is still very little consensus among us on these issues. Paradoxically, the most famous person in history is also the most elusive one.

This is not a book on the search for the historical Jesus. Neither is it a scholarly book on Christianity or the traditional doctrines and notions of Jesus. Rather, it is a book on the teachings of Jesus in the Gospels from a fresh perspective to recover the lost dimensions of his spirituality — joy, humor, and poetry. It is important for us to distinguish between what is said about Jesus and what Jesus has said.

11

To do so is to discover a brave new world full of color and vitality. It is the beginning of an eye-opening adventure.

We often misinterpret Jesus because we tend to take him too "seriously," or solemnly. Ironically, to take Jesus "seriously" is not to take him seriously. True spirituality begins with relaxation. In reading scriptures, "seriousness" is irreverence!

In order to understand Jesus' teachings, we must have a sense of humor. Indeed, humor is a key to Zen. Legend has it that the Zen was born in the midst of Mahakashyapa's smile. Mahakashyapa was one of Buddha's senior disciples. More will be said about his smile when we discuss the Sermon of the Flower in chapter 1.

Lest we think that the Judeo-Christian tradition is marked by a tight upper lip, it may help to remember that there is always a humorous, fun-loving side to God. For he made Moses, a man who was "slow of speech and tongue," the most important prophet of the Jews. It was also God who made Sarah bear a child in her old age. This is the reason why the child is named Isaac, which means "the Laughing One." And the apostle Paul gave us this portrayal of a prank-playing God:

> God chooses what is foolish in the world to shame the wise, God chooses what is weak in the world to shame the strong, God chooses what is low and despised in the world, even things that are not, to bring to nothing things that are. (1 Cor. 1:27–28)

Given the fact that God is fun-loving, it should not surprise us that seriousness is a major obstacle for spirituality. For relaxation is a prerequisite for humor. Jesus once exclaimed that God has "hidden these things [truths, secrets about the kingdom] from the wise and understanding and revealed them to babes" (Matt. 11:25). This is a most Zen-like utterance but is overlooked by laypeople, clergy, and theologians alike. The point is that little children are more spiritual than adults because they are much more relaxed and tend to rely on intuition rather than on intellect.

What most people refer to as "seriousness" is actually a sign of the ego. Most of us are "serious" because we are too self-obsessed — obsessed by our self-importance and our own notions of what is good, what is right, what is true, etc. I am not an advocator of frivolity, but seriousness is self-defeating to the extent that it is a reflection of a certain obsession. Obsessions obstruct both our vision and our adaptability. On the other hand, relaxation and humor, to the extent that they allow us to be more mindful and effective, are *real* seriousness.

There are other types of obsessions too. The most common one for most of us is what is called "common sense," of which rationality is a part. Most people will not take something "seriously" if it is not rational. In fact, this is what "non-sense" means. But as Albert Einstein has observed, our so-called common sense often turns out to be simply prejudices acquired through years and years of social conditioning. The point of Zen is not to defy reason but to recognize the limitations of rationality.

Unlikely as it may seem, humor is a way to truth. While many people often associate humor with lightness and a cavalier attitude toward life, the philosopher Georgias Leontinus sees things much differently:

> Humor is the only test of gravity, and gravity of humor. For a subject which will not bear raillery is suspicious; and a jest which will not bear a serious examination is certainly false wit.[1]

From now on let us define "humor" as the mental ability to discover, express, or appreciate what is ludicrous, incongruous, or absurd. This suggests a certain mental sharpness or quickness. Humor is closely related to *wittyness,* which is the mental ability to see illuminating or amusing relationships. Both are key mental qualities that are important for enlightenment.

True humor requires alertness — an alertness that is a result of relaxation and not of fear. Deep spiritual truths appear to be self-contradictory or even ridiculous when expressed in words. A ready example is Jesus' famous saying that "whoever seeks to gain his life will lose it, but whoever loses his life will preserve it" (Luke 17:33). The statement flies in the face of logic. As Simone Weil put it, "Contradictions are the criterion of the real."

We have been conditioned to treat rationality as sacred. But life itself is, in a very deep sense, absurd. It will not render itself to the tyranny of reason. Even the most wise cannot help but be flabbergasted by a three-year-old who keeps asking why. If you are not convinced, try asking yourself what is the reason for living. Life is basically a mystery that is not meant to be solved by our intellect. It cannot be "known" through the brain but through the heart. This is a basic message of Zen.

There have been a lot of confusions and misconceptions about

Jesus, often because he has been taken too seriously. He is more often worshiped (or attacked) than listened to. Zen is about relaxing, listening, and having a sense of humor while doing so. When we really listen to Jesus, we will find that he seldom preached or moralized. What he excelled at was relating to us through his colorful stories and enlightening us with his poetry.

We can certainly see Jesus as Savior, Messiah, Son of God, and miracle worker. But we may be missing the whole point if we do not recognize that he was, at heart, a poet, and his sayings are the songs of his soul. In the Zen circle, it is widely known that the Tao (Truth), being paradoxical in nature, cannot be preached or otherwise verbalized; it can only be hinted at. That's why Jesus resorted to poetry and humor. Where else but in poetry do we find contradictions coexisting and yet so gracefully harmonized?

If we are to understand the spiritual truth of the Gospels, we must begin to observe their poetry and cosmic jokes. Many Christians (and Buddhists also) have a tendency to undervalue joy, fun, laughter, and jokes, much to their own detriment. During one of my Zen classes, I asked my students to close their eyes and visualize Buddha. After that, I also asked them to visualize Jesus Christ. Then I asked them what their pictures of Buddha and Christ were like. Not surprisingly, most of them described Buddha as a smiling figure and Christ as a sober figure.

Part of what I am doing in this book is presenting the joyful Jesus. Laughter, particularly laughter in what we call the "real" (translated as the "joyless") world, is a key ingredient to our spiritual health. C. S. Lewis writing in the voice of a devil, made the following observation in *The Screwtape Letters:* "Laughter of this kind [joy] does us [the devils] no good and should always be discouraged. Besides, the phenomenon is of itself disgusting and a direct insult to the realism, dignity and austerity of Hell." Similarly, R. H. Blyth, one of the precursors of Zen in the Western world, observes that "enlightenment is always accompanied by a kind of sublime laughter."

Joy is an ability of the soul. It is not a natural instinct. If it were, we should find most people joyful. Rather, joy has to be learned. In this book, we will see how Jesus taught the art of joy through the Gospels.

Laughter is the beginning of liberation. We have to learn to be less serious and loosen up. In this context, humor is a key ingredient to spiritual awakening. Self-humor is particularly helpful because it loosens up our biggest attachment — our "self." People who cannot make fun of themselves and their own "holy objects" cannot make good Zen students. For enlightenment is largely a matter of seeing the cosmic joke on ourselves and giving it a hearty laugh!

Therefore, one of the first things we need to learn about Zen is that it is not solemn. There is no "holy object" in Zen, which is the same as saying that *everything* is holy for Zen. A famous Zen joke goes like this: "When you see the Buddha walking on the road, kill him!" Zen is deliberately "irreverent" or even "blasphemous" because our "holy objects" often turn out to be sources of our greatest attachments. They are the very things that are keeping us from being really spiritual. Is it a surprise then to find Jesus often being accused of blasphemy during his days?

Most of us know that the first two of the Ten Commandments have to do with idolatry. The problem is that we idolize all the time, often without being conscious of it. In fact, the most dangerous idolatries are those committed in the name of God. A ready example is the idolization of the words of Jesus by taking them literally rather than seeing the poetry of them. Our "punishment" for doing that is that we fail to recognize their beauty, joy, and insight.

As an illustration of the importance of reading the scriptures as poetry, let us take the following verses from the Sermon on the Mount:

> Blessed are you poor, for yours is the kingdom of God.
> Blessed are you that hunger now, for you shall be satisfied.
> Blessed are you that weep now, for you shall laugh.
> Blessed are you when men hate you, and when they exclude you,
> And cast out your name as evil, on account of the Son of Man!
> Rejoice in that day, and leap for joy,
> For behold, your reward is great in heaven....

> (Luke 6:20–22)

One of the saddest errors we have committed is to make the kingdom an event in the future. The apostle Paul has told us clearly that "now is the day of salvation" (2 Cor. 6:2). The word "shall" in the poem above is there to indicate necessity and not futurity. To interpret otherwise is to take away the mystery and the beauty of the kingdom, together with its liberating effect.

The kingdom is available *now;* this is what Jesus meant when he said that the kingdom of heaven is "at hand." Once our spiritual eye is opened, we will see that there is richness in poverty, fullness in hunger, joy in sorrow, and blessedness in trouble. All opposites are unified in the kingdom. They are all present realities. Jesus said "Behold, your reward is great in heaven." The kingdom is in the here-and-now — if we care to look. We will elaborate on this in the chapter titled "The Magic Kingdom."

Not only was Jesus a poet; he was also an artist. In a sense, this is already implied because a poet is an artist with words. But Jesus was not only an artist with words: *he was also a master artist of life.* He took life as the raw material to express his soul. He brought quality into life.

Zen is intricately related with art and poetry. In fact, Zen is nothing but the art of living. The practice of Zen means bringing beauty and quality into life — one's own and that of others. In the next two chapters, we shall see that some of Zen's basic elements are presence, ordinariness, zest, ease, gentleness, freedom, simplicity, and paradoxity. They also happen to be important elements of art. We shall see in the two chapters titled "What is Zen?" that the Sermon on the Mount is essentially an "art of living" lesson.

Let me give you a preview of the Zen element of "ordinariness." There is no doubt that modern civilization has made tremendous progress in science, technology, and material well-being. One of the big issues we will address in this book is why, given this "progress," we have not found happiness. An article in the *New York Times,* titled "A Rising Cost of Modernity: Depression" (December 8, 1992), is one of the many to lament this absurd fate of people today. Why are we so unhappy despite our material affluence? Basically my answer to this question is that the modern world has lost the *art of "ordinary magic"* — the art of transforming our ordinary, mundane, and perhaps humdrum existence into a life of beauty and joy.

This is precisely why Jesus is so relevant to our world. Jesus is a great teacher of "ordinary magic." But we have completely overlooked this great gift of his because we tend to be obsessed with his miracles and other supernatural feats. It might be fun to occasionally watch a faith- healing session, but it is more important to learn "ordinary magic" because it affects our daily life. The common mind looks for external wonders, but the most important wonder is an internal one — that of fundamentally transforming our way of perceiving the world. Without the latter, "ordinary magic" will not be possible.

Jesus was a powerful guru who taught "inner alchemy" through awakening the latent artist in us. Like in other arts, the objective in this "art of life" is not so much to change the external world but to come up with creative and constructive ways to relate to it. This alone is real miracle. Marianne Williamson offers us the following insight into the nature of miracles:

> It [a miracle] is a shift not so much in an objective situation — although that often occurs — as it is a shift in how we *perceive* a situation. What changes, primarily, is how we hold an experience in our mind — how we experience the experience.[2]

Even if we have a fantastical way to change the external world, our ego has a way to change its demand from one thing to another. For desires are endless. The only real solution is "inner alchemy," which means discovering the kingdom (or Quality, or Beauty) within. The initiation rite for the practice of "ordinary magic" is a kind of spiritual awakening. It is only after the awakening that one can be "born anew" and live like a new person.

True spirituality is art — for the practice of spirituality requires imagination and great sensitivity. Piousness is not the right approach to art or to the words of Jesus, which are the poetics of his inner spiritual experience.

The idolization and literalization of scriptures obscures the meaning of Jesus to many religious people. Remember that Jesus is an artist and a poet. Art is possible only if there is a genuine communication between two souls — that of the artist and that of the audience. The problem with an attitude of worship is that it tends to take the two souls apart rather than put them together. Sociologist Ellen Rosenberg makes the following observation about Bible worship: "As the code words have become 'Bible inerrancy,' the Bible itself is less read than preached, less interpreted than brandished.... The Bible has become a talisman."[3]

The fear of individuality or the urge to conform is another obstacle for genuine communication. One simply cannot "follow the party line" to spirituality. Bible illiteracy takes on a new meaning in certain Christian groups that believe in Bible inerrancy. Members of these groups are often quick to quote from the Bible, but their understanding of the Bible is often a result of indoctrination rather than a product of personal realization. As such, it lacks genuineness. Harold Bloom comments on this phenomenon:

One of the great ironies of Protestant history is that the exaltation of scripture, which in the seventeenth century endowed Baptists and other Protestants with freedom from institutional constraints and with spiritual autonomy, has become, as the twentieth century closes, the agent for depriving Baptists and other Protestants of their Christian Liberty, their soul competency to read and interpret the Bible, each person by her own Inner Light.[4]

The sayings of Jesus are spiritual poetry. We cannot get to their essence through the filter of institutionalized religion. Rather, we have to rely on our own "soul competency" to find resonance with them. Biblical knowledge through the intellect is not enough. We have to *feel* the truth and vibrancy of Jesus' words through our own heart. It is only when we can relate with Jesus through our "heart-connection" that we can really come to know him.

This book is also an attempt to clear away the negative images that some people have about Jesus. Some people may think of him as a fire-and-brimstone preacher. But this is unthinkable for a guru who was "outrageous" enough to ask us to seek spiritual guidance from little children rather than from the "religious and proper" Pharisees. Jesus says that the kingdom belongs to the children. Most of our mis-understandings about his teachings can be dispelled if we simply take a close look at how children behave. Children are alive, radiant, ener-getic, carefree, playful, and fun-loving. They live in the moment and are able to let themselves go completely in whatever they are engaged in. They are adventurous and live life to its fullest. They also practice spirituality without even being aware of it. These are the spiritual qualities of children that Jesus has asked us to learn.

The evidences are that the religion of Jesus is a *natural* one; there is not even a trace of artificiality or struggle in his spirituality. Just as art cannot be forced, Jesus saw that the way to God is *wu-wei* (action through no-action). We will see what this means in our chapter "My Yoke is Easy."

Another misconception about Jesus is that he was a moralist. A moralist advocates a set of explicit rules for goodness. But Jesus did not champion regulations because he realized that there can be no formula for Beauty (or Quality). In fact, the mere attempt to attain Beauty through obeying certain rules is the beginning of ugliness. As Lao Tzu has observed: "It is only after the Tao (Truth) is betrayed that there are talks of goodness and righteousness." Goodness, just like art, cannot be compelled; it has to be a spontaneous expression of the soul. Some people may look at this no-rules approach to goodness as some kind of moral laxity. But Jesus was really advocating a *higher* morality — a moral (or, better, a meta-morality) called art! We will explore the issues regarding goodness and evil in the chapter titled "What Defiles a Man."

Jesus was a lover. Above all, he was a lover of life. The first thing to learn about love is that it is a mystery, i.e., something that cannot be fully understood. In this book I have devoted an entire chapter to Love, but I realize how difficult it is for anyone to speak on this profound subject. In a sense, love is absurd. It follows neither rules nor reason. We know that true love is "unconditional," meaning that it is a free gift and not an investment or a reward. But "unconditionality" is a kind of irrationality in our world. For in the rational world, we do everything for a reason.

Love and fear do not mix: fear is driven by reason, love is not. But "religious" people often cannot distinguish between the two. When Jesus was asked what the greatest commandment in the law is, he answered, that "You shall love the Lord our God with all your heart, and with all your soul, and with all your mind."

In case you have not noticed, he was being immensely funny in giving this answer. He gave this answer to humor the religious authorities who confused love and fear. He even dropped us some hints by belaboring the point "with all your heart, and with all your soul. . . . " If we relax and listen to what he was saying, we will realize that this is one of his greatest "cosmic jokes": it is an *impossible* commandment! What can be commanded is not real love. Only fear can be commanded. In other words, the greatest and the only commandment that Jesus has given to the world turns out to be a statement of self-contradiction. This "Impossible Commandment" casts in sharp contrast Jesus' notion of ethics with that of the Pharisees. It reflects his spiritual insight that we are saved through grace, not through effort.

The way to true spirituality is graceful, effortless love, not rigid moralism. True love is art. It is not a restricted form of morality because it defies effort or rules. Love is spontaneous and creative; it is an art that frees the spirit. Moralism consists of rules that bind the spirit. This is precisely why Jesus had so much conflict with the religious authorities — the Pharisees, the scribes, and the like. A strict focus on morality undermines love.

A Gospel story perfectly illustrates Jesus' notion of moralism:

Now when Jesus was at Bethany in the house of Simon the leper, a
woman came to him with an alabaster jar of very expensive ointment,
and she poured it on his head, as he sat at the table. But when the
disciples saw it, they were indignant, saying, "Why this waste? For
this ointment might have been sold for a large sum, and given to the
poor." But Jesus, aware of this, said to them, "Why do you trouble
the woman? For she has done a beautiful thing to me. For you always
have the poor with you, but you will not always have me. In pouring
this ointment on my body she has done it to prepare me for burial.
Truly, I say to you, wherever this gospel is preached in the whole
world, what she has done will be told in memory of her." (Matt.
26:6–13)

Mark and John report a similar incident. John identified the woman
as Mary of Bethany, sister of Martha and Lazarus, who had a special
affinity with Jesus. It is also interesting to note that in St. John's account of it, it was Judas Iscariot who played the role of the moralist
and demanded: "Why was this ointment not sold for three hundred
denarii and given to the poor?" (John 12:5). Research shows that
three hundred denarii represented nearly a whole year's wage for a
working man at that time — a very large sum of money. In the eyes
of a moralist, this "waste" would simply be obscene. Hence, we have
the disciples' display of "moral" anger.

There is something ludicrous here. The disciples were raising a serious charge: they accused the woman of moral irresponsibility, and
Jesus of compliance. But the only defense Jesus gave for the woman
and for himself was apparently a weak one: "for she has done a
beautiful thing to me."

To understand this incongruence, we must remember that Jesus
was, first and foremost, an artist and not a moralist. Art is more important than morality because only art can bring true goodness. True
art is just "play"; it has no goal or self-consciousness. Morality, on
the other hand, is "serious," or solemn. That seriousness invites the
ego. That is why we see so much hypocrisy among so many moralists. Jesus, the artist of life, decided that what Mary did was right.
Like a good Zen master, he was able to see right into Mary's heart.
She should not be stopped because what she was doing was a beautiful and natural expression of her soul. Therefore, Jesus accepted it
with grace.

"The poor you always have with you, but you do not always have
me" is a beautiful verse from Jesus' poetry. Its spiritual dimension

should not be overlooked. "The poor" here refers to the heart's poverty, the inability of the soul to spontaneously express itself. The "me" here refers to those rare moments in our life when we simply let our love flow out in its abundance. Because these moments are few, they should be treasured and not suppressed.

Jesus, the artist, recognized a gem when he saw one. While the disciples focused on the social and economic significance of the event, Jesus focused on the spiritual significance. Therefore, he said that "wherever this gospel is preached in the whole world, what she has done should be told in memory of her." He concluded not only that the act should not be despised, but that it actually deserved to be eternalized. For it is within our moments of love that the kingdom exists!

The moralist's mistake was to put a price tag on art and love. The fact that the ointment could have been sold for three hundred denarii was quite irrelevant. Love, being an art, is not a matter of utilitarianism. Art should be done only for art's sake. It is an expression of the Taoist *wu-wei;* it is not a tool for serving any practical purpose. True art is "useless." The useless/aimless nature of art immunizes it against the corrupting influence of the ego. It is precisely when we try to assign a utility value to love that we debase it. Mary simply seized the opportunity to offer to her love the most precious thing she could offer. She did not calculate.

The story also presents Jesus, the humorist, at his best. Let us contemplate what the story might mean in today's terms. Imagine that you wake up one morning and you find this headline in the newspaper: "Woman spends $30,000 on bottle of perfume and uses it to wash her lover's feet." What vanity! What waste! What folly! The whole scene smells of earthliness and stupidity, and yet Jesus ordered it memorialized!

But it was precisely these elements that prompted Jesus to memorialize the event. Let's face it, the woman was not out for glory. This is exactly why Jesus chose to glorify her — for he had a way to treat "the first last and the last first." To common sense, there is nothing laudable about "wasting" money this way rather than using it to feed the poor. It just reflects the ordinary folly of love. Yet the discerning eyes of Jesus found beauty in such "vulgarness." To him, the act of an ordinary woman pouring out her heart without any consideration of earning praise or moral credit was much more laudable than the piousness of a Pharisee trying to become a moral superhero.

Jesus preferred "ordinariness" to heroism because the latter is often just another form of egotism. True spirituality has little to do with moral athleticism but has everything to do with being "ordinary" and letting one's feelings show.

Last, the story also teaches the importance of living in the moment, which is one of the key messages of Zen. Jesus said, "In pouring this ointment on my body she has done it to prepare my burial." The secret of living beautifully lies in living each day as if it were your last one. Only then will you treasure each moment.

As you can see, once we have learned to listen to Jesus with our heart, we will discover that what he actually taught is much different from what others have said he taught. What is important is to put aside our traditional baggage and prejudice, and start with a *beginner's mind*. Going through the Gospels this way has proved to be a very delightful and enriching experience for me. I hope that it will be the same for you.

— One —

What Is Zen? (I):
The Art of Living

My yoke is easy and my burden light.
—JESUS

The ordinary mind is the Tao.
—NAN CHUAN

Being a Zen teacher is a difficult job. In fact, it may be the most difficult job on earth. A carpenter, a dancer, or a physician can easily explain to others what she does for a living. But Zen teachers try to teach Zen without first telling people what Zen is. One of the requirements for teaching Zen is a kind of "holy outrageousness."

Jesus, one of the greatest Zen teachers, was no exception. When the multitudes followed him up a mountain, they expected him to deliver an earthshaking sermon. But Jesus simply asked them to watch the birds and pay attention to the lilies. He let nature do most of the talking and just made a few illuminating remarks here and there. Zen teachers understand the danger of talking too much. And, of course, we should not forget that God is the most outrageous Zen teacher of all. When Moses insisted that God give his name, God declared that his name is "I Am." Erich Fromm, the famous psychologist, got it right in translating this declaration of God as "My name is Nameless."

The most basic and important things in life are often the most difficult to talk about. Zen is one of them; others are quality, beauty, and truth. They tend to evade the rational mind. Just as a biolo-

23

gist cannot find life by dissecting it, an artist cannot find beauty by analyzing it.

The answer to "What is Zen?" is equally elusive. Our intellect can no better define Zen than it can define "whiteness" or "coolness." As we shall soon see, the difficulty has to do with the fact that these are direct experiences that fall under the domain of the right brain. As such, they tend to elude the left brain. The right brain is like an artist; it functions in a nonverbal, perceptual, intuitive, spatial, and concrete mode. The left brain, on the other hand, is like a scientist; it functions in a verbal, linear, analytical, logical, and symbolic fashion. Herein lies the difficulty. A scientist may be able to measure coolness in terms of the temperature registered on a thermometer; but no matter how accurate that measurement is, it still cannot capture the delight of a summer breeze.

The term "Zen" is the Japanese version of the Chinese word *Ch'an,* which in turn is derived from the Sanskrit word *dhyana.* Originally, *dhyana* means meditation. However, as we shall see, it would be a big mistake to define Zen in terms of meditation. As Zen scholar D. T. Suzuki has pointed out, Zen "is more than meditation and Dhyana in its ordinary sense."

Although the emergence of a Zen culture is relatively new in the United States, the term "Zen" is quickly catching on as a household word. Nevertheless, very few people really understand what it is. Some people think of it as a religion; others think of it as a philosophy. But neither characterization is correct. Zen does not fit well with the common notions of religion, for it has no object of worship and is short on rituals, formalities, and doctrines. Similarly, Zen does not fit well with the ordinary definition of philosophy, for it has a basic distrust of the intellect and language as a means for communicating truth.

Instead of calling Zen a religion or a philosophy, it is better to look at it as a *mental culture* — a culture that reflects a sensitivity to reality and an artistic approach to life. Quite a few people have remarked to me how elegant and tasteful the Zen arts and crafts are. This connection between Zen and beauty is not accidental. For what underlies this elegance is a keen attention to details, reflecting a sense of care and respect for the task at hand.

Obviously, no art is possible without care. In this context, we can regard Zen as a culture of *care* that makes art and quality possible. The importance of this culture goes far beyond the rarefied realms of spirituality and fine arts. It also has tremendous practical value. I am convinced that the Zen state of mind accounts for a big part of the Japanese success in the consumer goods market. For Zen implies a commitment to excellence, which is a key ingredient to quality work.

Although the Zen state of mind is a latent part of every human being, it is helpful to have a brief introduction to its development in Asia. For it is where Zen has blossomed to the fullest and become a cultural movement with its influence permeating all the social strata, all the way from the imperial courts to the ordinary person in the street.

The beginning of the Zen movement can be traced back to the arrival of its first patriarch, the fierce-looking Indian sage Bodhidharma, in China in 520 C.E. Although Buddhism was introduced to China around the time of Jesus (around 65 C.E.), the arrival of Bodhidharma has a special significance because he carried with him a unique approach to spirituality. It is an approach that recognizes the limitations of words, concepts, and thoughts and makes creative use of the power of silence. As the Zen people say, Zen is "a special transmission outside the scriptures."

From a historical point of view, it is important to realize that Zen is the child of a marriage between Buddhism and Taoism, drawing its strength and richness from China and India, two of the world's most ancient cultures. (As a later development, Zen also absorbs new qualities and colors from Japanese culture. Thus, the Indian genius, the Chinese genius, and the Japanese genius have all contributed to the Zen movement.) While Zen inherits its philosophical framework from the Madhyamika school of Buddhism, it derives its vitality, humor, beauty, and integrative-holistic nature from Taoism. The last element actually sets Zen apart from all other spiritual traditions of the world. Nowhere in human history have we seen such a seamless integration of the sacred with the mundane. Nowhere have we found the gulf between the spiritual world and the material world so gracefully bridged, through the miracle of artful living. As R. H. Blyth has observed, "When sacred really equals profane, we have Zen."

Zen is a product of the Chinese mind. The first thing to know about the Chinese is that they are a very down-to-earth people. Generally speaking, the Chinese do not have the same single-minded devotion to otherworldly ideals as their Caucasian counterparts do. Neither are they particularly drawn to metaphysical questions. When someone asked Confucius about afterlife, he answered: "If even the living is not fully known, why ask about the dead?" This answer is typically Chinese: it is nonspeculative and pragmatic, with an uncanny ability to focus only on what is relevant. In a sense, Zen inherits this down-to-earth attitude to life. It is not particularly concerned with whether there is a creator of the world, or with the existence or nonexistence of afterlife, or whether there is a supernatural entity that intervenes in worldly affairs. Zen is primarily interested in the quality of this life as we are living it now.

Religion, in the Western sense of the word, has never existed in traditional China. Surely, the common Chinese folks do go to temples. But they always have some practical purpose in mind when they do so — to divine the future, to pray for recovery from an illness, to petition for success in life. In Chinese folk religion, there are well over two hundred deities. But this doesn't make the Chinese a "religious" people because, in essence, these deities represent powers at the service of human beings and not supreme beings for human beings to surrender to. As theologian Hans Küng has observed, Chinese folk religion has been purely *utilitarian piety.*

Until quite recently, the notion of a supreme being as the ready-made answer to the problems of existence and as the savior of last resort has been totally foreign to the Chinese mind. Like other people, the Chinese have their moments of doubt, fear, sadness, and helplessness in their journey of life. But while Western people have traditionally turned to God on those occasions, the Chinese people have no such remedy for their plight. In the absence of an ultimate problem-solver, the Chinese have learned to turn their moments of darkness into opportunities for soul-making; they transform their existential angst into poetry and songs.

Thus, as an alternative to the path of religion, the Chinese have historically taken the path of the soul. This path is perhaps best understood through the Western tale of Tristan and Isolde. Author and psychotherapist Thomas Moore illustrates the path of the soul by retelling an episode where "equipped only with his harp, Tristan sails to Ireland in a small boat, without oar or rudder, a scene Joseph Campbell describes as a trusting to fate while armed with the music of the spheres."[1] The beauty of the story lies precisely in Tristan's carefreeness: he is not a victim to the neurotic culture of safety and control.

More than anything else, Zen represents a soulful approach to life in which one remains completely vulnerable and open to life, without

God as a security blanket. There is no attempt to eliminate the basic insecurity or unpredictability of life or to solve the mysteries of existence. Not only is this attempt unrealistic; it is also an anathema to soulfulness. Life is overcome, not by finding a strong ally (God), but through the soul's ability to develop a fresh perspective that enables the transformation of harsh realities into songs. Thus, the spirituality of the Chinese people has traditionally been expressed through poetry. In fact, the absence of a religious answer adds to the splendor of Chinese spirituality, as scholar Lin Yutang observes:

> Though religion gives peace by having a ready-made answer to all these problems, it decidedly detracts from the sense of unfathomable mystery and the poignant sadness of this life, which we call poetry. *Christian optimism kills all poetry.* A pagan, who has not these ready-made answers to his problems and whose sense of mystery is forever unanswered and unanswerable, is driven inevitably to a kind of pantheistic poetry. Actually, poetry has taken over the function of religion as an inspiration and a living emotion in the Chinese scheme of life.[2]

This notion of substituting poetry for religion is not so far-fetched. America, in the aftermath of the decline of its traditional religions, may have come to the same crossroad. In fact, this may be precisely what the contemporary literary critic Harold Bloom has been trying to do all his life. The *New York Times Magazine,* in its September 25, 1994, issue, did a special feature on the life of Bloom, who has just published another major work, *The Western Canon.* As Linsay Waters, executive editor at Harvard University Press, said of him: "Bloom is always asking what could it mean for America to have a spiritual life that is not identified with or rooted in organized religion." According to Waters, the goal of Bloom's criticism "is to goad us into living that life." In a nutshell, Zen is a poetization of life and a vivid expression of the human soul, albeit without the formality, rigidity, and superficiality associated with organized religions. R. H. Blyth remarked that "Zen is poetry and poetry is Zen."[3] As such, it is always fresh, genuine, and highly individual. Zen is a tradition where conformity and the herd instinct have no place. As an art form, it demands originality. For unlike some commodified spiritual product, Zen is an inward search for beauty and meaning, in the uncompromising ruggedness of "real life."

Much of Zen's character, insight, playfulness, and artistic quality can be traced back to Chuang Tzu, China's great philosopher, literary genius, and master-artist of life. Thomas Merton made this observation about the family tree of Zen:

> There is no question that the kind of thought and culture represented by Chuang Tzu was what transformed highly speculative Indian Buddhism into humorous, iconoclastic, and totally practical kind of Buddhism that was to flourish in China and Japan in the various schools of Zen. Zen throws light on Chuang Tzu, and Chuang Tzu throws light on Zen.[4]

Chuang Tzu's humor, earthly spirituality, and anti-establishment sentiment can be felt in the entire Zen tradition. Another source of Taoist inspiration comes from Lao Tzu, who captured much of his spiritual insight in his short but brilliant masterpiece, the *Tao Te Ching*. One of the most common Zen words, *Tao*, comes directly from this Taoist classic. The term has multiple layers of meaning. It can be taken to mean "Way," "Truth," or "ultimate reality." What is particularly notable about this word is that it is the closest Chinese equivalent to the Christian notion of God. In fact, the Chinese version of St. John's Gospel begins with these astounding words:

> In the beginning was the Tao.
> The Tao is with God.
> Tao is God. (John 1:1)

Even today, Chinese Christian ministers still refer to their sermons as "Tao-talk." I will henceforth treat "Tao" and "God" as equivalent terms and use them interchangeably. Both reflect a human attempt to name the Unnameable. There are many other Taoist terms that are borrowed by Zen teachers, including *wu-wei*, "spontaneity," "the use of uselessness," the "True Man," and *yin-yang*. We will introduce them whenever appropriate.

Zen is more Taoist than Buddhist, more Chinese (and Japanese) than Indian. Actually, by the time of its sixth patriarch, Hui Neng (636–712 C.E.), whatever Buddhist elements that came along with Bodhidharma had already been assimilated into Chinese culture. The otherworldly spiritual orientation, so prominent in the Indian version of Buddhism, had vanished without a trace. *The gospel of Hui Neng is that one can be at once spiritual and earthly.* Carrying water and chopping wood are just as much spiritual practices as reading scriptures.

Hui Neng's vision is that a spirituality that is not firmly grounded in the ordinariness and concreteness of everyday life is not even worth its name. To avoid the pitfalls of idealism and spiritual heroism, Hui Neng, acting in the spirit of Mahayana Buddhism, advocates doing away with all kinds of distinctions. Thus, he equates nirvana with the here-and-now, passions with *bodhi* (wisdom), and sages with ordinary people. The true practice of spirituality, according to Hui Neng, is the *asceticism of being ordinary* — living in the moment and not making anything special about oneself. For any attempt to become special is an open invitation to the ego. With Hui Neng, the characterization of Zen as a practical art of living, equally accessible to the aristocrats and to the proletariat, is firmly established. Spirituality is no longer a prized good of the monasteries but has become a common heritage and culture of the ordinary folks.

A comparison of Zen with fine arts is provided in the table on the following page. One element shared by both is *creativity.* Creativity implies the absence of formula and the need for improvisation and originality. Every once in a while, the students in my Zen class will ask me to give them more concrete and specific instructions for the practice of Zen. That reflects a very basic misunderstanding. In reality, Zen is a "pathless path."

A very common misconception about the practice of Zen is that it has a "system" for the students to follow. Zazen (sitting meditation) has become almost a symbol for Zen. But the fact is that systems and formulae are exactly what Hui Neng vehemently protested against, for they tend to induce pretense and stifle creativity. One of Hui Neng's major accomplishments was to revolutionize the whole concept of meditation (*dhyana*) and return to the original mental culture that Buddha advocated.

Prior to Hui Neng, the dominant idea of meditation was that it was a form of *quietism*: the practitioner is supposed to purify his mind through keeping still so that the "dust" of his inner world can settle. The pitfall of this is that the practitioner may become attached to the notion of purity, thus making meditation another form of bondage that deadens the senses. Hui Neng reversed this trend of mind-killing by proclaiming that true meditation has nothing to do with sitting or keeping still; it is "neither to cling to the notion of a mind, nor cling to the notion of purity, nor to cherish the thought of immovability." True practice, according to Hui Neng, is "not to be obstructed in all things." For spirituality is an expression of creativity and not an expression of attachment.

Discipline is another often misunderstood concept in Zen. One

COMPARISON OF ZEN WITH FINE ARTS

ZEN	FINE ARTS
Presence	Seeing/listening/feeling/tasting...
Ordinary magic	Transformative power
Zest/radiance/joy	Vitality/playfulness/fun
Insight	Depth
Wu-wei	Effortlessness/aimlessness/uselessness
Gentleness	Easiness/grace/efficiency
Freedom	Childlike/artful stupidity/carefreeness
Simplicity	Simplicity
Paradoxity	Unification of opposites, poetic fuzziness
"Mindlessness"	Right-brain orientation/nonintellectual
Inner quest	Self-discovery/self-expression/soulfulness
Creativity	Creativity
Individuality	Character
Pathlessness	No system or formula
Middle Way	Balance/harmony
Openness	Openness
Spontaneity	Spontaneity
Nonmoralistic	Nonjudgmental
Quality	Beauty; good taste
Genuineness	Genuineness
Discipline	Discipline
Concentration/absorption/ egolessness	Concentration/absorption/ loss of self

dictionary definition of "discipline" is "control gained by enforcing obedience or order." Unfortunately, this notion of "discipline" is practically synonymous with punishment.

Zen discipline has nothing to do with control, obedience, rules, or punishment. Neither is it a militant display of will power. Rather, it has to do with the cultivation of awareness and sensitivity, which are critical in the practice of any art. Above all, Zen discipline means complete openness to what is and the ability to be totally immersed in whatever one is doing. This openness implies a dynamic and fluid adaptability that is the direct opposite to rigidity. For Zen discipline is the discipline of nonattachment. It certainly does not mean some kind of dogged obedience to a given set of rules.

The bottom line is that Zen has no formula. It does not tell us *what* to do; it is concerned about *how* we are going about doing whatever it is that we are doing. An art teacher may ask a group of young children to draw a butterfly. Each child will have his or her own way of drawing it: some may draw a butterfly with no legs, some may draw it with an extra pair of legs, etc. The point is that there is no "correct" way to draw it. The quality of a drawing does not depend on whether the child has drawn the right number of legs for the butterfly; it depends on whether the child has expressed genuine feelings about the object at hand.

Many people cannot see any relationship between Zen and the teachings of Jesus. But Reginald H. Blyth, who ranked with D. T. Suzuki as one the leading interpreters of Zen, has a little surprise for us. Here is how he sees the relationship between Zen, Christianity, and Buddhism:

> In some ways there is more Zen about Christianity than Buddhism; certainly there is more Zen to be found in English literature than in Japanese or Chinese literature, and in Indian literature Zen is painfully absent.... Zen may be called the ultimate simplification of both Christianity and Buddhism, the former being clobbered up with emotionalism and theology, the latter entangled in morality and a more or less scientific philosophy.[5]

All we need to do is to listen to the way Jesus talked. His Zen qualities are obvious. In contrast to the teachings of many Buddhist philosophers who are often caught up with abstractions and abstruse metaphysics, Jesus' teachings are poetic and not pedantic, simple and not laborious, intuitive and not analytical, humorous and not stodgy.

The most tell-tale sign that Jesus was a Zen teacher and an artist is the well-known fact that he often used children as role models for the Tao (Way). While traditionalists and moralists exhort us to "grow up," Jesus says "Be like a child!" Childlike audacity, simplicity, openness, and carefreeness have always been key elements in art. In fact, to be artistic is to be child-like! Picasso showed his understanding of this when he said: "I used to draw like Raphael, but it has taken me my whole life to draw like a child."

Zen cannot be explained; it can only be "shown." The easiest way to teach Zen is to illustrate by example. One of the best Zen lessons was actually given by Sidhartha Gotama the Buddha himself in the legendary Sermon of the Flower. The following is my adapted version of this exquisite sermon:

> One day the Buddha was about to give a sermon to a large congregation of fifteen hundred monks and nuns. When the Buddha came to the front, sending his greetings to the audience, someone offered him a flower. The Buddha picked up the flower and showed it to everyone. For a long time, he did not utter a word. This is very unusual because the Buddha was usually very eloquent. After a while, the congregation began to feel uneasy.
>
> "The Master must have lost his memory due to his old age," some speculated. Others thought differently: "The Master must be trying to tell us something extremely profound. I must try hard to figure it out!" Among all those present, only one disciple, Mahakashyapa, was able to stay cool. He seemed to have gotten the point and smiled at the Buddha. Seeing that, the Buddha was overjoyed, and he said to the congregation:
>
> I have a treasure of insight and a heart of bliss.
>
> Since Ultimate Reality has no form, I have come up with a wonderful method of conveying it.
>
> This method does not depend on words.
>
> In fact, my teaching is less important than the student's self-realization.
>
> I hereby transmit this method to Mahakashyapa.

Do you get the message? Before discussing this sermon in detail, I would like to quote from the Sermon on the Mount a passage that I think is a direct parallel to the Sermon of the Flower. It is also one of the most beautiful and poetic of Jesus' teachings. We will henceforth refer to this as his Nature Sermon:

> Therefore, I tell you, do not be anxious about your life, what you shall eat or what you shall drink, nor about your body, what you shall put on. Is not life more than food, and the body more than clothing? Look at the birds of the air; they neither sow nor reap nor gather into barns, and yet your heavenly Father feeds them. Are you not more value than they? And which of you by being anxious can add one cubit to his span of life?
>
> And why are you anxious about clothing? Consider the lilies of the field, how they grow; they neither toil nor spin; yet I tell you, even Solomon in all his glory was not arrayed like one of these. But if God so clothes the grass of the field, which today is alive and tomorrow is thrown in the oven, will he not much more clothe you, men of little faith? Therefore, do not be anxious, saying, "What shall we eat?" or

"What shall we wear?" For the Gentiles seek all these things; and your Father knows that you need them all. But seek first his kingdom and his righteousness, and all these things will be yours as well.

Therefore, do not be anxious about tomorrow. For tomorrow will be anxious for itself. Let the day's own trouble be sufficient for the day. (Matt. 6:28–34)

Where are the similarities? For starters, both masters were asking their audience simply to look and pay attention. Art is about *seeing*. To be an artist, one must be sensitive to reality. Picasso once said, "I see for others." Attentiveness is the key in Zen, as in all other arts. When Buddha picked up the flower and showed it to the congregation, he was trying to draw everyone's attention to the flower. Similarly, when Jesus said, "Consider the lilies, see how they grow," he was asking his audience to pay attention to whatever was in front of their eyes.

The first and most important element of Zen is presence. Presence refers to a person's ability to be fully aware of what is going on within the self and in the environment. In the Theravadic tradition of Buddhism, which is the dominant form of Buddhism in Thailand, Sri Lanka, Cambodia, Laos, and Burma, it is referred to as *sati*, or mindfulness. The practice of mindfulness is, without question, the most important spiritual practice in this tradition. The Satipatthana-sutta, the most revered discourse given by the Buddha on mental development, is totally devoted to the discussion of this subject. A passage from the sutta reads as follows:

> ...a bhikkhu [monk] applies full attention either in going forward or back; in looking straight on or looking away; in bending or in stretching; in wearing robes or carrying the bowl; in eating, drinking, chewing or savoring; in attending to the calls of nature; in walking, in standing; in sitting; in falling asleep, in waking; in speaking or in keeping silence. In all these he applies full attention.[6]

Thus, a Theravadic monk is supposed to be mindful of every aspect of daily life. It is a key Buddhist belief that the seeds of enlightenment are sown in mindful living.

The Sermon of the Flower is first and foremost a story that illustrates the importance of mindfulness. What do you think is the reason that no one in the congregation except Mahakashyapa was able to get Buddha's message? The answer is incredibly simple: most of us do not have presence. We tend not to live in the moment. When Buddha lifted up the flower and showed it to everyone present, he simply wanted them to see its beauty and smell its fragrance. This is straightforward enough. Yet only Mahakashyapa got the point! All others failed to get it because they were too busy speculating, thinking, and worrying. By not living in the moment, they failed to notice and appreciate the beauty in the here-and-now. Unfortunately, this is exactly what we are doing all the time.

It will be fair to say that "presence" is the cornerstone of all true spirituality, regardless of ethnic or cultural origin. Presence is something that Jesus emphasized over and over again. The Gospels are filled with statements of Jesus that begin with words like "Beware" (be aware), "Look," "Hear and understand...." " In this sense, the teaching of Jesus is very close in spirit to that of the Buddha. After all, Buddhism is a culture of awareness. The word "Buddha," for example, means the "Awakened One." Similarly, Jesus is called "the Light of the World" in the Gospel of John. In the Sermon on the Mount, Jesus alerted his disciples to the importance of awareness:

> The eye is the lamp of the body. So, if your eye is sound, your whole body will be full of light; but if your eye is not sound, your whole body will be full of darkness. If the light in you is darkness, how great is the darkness! (Matt. 6:22–23)

Certainly, if the eye is not sound, one can see neither truth nor beauty. Here Jesus is explicitly stating that awareness is a requirement for spirituality.

To reinforce this point, consider Jesus' remark about the lilies of the fields. There is no doubt that Jesus was addressing a basic and universal human problem — our sense of insecurity. He was talking to people experiencing existential anxiety just as we do. In fact, that section of the sermon opens with the following words: "Therefore, I tell you, do not be anxious about your life, what you shall eat or what you shall drink, nor about your body, what you shall put on" (Matt. 6:25). After asking his audience to look at the birds of the air, he then asked them to consider the lilies of the fields. It is as if he were saying to them something like this: "Drop what you are doing for a moment. There is a very important lesson that you can learn from nature. But you cannot get the message until you have managed to quiet down and really listen to her." Thus, just like the Buddha in the Sermon of the Flower, Jesus was illustrating the *power of silence.*

Until we have learned the art of silence, we cannot develop presence. Silence requires deep relaxation, which in turn requires dropping all preoccupations, whatever they may be. These preoccupations may be physical or mental in nature. Most of us are preoccupied with our anxieties, our desires, our fears, and our thoughts. The noise generated from these anxieties, fears, and thoughts is precisely what is preventing us from enjoying the present moment. In the Sermon of the Flower, many people in the audience were preoccupied with figuring out Buddha's meaning and hence failed to become silent. Similarly, in Jesus' Nature Sermon, Jesus noted that most people are preoccupied with their worries. The problem is that unless we relax, we cannot see truth.

The second key element of Zen is "ordinariness." In both the Sermon of the Flower and the Nature Sermon, the teachers use common and natural objects as teaching tools. Buddha simply picked up a flower. Likewise, Jesus did not say something like "Watch, everyone, I am going to show you an awesome miracle!" He simply drew his audience's attention to something ordinary and mundane — the birds in the air and the lilies of the fields. Yet an important spiritual lesson is taught through something so plain and apparently unremarkable. This ability to transform something that is ordinary and familiar into something wonderful is an unmistakable trait of art.

In the Introduction we discussed the notion of "ordinary magic," with an emphasis on the adjective "ordinary." The extraordinary and the miraculous have been grossly oversold in popular Christianity. Some Christians even think that their faith depends critically on the evidences for the occurrence of certain extraordinary or supernatural events. It should be noted, however, that this obsession with the supernatural and the extraordinary contradicts the original spirit of Jesus' teachings. When the Pharisees and the scribes came to Jesus and asked for a sign, Jesus denied their request (Matt. 12:39; 16:1–4). He renounced such an approach to spirituality. The danger about signs, miracles, and psychic power is that they are often abused and misinterpreted. The Gospels record that Jesus did use his psychic power to heal. But we should also note that he did it out of compassion, not out of a desire to impress, to make converts, or to teach spirituality. Besides, the world is full of faith-healers and psychics, both fake ones and authentic ones. The mere display of psychic ability may not mean much.

Many Christians have put a heavy emphasis on Jesus' supernatural ability. They emphasize that he was capable of performing all kinds of superhuman feats, including rising from the dead. I do not intend to throw doubt on these claims. But I think the relevant question is not whether he performed miracles. Rather, assuming that he did actually do all these amazing things, the key question is what specific impact such deeds had on the people around him. Did these deeds simply create a sensation, or did they transform the lives of those who saw them and put them on a path of inner peace and joy?

Many people conceive of Jesus as a miracle worker, but very few come to know him as an artist and a master of "ordinary magic." John Welwood, writer and psychologist, provides us with this insight:

> Magic, as I use this term, is a sudden opening of the mind to the wonder of existence. It is a sense that there is much more to life than we usually recognize; that we do not have to be confined by the limited views that our family, our society, or our own habitual thoughts impose on us; that life contains many dimensions, depths, textures, and meanings extending far beyond our familiar beliefs and concepts.[7]

Zen is called "ordinary magic" for two reasons. First, it induces spiritual awakening in the student through natural and ordinary means. Supernatural power is never part of the Zen tradition. Second and more important, Zen calls our attention to the wonders of the ordinary. There is a hidden dimension of beauty, richness, and harmony in the common world surrounding us, but we seldom take notice. Zen tries to stimulate our sensitivity to these natural wonders and hence to recover the joy in our daily lives.

Art is ordinary magic. In photographic art, for example, the object is often one of the most usual things in life — an old run-down house, a window, linen hanging on a clothesline. But because of the photographer's ingenious choice of perspective, lighting, texture, distance, and contrast, the ordinary is turned into a wonder. Author Dorothea Brande made the following observation:

> The author of genius does keep till his last breath the spontaneity, the ready sensitivity, of a child, the "innocence of eye" that means so much to the painter, the ability to respond freshly and quickly to new scenes, and to old scenes as though they were new; to see traits and characteristics as though each were newly minted from the hand of God instead of sorting them quickly into categories and pigeonholing them without wonder or surprise; to feel situations so immediately and keenly that the word "trite" has hardly any meaning for him; and always to see the "correspondence between things" of which Aristotle spoke two thousand years ago.[8]

The "innocence of eye" mentioned by Dorothea Brande is the

equivalent to the *beginner's mind* discussed earlier. Zen is an art of seeing. Just as in other arts, the objective in ordinary magic is not so much to change the external world as to see the world in a different light. If Zen can be said to have any goal at all, it is *satori* (enlightenment). D. T. Suzuki, one of the pioneers of American Zen, defined *satori* as the acquisition of a new perspective. In Zen as well as in other arts, it is the "beginner's mind" that makes the magic possible by seeing everything afresh.

The fact is that Jesus was far more powerful and effective with his "ordinary magic" than with his miracles. The Pharisees and the scribes were supposed to have seen or heard about the miracles that Jesus had performed, but they put him on the cross anyway. His "ordinary magic," however, is able to make a positive and lasting impact on those who pay attention. In the Nature Sermon, for example, Jesus taught peace in the present through the "birds of the air" and the "lilies of the field." Despite the fact that these are just ordinary objects, Jesus was nevertheless able to make a heavy impact because he used these objects not to impress but to awaken something that lies deep in the hearts of listeners.

In any case, it is a characteristic of Zen to teach the spiritual through the ordinary and mundane. To the Western person who is used to drawing a clear line between the spiritual and the mundane, this is unthinkable. But this is what makes Zen so interesting and poetic. D. T. Suzuki makes the following comment:

> For Zen reveals itself in the most uninteresting and uneventful life of a plain man in the street, recognizing the fact of living in the midst of life as it is lived. Zen systematically trains the mind to see this; it opens a man's eye to the greatest mystery as it is daily and hourly performed; it enlarges the heart to embrace eternity of time and infinity of space in its every palpitation; it makes us live in the world as if walking in the Garden of Eden; and all these spiritual feats are accomplished without resorting to doctrines but by asserting in the most direct way the truth that lies in our inner being.[9]

The third element of Zen is zest, which is closely related with presence. Zen is art, and art is about having fun. Those who have lost their ability to have fun will gradually lose zest in life. We have observed that contemporary men and women seem to be more and more depressed despite the material affluence of modern society. What has gone wrong? Why have we lost our zest for life while our civilization has become so highly developed and sophisticated?

Aren't we supposed to be happier as our society makes more and more "progress"?

But perhaps we should not be dismayed. For what has happened on a social level has a parallel on an individual level. As we progress from childhood to adulthood, we also lose some of our zest for life. I have two young children, and I have always been amazed by their energy level. They are so full of life! My own energy level cannot match half of theirs. I am sure that age and biology have something to do with it. But I am also sure that they are only part of the story. The difference has to have something to do with adult psychology.

Jesus' love of children is well known and reflects his insight into the connection between psychology and spirituality. He says that the kingdom belongs to the children (Mark 10:14). He also says that unless we return and become like children, we can never enter the kingdom of God (Matt. 18:3). "To become like children" is the *sole* requirement that Jesus specified for entry into the kingdom! And this is not so surprising, for children are great artists of life. It is a delight to watch small children interact with their environment. Children have amazing abilities to wonder, to play, to appreciate beauty and mysteries, to be joyful, and to be carefree. Unfortunately, we gradually lose those abilities as we grow older.

Why have our lives become duller and less enjoyable as we grow older? To answer this requires looking into the complex interactions between our culture, our upbringing, and our consumeristic economy. We have to see how our society has conditioned us to be unhappy. But there is also a simpler answer: we lose our zest for life because of the deterioration of our mindfulness and the increase of our attachments as we grow up.

Small children have few attachments. Unlike adults, they have not yet been conditioned into tying themselves to certain concepts, opinions, values, or specific ways of doing things. Therefore, they are more creative and are more able to enjoy themselves even with simple things. Just look at how they can make a toy out of virtually anything! Every child is a wizard. Through the magic of imagination, children can turn a broomstick into a toy horse in no time. But as we mature, our attachments and obsessions also grow. They lead to distracting emotions such as worries, anxieties, desires, and anger, and our ability to be mindful and creative suffers. When I was a child, I used to enjoy the smell of fresh bread as I passed by a bakery in the morning. But I lost that ability a long time ago and did not manage to recover it until I discovered Zen. When the mind is all clogged up with all kinds of worldly concerns and worries, it is difficult to experience the simple pleasures of life.

The fourth element of Zen is insight, which comes together with mindfulness. Ordinary magic cannot happen without insight, which means the ability to see deeply into the nature of things. Surely, the appreciation of humor and poetry requires insight. Both the laughter associated with a joke and the joy associated with *satori* are triggered by an "Aha!" experience. There can be no art without insight. The ability to discern (to look beyond what is obvious) is a key skill for an artist. The painter Paul Klee observed that "the artist does not reproduce the visible; rather he make things visible."

Jesus consistently maintained that liberation is a matter of spiritual insight. The primacy of spiritual insight in the salvation process is crystalized in Jesus' statement that "the truth will make you free" (John 8:31). In fact, given the prevalence of terms like "truth," "light," "eye," "ear," and "blindness" in the Gospels, it is difficult to conceive why the church has so far failed to recognize that liberation is a matter of discerning and not a matter of believing. Jesus praised his disciples for their spiritual insight and understanding: "Blessed are your eyes, for they see, and your ears, for they hear" (Matt. 13:16). He saw the spiritual problem of human beings as the lack of insight and mindfulness.

Note how Jesus distinguishes between "looking" and "seeing." "Looking" can be superficial, but "seeing" requires depth. True spirituality is not possible without deep spiritual insight. In his Nature Sermon Jesus demonstrated how inner peace can result from the development of insight into the nature of things. He offers us three key points:

First, the birds do not worry for their food and the lilies do not worry about their clothes. Things have been working amazingly well even without our intervention or worry. The birds and the lilies simply "trust in God." (This, of course, is just a poetic expression. For birds and lilies do not even think. But they are metaphors for those who submit their wills to God's.)

Second, many important things in life are simply not up to us to control. We do have serious limitations as human beings. It is time that we recognize that. Jesus asked rhetorically, "Which of you by being anxious can add one cubit to his span of life?" (Matt. 6:27). This is the central fact of life—that our own life, precious as it may be to us, is not in our control. The acceptance of this truth leads to inner peace; the denial of it leads to unnecessary anxiety and frustration.

Third, we already have enough to do without having to worry about tomorrow. Jesus advised us to "let the day's own trouble be sufficient for the day." Worrying about the future is self-defeating because it simply makes it harder for us to get our current jobs done.

Jesus taught the importance of insight in his Nature Sermon. True spirituality, with its concomitant joy, peace, and freedom, is a matter of seeing. It is not a matter of believing. When there is seeing, there is no need for argument, belief, or persuasion. Therefore, the priority is to see reality as it is. Nobel laureate and author Albert Camus made the following observation: "A man is always a prey to his truths. Once he has admitted them, he cannot free himself from them. One has to pay something."[10]

The good news, however, is that while truths are binding once they are recognized, they also liberate and tend to take the heat off us. With reference again to the Nature Sermon, those who are always trying to control everything and eliminate all uncertainties are miserable. For they are fighting against nature. On the other hand, those who come to accept uncertainties as inevitable live lives of peace. There is plenty that we can learn from the birds and the lilies.

Many people have interpreted Jesus' Nature Sermon as a teaching about providence. According to this interpretation, a person's peace is based on the belief that "God will always provide." If so, it is clear that this peace is based on future belief and not on present insight — for there cannot be any concrete proof that God will indeed provide. Another problem is that those who are constantly counting on God's provision are still expecting God to serve their self-interest. They are putting themselves before God.

But in the passage Jesus asks that we "seek first his [God's] kingdom and his righteousness," meaning that we put God in the first place. Effectively, he is saying that once we have managed to do that, everything else will be automatically taken care of. His position is clear: ultimately, joy and peace are not the result of having the guarantee that God will always grant our will or take care of our needs. It is more a matter of subjecting our will to God's, meaning a total and unconditional acceptance of reality.

Therefore, the Nature Sermon need not be interpreted as a teaching about providence. In fact, the essence of the sermon can be grasped without any supernatural undertone. One does not even have to believe in the existence of a personal God. It will suffice just to have the insight that worrying is futile and that true peace is the result of one's ability to accept reality as it is.

The fifth element of Zen is "wu-wei." Literally translated, *wu-wei* means "doing nothing." But, in a sense, it is almost the direct opposite of inaction. The best English translation of *wu-wei* that I have come across is that of Huston Smith, who translates it as "creative quietude." It points to the paradoxical state where supreme activity coexists with supreme relaxation. Smith elaborates on the meaning of the term as follows:

> Wu-wei is supreme action, the precious suppleness, simplicity, and freedom that flows from us, or rather through us, when our private egos and conscious efforts yield to a power not their own. In a way it is virtue approached from a direction diametrically opposite to that of Confucius.[11]

Instead of talking about *wu-wei* in the abstract, I will illustrate it with an incident. Not long ago, I was invited to my friend's house for dinner. Hanging in the middle of her living room was a framed piece of calligraphy, artwork done by my friend's grandfather. In fact, it was her grandfather's favorite piece. What is interesting, however, is that the calligraphy was done on a piece of scrap paper — not the kind of paper normally used for calligraphy. It turns out that her grandfather was simply practicing when he did this. There was no intention of achieving excellence at all. Ironically, it turned out to be his best work ever.

This is a typical case of *wu-wei*, accomplishment with no special effort. It is amazing how many masterpieces and peak performances are done in this carefree, unintentional manner. As we said earlier, relaxation is a prerequisite for spirituality. One problem with our modern society is that it has become too achievement-oriented. We tend to exert ourselves even in areas where exertion is not appropriate. Art is not a matter of achievement; neither is spirituality. If we try to make it a matter of achievement, it will become a means for something else — fame, money, respect. When that happens, it turns ugly; it is no longer art. Real art is about having fun and enjoying oneself. It should be an end in itself.

Zen, being an art, is "aimless" and "useless." But herein lies the great use of its "uselessness" — to allow us to relax and enjoy life as it is. This is precisely why Jesus said that "my yoke is easy, and my burden is light" (Matt. 11:28–30). Things are "easy" if you know when to leave matters in God's hands.

Jesus illustrated the principle of *wu-wei* beautifully in his Nature Sermon. The wild birds neither sow nor reap nor gather into barns, yet they are fed; the lilies of the field neither toil nor spin, yet they are clothed. *Wu-wei* is not about being lazy and doing nothing. Rather, it is about following the way of nature and not wasting energy. It is about the beauty of "letting it be"!

These are the first five key elements of Zen: presence, ordinariness, zest, insight, and *wu-wei*. Let us now consider the remaining key elements (gentleness, freedom, simplicity, paradoxity, right-brain orientation, and soulfulness).

Two

What Is Zen? (II):
The Heart of the Matter

Unless you turn and become like children,
you cannot enter the kingdom of God.
　　　　　　　　　　　　　　　　　–JESUS

Superior goodness is like water.
　　　　　　　　　　　　　–LAO TZU

Zen is like motherhood and apple pie: we grow up with it, but whether we recognize it is another matter. Robert Fulghum, author of the wonderful little book *All I Really Need to Know I Learned In Kindergarten,* made the following observation:

> And then remember the Dick-and-Jane books and the first word you learned — the biggest word of all — LOOK.
> Everything you need to know is in there somewhere. The Golden Rule and love and basic sanitation. Ecology and politics and equality and sane living.[1]

Zen is virtually everywhere. In traditional Chinese culture, there are six classical arts — music, chess, archery, horsemanship, calligraphy, and painting. We could learn much about Zen if we really put our hearts into learning any one of these. The same principles apply. Similarly, in Japanese culture, there are *chado, kendo, judo,* and *bushido.* The "-do" ending of these words is the Japanese equivalent to the Chinese magic word "tao." The words stand, respectively, for the art of tea, the art of swordsmanship, the art of gentleness (for judo is based on the principle of borrowing strength from the oppo-nent), and the art of the warrior. Each of these arts is considered as a way to practice Zen. Indeed, you can discover Zen in whatever you do, if you are mindful. For Zen is the art for excellence.

In this chapter, we will continue to explore a few more elements of Zen. In a way, it is most un-Zenlike to get into a long discussion like this. But I have already said enough about the subject to disqualify myself from being a Zen master, so I do not mind saying some more to satisfy your intellectual curiosity. In what follows, we will continue to use Jesus' Nature Sermon as our main reference.

The sixth element of Zen is gentleness. To understand gentleness in Zen, it helps to have some background about the Taoist notions of *yin* and *yang*. The *yin* and the *yang* literally mean the masculine and feminine principles. They are expressed in the contrasts between man and woman, good and evil, light and darkness, day and night, positive and negative, explicit and implicit, strong and weak, etc. The couplet, expressed as *yin-yang*, is actually the emblem of Taoism. It shows the two cosmic forces merging into each other, with a little bit of *yin* in the *yang* side and vice versa. The Taoist notion is that it is the interaction between the *yin* and the *yang* that sets the universe in motion and creates all lives.

While the mainstream Western mind visualizes the good and the evil as two opposite forces, each attempting to annihilate the other, the Taoists envision them as interdependent and complementary. The *yin-yang* is the primordial symbol for *creative tension,* without which life and growth are not possible. This understanding that the opposites are complementary is essential to Zen's gentle attitude toward life.

Gentleness is one of the prime Taoist virtues. It is what distinguishes a real artist from a mere craftsman. Lao Tzu also considers it critical for survival. The Taoist master Chuang Tzu taught the art of gentleness in his story about Butcher Pao:

> Pao was a butcher with wonderful skills. When Butcher Pao was carving up a cow with his knife, his physical movements were so well coordinated that the whole process was like a dance, with the dancer and the dance merging into one. Once, the emperor saw Butcher Pao in action, and he exclaimed: "Your skills are absolutely adorable. I can't believe my eyes!"
>
> Butcher Pao replied: "What I use for carving up the cow are not skills; it is the Tao itself! When I was learning butchering, I still saw a cow as a cow. But after three years, I did not see the cow anymore—all I saw was a well-ordered structure of muscles and bones.

Ever since that time, I no longer have to use my eyes to watch what I am doing. I simply rely on my instincts to feel it. Other butchers use their knives to chop; for me, no chopping is necessary. This knife that I have here is already nineteen years old. It has gone through thousands of cows, yet it is as sharp as new. It is because my knife simply "swims" through the gap between the bones...."

Upon hearing this, the emperor said, "Now, I have learned the art of living."

Butcher Pao's knife did not wear out because of his gentleness, which stems from his knowledge of the way of nature. This gentleness is the key to the beautification of life and the sanctification of work. Gentleness means following the way of nature, not going against it. It prevents wastage of energy and improves productivity.

The opposite of gentleness is violence, which means any action that opposes reality. Spiritual violence is prevalent in our society. Most of us are violent in one way or another because we do not have good insights into the nature of reality. We are often not even aware of our violence. One ready example is our antagonistic attitude toward death. We simply cannot accept death as an inevitable fact of life, and our medical technology is oriented toward fighting it at all cost. Such violence has generated much misery for patients and for society as a whole.

C. S. Lewis referred to Christianity as a "fighting religion." This characterization is most misleading. What Jesus actually taught was the art of "winning through losing" — a kind of spiritual judo. In the Nature Sermon, Jesus used the birds of the air and the lilies of the field to illustrate the art of gentleness. Note that although the birds are fed and the lilies are clothed by the invisible hand of God, they are also exposed to the elements and other unknown factors. The birds have natural predators and the lilies experience droughts and floods. Also, just like us, they are not immune to the central facts of life — sickness, aging, and death. Indeed, Jesus described the lilies as living beings that "today are alive and tomorrow are thrown into the oven." Certainly, providence does not mean security or long life.

Yet the birds and the lilies seem to be able to adapt amicably to their environment and live gracefully — without worries, protests, or complaints. Therefore, Jesus asked if these "lower lives" are able to do it, why is it so difficult for us to do the same as human beings? Jesus praised the birds and the lilies for their special way of gentleness. It is this gentleness that allows them to live beautifully despite everything.

The main thrust of the Nature Sermon is *not* on providence. Rather, it is on the *power of weakness*. As Alan Watts has remarked, the lilies are "frail and frivolous, gentle and inconsequential, and thus have those very qualities of vegetative wisdom so despised by those who have wills of iron and nerves of steel to fight the good fight and run the straight race."[2]

Jesus taught that spirituality is not a matter of toughness or a display of will power. Lao Tzu, the founder of Chinese Taoism, remarked that "superior goodness is like water." In fact, water is the perfect teacher of gentleness. Whatever container you pour it into, water will immediately take the shape of that container. Water does not resist reality; it adapts to it. It is in this adaptability that superior strength lies. Lao Tzu remarked in the *Tao Te Ching* about the strength of water:

> The weakest things in the world can overmatch the strongest things
>   in the world.
> Nothing can be compared to water for its weak and yielding nature;
> Yet in attacking the hard and the strong nothing proves better than it.
> For there is no other alternative to it.
> The weak can overcome the strong,
> And the yielding can overcome the hard.

The seventh element of Zen is freedom. "Freedom" is a much-abused term in this country. When I ask my children to do something they would rather not do, they often invoke freedom as a talisman and say: "This is a free country!" To them, freedom means the absence of constraints and limitations.

On my bookshelf there is an interesting book titled *Teaching Young Children How to Draw* by art teacher Fei-tung Chen. I bought it many years ago because I have always been fascinated by children's art. It is only recently that I got a chance to read the text of the book carefully. What I discovered was that the author is not only a teacher of art, but also a teacher of Zen.

One of the chapters is called "A Guide to Random Art." In a "random drawing" session, children are asked *not* to draw any natural object, but to freely express themselves and draw whatever comes to mind. The result of such a drawing exercise is usually some kind of "chaos." But here the author makes a remarkable observation: even in these "chaos" drawings, he can identify the ones that are drawn with boldness and those drawn with timidity. In other words, "chaos" (or lawlessness) does not necessarily mean freedom.

Contrary to what many of us may think, freedom is not the absence of constraints. Freedom is a relative concept; there is no such thing as "absolute freedom." In fact, freedom can exist only relative to its associated constraints. In this sense, freedom and constraints are just two sides of the same reality. One cannot exist without the other.

In the United States, people tend to take a warrior's approach to freedom. A common American expression is to "fight for one's freedom." But spiritual freedom is not a matter of fighting. It is a matter of *letting go*.

We can learn much about freedom by watching children play. There is a lot more fun in children's play than in the play of adults. Little children are not afraid to make fools of themselves or to express their real feelings. Their play is accompanied by much laughter, yelling, and screaming — a sign that they can let go of themselves completely. As we grow older, we lose this carefreeness because our sense of self-importance has grown within us like a cancerous cell. As we become more and more egocentric and controlling, our inner freedom and joy dwindle.

Spiritual freedom does not mean the absence of physical constraints, but it does mean the ability to loosen oneself from the bondage of one's own ego. True freedom is a mirror image of one's gentleness — the ability to follow nature's way and the willingness to give up one's insistence when it is not appropriate. In the context of the Nature Sermon, the birds and the lilies are "free" because they do not have any anxieties or worries, both of which are expressions of ego. Unlike most human beings, they do not resist reality or rebel against nature. Most of us, on the other hand, feel oppressed because we have not learned to accept the realities of uncertainties, aging, sickness, and death. We tend to resist them, as if we could avoid them. This blind resistance costs us much misery.

The eighth key element of Zen is simplicity. Remember Mrs. Marcos, the widow of the president of the Philippines and the owner of three thousand pairs of shoes? You may find her extravagance amusing, but she accurately reflects the acquisitive/consumeristic modern culture that we live in. Intelligent as we are as modern men and women, we nevertheless find it difficult to distinguish between quality and quantity.

Zen is a discipline to make life simple. The Chinese character for the word "Zen" is composed of two radicals — one representing revelation, and another representing simplicity. Thus, Zen means the truth that is revealed through simple living. In the acquisitive society, we tend to have too many personal possessions, responsibilities, engagements, and entertainments. The big secret is that our quality of life has deteriorated because we are crushed by the weight of all these. There is so much to do and so little time to do it! Our situation is not unlike going on a tour where the tourist guide has scheduled too many sites to visit. Instead of increasing our enjoyment of the tour, the cramming actually diminishes it.

Yes, there can be too much of a "good" thing. If we have not learned this yet, we may learn it from the *Cosmo*-girl. *Cosmopolitan* magazine, catering to the market of young, "sophisticated" urban women, once ran an article with this headline: "FOR GREAT SEX, LESS IS MORE. Preserve the *mystery,* go *slow.* Make love the old-fashioned way. Make him earn it."[3] The article quoted Nathaniel Brandon, clinical psychologist at the Biocentric Institute in Beverly Hills: "You build up much more of a charge by deferring sex than by instant gratification. It's erotic to contain sexual feelings and take time to know the person." Apparently, Zen teachers are not the only ones who appreciate the *magic of thinking small.*

Simplicity also has an impact on the depth and richness of everyday experience. Thomas Moore, a former monk turned psychotherapist who has done substantial research in medieval spirituality, observes that one reason that our generation has lost its soul is because we are living such a hectic lifestyle. He says in his *Care of the Soul,* that "living artfully, therefore, might require something as simple as pausing."[4] He further comments that "the soul cannot thrive in a fast-paced life because being affected, taking things in and chewing on them, requires time." We find the experts agreeing on one thing: spirituality has much to do with the development of depth in everyday experience, which requires slowing things down and demanding less.

This is precisely why Jesus made the rather shocking statement that "it is easier for a camel to go through the eye of a needle than for a rich man to enter the kingdom of God" (Matt. 19:24). Many people misinterpret this as an indication that material life and spiritual life have some kind of inherent conflict. If this were so, all the hungry souls in Africa would be saints!

Material life and spiritual life are not mutually exclusive. Jesus' statement about the poor simply highlights the relationship between spirituality and simplicity. The life of the rich is seldom simple. Their high purchasing and acquisition power turns out to be more a curse than a blessing. They are prone to become slaves to their possessions and earthly pleasures, which tend to distract them from their inner life. Therefore, their chance for liberation is extremely slim.

Thus, the adjective "rich" must be understood figuratively. A person's possessions may be material, psychological, intellectual, or even religious. Whatever their nature, so long as they are attachments, they will be an obstacle to liberation. Jesus makes this point clear in the beatitudes: "Blessed are the poor in spirit" (Matt. 5:3). He did not say here that the poor are blessed. Certainly, there is a big difference between the poor and the *poor in spirit*. The poor are those with few or no material possessions, whereas the "poor in spirit" are those with no baggage (attachments) of any kind. A person can be poor and yet have many obsessions. Alternatively, a person may have substantial possessions and yet little attachment (although this is rare).

The ninth key element of Zen is paradoxity. As you recall, the Cosmopolitan Girl teaches that "less is more" in sex. The statement is illogical, but most of us can understand what it means.

A paradox is a statement that seems to defy logic or common sense but is nevertheless true. A famous Zen koan goes like this: "If you have a stick, I will give you one. If you do not have a stick, I will take it away from you." Directly corresponding to this is Jesus' paradoxical expression: "For to him who has will more be given; and from him who has not, even what he has will be taken away" (Mark 4:25).

Zen paradoxes are not to be take lightly. For they have something important to tell us about the nature of reality. The understanding of them is a key to one's enlightenment and liberation. R. H. Blyth made this observation about them:

> A paradox is not a kind of pun, to be resolved by explaining the double meaning of the word. It does not spring from a desire to mystify the hearers or oneself. It arises from the inability of language to say two things at once. A doctor cuts off a leg causing pain and loss, which is evil, but saves a life, which is good. If we speak of the good-bad action, the mind unavoidably interprets this as partly good and partly bad. In this way music is greater than language. We can say two things at once, and the two separate melodies become one single indivisible harmony.[5]

Paradoxes tend to be ignored in our society because we live in
a world where rationality is king. Here it is important to note that
both Zen and Christianity seem to have a very anti-intellectual and
irrational tradition. There is a mystical saying of Jesus that is seldom quoted and rarely understood. Referring to the "intelligent"
men and women of the world, Jesus said, "I thank thee, Father, Lord
of heaven and earth, that thou hast hidden these things from the wise
and understanding and revealed them to babes; yea, Father, for such
was thy gracious will" (Matt. 11:25–26).

This is outrageously illogical and radically anti-establishment.
How can babes know things that the wise and the understanding
do not know? Was Jesus out of his mind? How could the unlearned
be better off than the learned? To the rational mind, this is pure
non-sense.

But such "craziness" is a consistent thread that runs through
the Christian tradition. The apostle Paul, for example, occasionally
talked like a mad Zen monk. Here is a sampler:

> Where is the wise man? Where is the scribe? Where is the debater of
> this age? Has not God made foolish the wisdom of the world? For
> since, in the wisdom of God, the world did not know God through
> wisdom, it pleased God through the folly of what we preach to save
> those who believe.... For the foolishness of God is wiser than men,
> and the weakness of God is stronger than men. (1 Cor 1:20–25)

Thus, the Zen world is a world of *poetic craziness*. It is a twilight
zone where knowledge becomes ignorance, folly becomes wisdom,
weakness becomes strength, and vice versa. Everyday logic simply
does not apply here.

The Buddhist tradition is not any less illogical. The Heart Sutra, a
Zen classic, opens with the statement that "form is emptiness, and
the very emptiness is form." The Diamond Sutra, another classic,
is even more blatantly illogical. It quotes Buddha saying that "the
dharma [truth] teacher has nothing to teach; precisely this is called
teaching the dharma." How outrageous! How crazy! Yet there is an
unmistakable sense of poetic beauty and a subtle ring of truth in
all these.

To understand this seemingly irrational side of Zen, we must
have some insight about the functioning of our intellect. As modern people, we are wary of various forms of addictions — addiction
to television, addiction to gambling, addiction to sex, addiction to

alcohol and drugs. But one thing that we seldom notice is our addiction to logical thinking, which can be very detrimental to our spiritual and mental health if we are not aware of its limitations and pitfalls.

The limitations and pitfalls of logic are best shown by some of the recent developments in computer science. The computer is the quintessential symbol of the rational-logical side of the human mind. Many of the scientific and technological advances made in this century would not have been possible without the aid offered by the computer. The computer is the modern hero with an indisputable track record. Its awesome accomplishments in the past have led scientists to strive to make it emulate even more of the brain functions. One of the more recent efforts has been to try to make the machine understand human language. Research in this area, named "artificial intelligence" (AI), is deemed to hold tremendous promise.

Unfortunately, artificial intelligence turns out to be a pie in the sky. After thirty years of research and billions of dollars have poured into these projects, our scientists are coming to realize that we have grossly underestimated the complexity of the problem. In one of these AI experiments, the English-language statement, "The spirit is willing, but the flesh is weak," was first translated into Russian, and then translated back into English. The outcome was "The vodka is agreeable, but the meat is too tender."

Such blunders highlight a key problem in logical thinking. Logic dictates that we think in an either-or mode: something can be either A or not-A, but not both. This, in turn, is a reflection of our rational mind, which tries to pigeonhole life into neat little boxes — classifying, labeling, and discriminating.

But the fact is that the real world is not "neat"; fuzziness is the way of nature. The computer, operating on a binary either-or mode, will not perform well on tasks involving ambiguities. While the machine has no problem projecting the trajectory of a spacecraft, it does have considerable difficulty handling even very simple conversations, which typically entail understanding multiple layers of meaning. As Steven Pinker, director of the Center for Cognitive Neuroscience at MIT, pointed out, "a robot can't tell that 'Mary had a little lamb' means only that she owned it, not that she ate it, gave birth to it or had an affair with it." The basic problem is one associated with the usage of logic in general, which is summarized by a logician as follows:

All traditional logic habitually assumes that precise symbols are being
employed. It is therefore not applicable to this terrestrial life, but only
to an imaginary celestial one. The law of excluded middle (A or not-
A) is true when precise symbols are employed but it is not true when
the symbols are vague (fuzzy), as, in fact, all symbols are.[6]

Unlike computers, Zen logic allows for fuzziness. It does not object to the coexistence of A and not-A. But it would be a grave
mistake to think that Zen masters are irrational people. Were they
not believers in rationality, they should not teach and they would
have nothing to teach. What the Zen masters are really getting at is to
inspire a higher logic that transcends the binary either-or world — a
logic that is more flexible and can allow for multiple interpretations
and possibilities. The problem with everyday logic is that it is too
rigid and cannot accommodate the fluidity and amorphous nature of
real life.

So Zen logic blatantly says that "A is not A." It is just another way
of saying that "things are not what they may seem" and that "the
conventional way of looking at A has no finality." Beyond its ingenious arguments and rude shocks, Zen does point to a deeper reality
beyond opposites and dualities where we may find our liberation.

Zen is about creativity. The heart of creativity is the realization
that there is more than one way to look at or to operate on the same
thing. Therefore, Zen masters use paradoxes to shock students into
seeing the world in radically unconventional ways. After all, enlightenment (*satori*) is a matter of creative visualization. In this sense, Zen
is both maverick and deviant. It is maverick because Zen has to be
practiced with an independent mind and not with a herd instinct. It is
deviant because the conventional way can never be taken for granted.
The Zen path is a lonely path that takes both courage and creativity
to tread.

Jesus praised the babes because their minds had not yet fossilized
into fixed modes of dualistic thinking. It is the *beginner's mind* that
can wonder, appreciate, and discover new possibilities.

Not enslaved by everyday logic, Jesus was an adept user of paradoxes. His Nature Sermon, for example, is effectively a hidden
paradox. On one hand, the birds and the lilies are at the mercy of the
laws of nature. Being exposed to the elements and other unknown
factors, they are prisoners of life. On the other hand, they can be
viewed as totally free — for they do not resist what reality dictates.

Thus, they are both free and not-free, depending on how we look at them.

The tenth key element of Zen is right-brain orientation. Art is not about thoughts. Rather, it is about seeing, listening, feeling, and touching. It prefers the concrete over the abstract. Philosopher George Santayana once remarked: "Art critics talk about art. Artists talk about where you can buy good turpentine." As we recall from Buddha's Wordless Sermon (the Sermon of the Flower), those who missed the point were those who were too busy thinking. Seeing and thinking do not go well together. True artists do not spend much time on talks or thoughts. They prefer to be absorbed in the concrete and direct experience of beauty instead of working with its abstractions.

This nonverbal and nonintellectual orientation of art (and Zen) can be more simply referred to as *right-brained*. According to recent findings in neuroscience, the left hemisphere of our brain controls our analytical, conceptual, linear, verbal, disciplined, and goal-oriented brain activities; they are called activities of the *intellect* and are critical in determining how effective we are in dealing with the external world. The right hemisphere of our brain, on the other hand, is responsible for our intuitive, visual, artistic, integrative, emotional, spontaneous, and holistic brain activities; they are referred to as the activities of the *unconscious*. The two categories of brain activities are complementary to each other. They are the *yin* and *yang* sides of our mind. A comparison between left-brain and right-brain activities is provided in the table on the following page.

The activities of the two hemispheres of the brain relate to spirituality in the following manner: The left brain is "masculine"; it is the seat of the ego and the hub of our external actions. Its character is to take charge, acquire, and dominate. Being goal-oriented and outward-seeking, it drives our will, desires, and ambitions. The right brain is "feminine"; it is the home of the soul. Its nature is to receive, imagine, balance, and adapt. Being inward-oriented, it enables us to feel, perceive, listen, and appreciate. Obviously, we need both types of capabilities in order to function well as human beings. Since most of the activities of people today are left-brained, Zen seeks to restore the balance by being right-brain-oriented, emphasizing nonverbal and integrative activities.

Because the Zen experience is right-brained in nature and cannot be verbalized, it tends to be mystified. It is, however, no more mystical than the feeling of the coolness of water on one's hand. Modern

LEFT-BRAIN VERSUS RIGHT-BRAIN
THINKING MODES

LEFT	*RIGHT*
Analytical	Synthetic
Precise	Fuzzy
Dichotomous	Holistic/relational
Systematic	Playful
Sequential	Simultaneous
Verbal	Nonverbal
Symbolic/abstract	Concrete
Rational/logical	Artistic/intuitive/emotional
Planned	Spontaneous
Goal-oriented	Process-oriented
Syntactical	Perceptual

master Shree Rajneesh talked about the Zen experience in the most ordinary terms:

> A distant call of the cuckoo...and for a moment you forget all your thoughts. The call of the cuckoo is so beautiful, so penetrating; it goes like an arrow into your heart. For a moment everything stops...and suddenly you have a taste of the Tao. You call it beauty because you don't know what it is. Yes, beauty is one of its aspects.... This night full of stars, you lying down on the grass looking at the sky, struck by the splendor of it — you call it splendor — that is another aspect of Tao. Listening to music, something stirs very deeply in your being; a synchronicity happens. You have become attuned to the music, a subtle dance arises in you. You call it music? You call it poetry? It is Tao, another aspect of Tao.[7]

The Zen experience is what happens when you lose yourself in the moment. It feels as if the whole world stops, and you have a supreme sense of harmony and peace. But in fact what actually stops is your ego-process. When the ego-process stops, so stop your expectations, desires, worries, and anxiety. Then you find yourself living in the present, overtaken by joy and filled with peace.

The Nature Sermon actually has two parts — one with words, one without. The part without words was taught by nature herself. Note that the sermon actually took place on a mountain. In the midst of natural beauty, Jesus asked his disciples to see and to contemplate what was present and real. Actually, no word is necessary. For nature soothes, heals, and teaches with her silence. All Jesus did was to let the right brains of his audience do their work — to listen, to see, to appreciate, and to be.

But for the benefit of those who were weak in their right-brain abilities, Jesus supplemented nature's silent lesson with his words. That was when he resorted to reason and logic to soothe and pacify. We should consider the verbal part and the nonverbal part of the sermon as being complementary, each lending strength to the other. It is here that we see Jesus' superb skill as a spiritual teacher.

The last key element of Zen is soulfulness. In order for something to be art, it has to go beyond the superficial. The key difference between beauty in art and prettiness is that the former has depth and the latter doesn't. What is art may not be pretty, and what is pretty may not be art. A true artist can coax beauty out of ugliness, just as a true Zen person can turn the mundane into spiritual. A key determinant of the art content of an object is its *soulfulness* — the degree that it reflects the inner life of the artist. For art is a process of self-discovery and self-expression.

This inward orientation is what distinguishes spirituality from religion. Though many people confuse the two, they are not the same thing. Often, religion is identified with a specific set of dogmas, beliefs, rules, and rituals. As such, it tends to be formal, institutional, and political in nature. Spirituality, on the other hand, has to do with what is deep and individual. It has less to do with what is imposed on us from the outside than what we bring out from within. In fact, many aspects of popular religions, to the extent that they are outward-seeking, are actually obstacles to true spirituality. Robert Linssen makes the following observation:

> The depth of the unconscious and of the conscious are to us the fertile soil into which the roots of our being must spread, in order to obtain the vivifying contact of its essence. It is a strictly individual process. All expectation from outside, all cult of authority, all hope of a miracle, are just so many elements which paralyse the development of our psychic roots towards the buried center which is the source of Life in us.[8]

Jesus emphasized the importance of this inward orientation when he asked rhetorically. "For what will it profit a man, if he gains the whole world and forfeits his soul? Or what shall a man give in return for his soul?" (Matt. 16:26). By contrasting the soul (*psuchē* in Greek) with the world, Jesus clarified that spiritual life has nothing to do with the acquisition of external things. Rather, it is an inner quest of finding and knowing one's true self. As Jesus pointed out elsewhere, it is within us that the kingdom lies. Again, we see the perfect agreement between Zen and Jesus' spirituality.

In a nutshell, Zen is about cutting through what is superfluous and peripheral and getting to what is truly important, which is self-knowledge. The key is to understand the seeker, who is constantly demanding gratification and happiness outside of the self. A story in the ancient Buddhist scriptures makes the same point:

> The Buddha was once seated under a tree on the way to Urela from Benares. On that day, thirty friends, all of them young princes, went out on a picnic with their young wives into the same forest. One of the princes who was unmarried brought a prostitute with him. While the others were amusing themselves, she purloined some objects of value and disappeared. In their search for her in the forest, they saw the Buddha seated under a tree and asked him whether he had seen a woman. He enquired what the matter was. When they explained, the Buddha asked them: "What do you think, young man? Which is better for you? To search after a woman, or to search after yourselves?"[9]

So, without further delay, let our search begin!

— Three —

The Magic Kingdom

The kingdom of God is not coming with signs to be observed.
                                                              —LUKE 17:20

If you approach it, you will certainly miss it.
                                                              —NAN CHUAN

Have you ever wondered about that familiar stranger, time? To see the beauty of the kingdom, one has to develop an appreciation for the wonder of time. But what is time? When people asked St. Augustine of Hippo this question, he answered: "I know what it is, but when you ask me I don't know." Amazingly, the most familiar and ordinary things often turn out to be difficult philosophical puzzles.

Albert Einstein told us that our notion of time as an absolute is just an illusion. Other scientists and philosophers have concluded that time has no objective reality. German philosopher Immanuel Kant remarked: "Time is not something objective. It is neither substance nor accident nor relation, but a subjective condition necessary owing to the nature of the human mind."

This is most interesting: time as a phenomenon of the mind. But perhaps it is not such a strange notion when we consider that for thousands of years Hinduists and Buddhists have consistently treated everything as a creation of the mind and that the modern quantum physicists are finding that there may not be such a thing as "objective reality" (i.e., a reality independent of consciousness) at all!

We are used to dividing time into past, present, and future, with the present being the dividing line between the past and the future. "The present," of course, is as elusive as a phantom. The moment I say "Now," the nowness is gone. The Chinese philosopher Chuang

Tzu commented: "Just when the sun is in the middle of the sky, it is no longer in the middle of the sky." Time tends to be self-contradictory. There is always this fuzziness about the now-moment. But if the present moment cannot be well defined, it means that the past and the future cannot be well defined either.

Jesus, the great mystic and poet, said, "Truly, truly, I say to you, before Abraham was, I am" (John 8:58). He fully appreciated the mystery of the now-moment. His statement does not seem to distinguish between the past and the present.

There are at least two kinds of time: *clock time* and *psychological time*. The latter has a direct bearing on spirituality and is the focus of our foregoing discussion.

Recall a moment when you had an experience of immense joy. During that experience, were you aware of time? Can joy and time coexist?

I have always been intrigued by the elasticity of time. In the last few years, I have given many public talks and seminars. One thing that I have noticed is that in a good talk, I tend to lose my time awareness. By "good," I mean those instances where I feel so comfortable that the talk evolves into some sort of *play:* I "play" with my material, I "play" with my audience. When I finally look at my watch, I cannot believe my eyes. On other occasions, however, time seems to be a crawling snail. It is very temperamental.

Thus, time seems either to speed up or to slow down, depending on our inner state. Consider the common expression: "Time flies when you're having fun." Conversely, time drags when you're bored. In Chinese and Japanese folklore we find a common theme that is eerily similar to Einsteinian time-travel: A young man goes into a magic mountain for a few days and becomes shocked when he returns to the mundane world. He discovers that dynasties have changed and his contemporaries are now all white-haired and toothless. It was once said that a day in heaven is equal to ten years on earth. Apparently, the speed of time depends on where you are.

To live in God's kingdom is to live in eternity. So let us first find out what eternity means. Many people take eternity to mean a very long duration of time. But is this true? Is eternity the indefinite extension of time? Jesus offers us some insight on this subject:

> The same day Sadducees came to him, who say that there is no resurrection; and they asked him a question, saying, "Teacher, Moses said, 'If a man dies, having no children, his brother must marry the widow,

and raise up children for his brother.' Now there were seven brothers among us; the first married, and died, and having no children left
his wife to his brother. So too the second and third, down to the seventh. After them all, the woman died. In the resurrection, therefore,
to which of the seven will she be wife? For they all had her."

But Jesus answered them, "You are wrong, because you know neither the scriptures nor the power of God. *For in the resurrection they
neither marry nor are given in marriage, but are like angels in heaven.*
And as for the resurrection of the dead, have you not read what was
said to you by God, 'I am the God of Abraham, and the God of
Isaac, and the God of Jacob'? *He is not the God of the dead, but of
the living.*" And when the crowd heard it, they were astonished at his
teaching. (Matt. 22:23–33)

We must first have some background about this story. Before Jesus
was questioned by the Sadducees, he was also questioned by the
Pharisees. The two groups represented the religious establishment
at the time. The Sadducees were fewer in number, representing the
wealthy and educated religious elite. Compared to the Pharisees, the
Sadducees were more conservative in their Jewish belief; they accepted the authority of only the first five books of the Old Testament
(the Pentateuch). While the Pharisees believed in the existence of
an afterlife, the Sadducees denied it because they saw no convinc-
ing evidence from the Pentateuch to support it. The Pharisees were
more "liberal" in these matters; not only did they believe in afterlife,
they also believed in the bodily resurrection of the dead. They would
even argue among themselves whether the dead will be clothed or
unclothed when they do resurrect.

In an attempt to ridicule the Pharisees' doctrine of bodily resurrection, the Sadducees asked Jesus this question: Whose wife would
a woman be in the resurrection, given that she had been married to
seven different men while living? And Jesus answered that "in the resurrection they neither marry nor are given in marriage, but are like
angels in heaven."

What did Jesus mean by his answer? Was he confirming or refuting
the existence of an afterlife? The problem is that no one really knows
what it is like to be "like angels in heaven"! So where does this leave
us? Was Jesus trying to tell us something about the kingdom of God
and the nature of eternity?

From a Zen perspective, it would be helpful to meditate on Jesus'
answer for a few days and not jump to any quick conclusion. Muse
over it and see what you can come up with.

You might be surprised to discover that this sermon of Jesus on resurrection and afterlife is the equivalent of Buddha's Sermon of the Flower discussed before. Remember how Buddha simply held up the flower without saying a word? To answer that there is or that there is not an afterlife is to miss the point entirely. The proper response to the question is not to think!

During Buddha's time, many spiritual people came to him and asked various metaphysical questions: Does the world have an end or not? Do saints exist or not exist after their death? Is there a boundary to the universe? In these situations, Buddha's typical response was to maintain a golden silence; mum was the answer. The Buddha refused to answer them because they are *questions that tend not to edification.* In one instance, a seeker by the name of Malunkyaputta asked a series of such questions, and Buddha replied: "The religious life, Malunkyaputta, does not depend on the dogma that the world has an end, nor on the dogma that it does not have an end."

Jesus said that "in the resurrection they neither marry nor are given in marriage, but are like angels in heaven." A word of caution is in order here: whenever we hear Jesus speak, we have to pay close attention. Look for the twinkle in his eye or the secretive smile on his face. Just like any Zen master, Jesus can be quite "naughty" in his way of teaching. What does it mean to be "like angels in heaven"? We may think until the day we die and still not have an answer.

Mercifully, Jesus also dropped us some hints: "He is not God of the dead, but of the living." Why worry about matters of the dead now? And how can we find out whether there is afterlife while we are still living?

This question about afterlife actually turns out to be one of Jesus' greatest koans, and there is no solution to it. The koan is similar to the one brought up by Buddha in his Sermon of the Flower. Its purpose was simply to get the students frustrated in trying to come up with an answer. For it is only when they were exhausted would they finally realize that it is futile even to think about such matters.

Thinking is not the way to the Tao; the Tao is "approached" through not thinking. All sages and mystics agree on this point. When asked about the afterlife, Confucius answered: "If even matters of the living cannot be fully known, why bother yourself with matters of the dead?"

The kingdom is the state of joy, but joy vanishes once one starts thinking unproductive thoughts. We have already mentioned that spirituality has to do with living in the moment. Consider this:

> A man was dating a woman whom he fell in love with. In the middle of a candlelit dinner, charmed by soft music, he asked his companion: "When can I see you again?"

What happened here? A beautiful moment assassinated by a nasty little thought! The couple were bathed in an atmosphere of serenity and love until the disturbing thought entered. With that all is lost; joy turns into anxiety.

The kingdom is in the *thoughtless zone.* Quality living begins with the ending of our addiction to the left-brain. It is not necessary, however, to deliberately try to stop thoughts. For the attempt to stop thoughts is itself "thought-provoking." To tell someone not to think of a pink elephant, for example, is to create the opposite effect. So stop thinking about stopping thoughts. Just immerse yourself in the task at hand, whatever it is: washing dishes, doing homework, cutting grass, making love....

To live in the *thoughtless zone* is the same as to live in the *timeless zone.* There is no time if there is no thought. Therefore, the kingdom of God is also called eternity. Eternity is not the indefinite extension of time; it is the disappearance of time.

Have you ever wondered why some perfectly sensible people nevertheless engage in risky sports? What exactly is the appeal of mountaineering, car racing, scuba diving, and testing of fighter aircraft? If you ask these risk-lovers why they get into these potentially life-threatening situations, they will answer that these experiences are exhilarating: they cheer, enliven, excite, refresh, and bring us a sense of power and joy. What most people are not aware of, however, is that on a deeper level these high-risk, high-stake endeavors are *spiritual* in nature. They provide an opportunity for us to catch a glimpse of eternity. Lucy Oliver, a teacher of spontaneous meditation, provides us with this insight:

> What compels people towards all kinds of challenging, dangerous or emotionally demanding pursuits is that, under extreme conditions, the normal modes of functioning which shield us from immensity may cut out. Such situations knock out personality and force people to the edge of themselves, the edge of endurance or the edge of death where something else takes over. The results are well documented: a surge of power; renewal of energy; an opening out into a space of clarity, insight, carefreeness and detachment; intimations of immense

potential, of joy, of peace, of feeling more alive. These states are of ultimate value to those who encounter them.[1]

So perhaps these high-risk games and challenging sports are the Western way of meditation. By forcing us to be fully engaged in the situation, they satisfy our highest need: the need for self-actualization. According to humanist psychologist Abraham Maslow, "self-actualization" means "experiencing fully, vividly, selflessly, with full concentration and total absorption."

It should be noted that such intense experiences are exhilarating because they enable us to forget ourselves. Ordinarily, we tend to clutch on to our ego: we try our utmost to bolster it, gratify it, and defend it. Few of us realize that the secret of happiness is in letting go. The forgetting of self means the ending of thoughts, which in turn means the dissolution of psychological time. When this happens, it is as if the world has come to a standstill and we experience a glorious moment of bliss. Abraham Maslow refers to these transient moments of egolessness as "peak experiences." They are fleeting glances of the kingdom.

But we should not think of peak experiences as rare occurrences enjoyed only by meditation practitioners, world-class athletes, and players of high-risk games. The empirical research of Abraham Maslow shows that they are actually rather commonplace. Maslow conducted his research by asking his subjects these questions: What is the single most joyous, happiest, most blissful moment of your whole life? How did you feel differently about yourself at that time? How did the world look different? How did you change if you did? He found that peak experiences can be triggered by rather ordinary events and that the two easiest ways of getting peak experiences are through music and through sex. These are the common folks' doorways to the eternal. With regard to sex, Maslow has the following insight:

> I am sure that one day we will not giggle over it [sex], but will take it quite seriously and teach children that like music, like love, like insight, like a beautiful meadow, like a cute baby, or whatever, that there are many pathways to heaven, and sex is one of them, and music is one of them. These happen to be the easiest ones, the most widespread, and the ones that are easiest to understand.[2]

Sex means different things to different people. To some, it means something filthy that has to be avoided at all cost. To others, it means another situation where "performance" is required; hence the popularity of aphrodisiacs, sex manuals, how-to videos. To me, however, sex means total let-go. It is the abolishment of ego. It is only when we abolish our ego that we can really enjoy ourselves. Have you ever heard of anyone who gets pleasure out of sex while his or her "performance" is constantly monitored? Shree Rajneesh, a creative modern master, has this advice: "Approach the sexual act as if you are approaching the temple of the divine." This means reverence and complete surrender. For eternity is the death of the ego.

Unfortunately, most of us do not think of the kingdom this way. For many "religious" people, the kingdom is otherworldly and a matter of eager anticipation. In traditional Jewish theology, the arrival of the kingdom, the advent of the Messiah, and the resurrection of the just and unjust are tied together as one single historical event that is supposed to happen in the "latter end of the days." That is why many people are interested in finding out when "the end" will come. The following passage shows how Jesus approached the issue:

> Being asked by the Pharisees when the kingdom of God was coming, he answered them, "The kingdom of God is not coming with signs to be observed; nor will they say, 'Lo, here it is!' or 'There!' for behold, the kingdom of God is in the midst of you." (Luke 17:20–21)

Here we can see clearly how radical Jesus' position is. For him, the kingdom is not an event to be anticipated; it is in the here-and-now. Precisely this is the "good news": the kingdom is already here! It is not a promise; it is a present reality. Jesus said that "the kingdom of God is in the midst of you." This means that we are currently living in it. But whether we are aware of it is another matter.

A beautiful parallel is seen in the conversation between two famous Zen masters, Chao Chou and Nan Chuan:

> Chao Chou asked Nan Chuan, "What is the Tao?"
> Nan Chuan answered, "The ordinary mind is the Tao."
> Chao Chou pressed further, "How can one approach it?"
> "If you want to approach it, you will certainly miss it," Nan Chuan replied.
> But Chao Chou countered, "If you do not approach it, how do you know it is the Tao?"
> Nan Chuan answered, "The Tao is not a matter of knowing, nor a matter of not knowing. To know is a delusory way of thinking, and not to know is insensitive. If one can realize the Tao unmistakably,

his mind will be like the great space — vast, void and clear. How then can one regard this as either right or wrong?"

Upon hearing the remark, Chao Chou was immediately awakened.[3]

Jesus said that the kingdom of God is "in the midst of you." This means that it cannot be sought. We can seek only what we don't have. For things we already have, why seek? In fact, it is the seeking that obstructs our path toward the eternal — for it reinforces the ego. Remember, Beauty can be experienced only in the timeless, thoughtless zone where ego disappears.

But many people are still seeking the kingdom because they do not recognize its immediate presence — right now — in our midst. Such pursuits are futile. The situation is like a fish in the ocean looking for water, not realizing that it is already surrounded by it! How odd that the closer something is to us, the more difficult it is for us to detect it!

Jesus neither confirmed nor denied the existence of afterlife. The kingdom means the ending of thoughts. Both assertion and denial imply thoughts. Zen transcends both dualities. The kingdom of God is in the *thoughtless zone,* out of reach of the rational/logical mind, which cannot break the habit of thinking in either-or terms.

On the surface, Jesus appeared to be answering people's questions about the kingdom. But in reality he pointed to a greater truth. Given that all these questions are misframed, to answer one way or another is ludicrous. If you were to ask me whether a certain table is male or female, the only appropriate response that I can make is to laugh. No discussion or debate on this subject will be worthwhile. As the ancient philosopher Chuang Tzu observed, "It is futile to talk snow with a summer insect that has never seen it."

The kingdom is not a matter of thought. As such, it is not a matter of time either (for there is no time without thought). Yet traditionally people have been talking about it as if it were an event in the future. Why?

The answer is simple. The kingdom is always conceived to be a future event because it is a habit of the left brain to live in the future and not in the present. Bhagwan Shree Rajneesh gives a beautiful diagnosis of the situation:

Human mind disappears in the present. It lives in the future, in the hope, in the promise of the future; it moves through desire. Desire needs time, desire cannot exist if there is no time. If suddenly you come to a moment where you realize that the time has disappeared, now there is no time, no tomorrow, what will happen to your desire? It cannot move, it disappears with time.[4]

The kingdom of heaven — in the midst of us — is the land of bliss where there is no greed, lust, anger, fear. But how can we enter it? Jesus unlocked the door, by showing us that there is no door, in the following passage from the Gospel of Luke:

> Now, as they went on their way, he entered a village; and a woman named Martha received him into her house. And she had a sister called Mary, who sat at the Lord's feet and listened to his teaching. But Martha was distracted with much serving; and she went to him and said, "Lord, do you not care that my sister has left me to serve alone? Tell her then to help me."
>
> But the Lord answered her, "Martha, Martha, you are anxious and troubled about many things; one thing is needful. Mary has chosen the good portion, which shall not be taken away from her." (Luke 10:38–41)

Here again Jesus was teaching the art of living. The one thing that Mary had that Martha did not have was *concentration.* The art of living, just like other arts, requires concentration. To be an artist, one has to lose oneself in art. Without losing oneself, one simply cannot truly listen, see, or be. Jesus praised Mary because she listened — she paid attention *without effort* on the now-moment. When one is aware of the moment, there is no thought and no time. One is in the kingdom.

On the other hand, Martha was distracted. Because she was busy with various worldly matters, she did not pay attention to the moment. As a result, all kinds of thoughts and anxiety troubled her. Jesus told Martha that while she might have many things on her mind, only one thing is needful: to concentrate on the task at hand.

Many of us think that in order to enter the kingdom we have to fight the anger, violence, and lust within our mind. But Jesus taught a much different method: living in the moment. When one is truly focused on the task at hand, no negative emotions can arise.

The kingdom exists in the timeless zone. The practical implication of this is that happiness is not a product of time. Master Jesus revealed a big secret: the gateway to eternity is to be found in the moment. Most of us, however, think of happiness as materializing in time. This misconception is the cause for much misery.

In the seventy-fifth anniversary issue of *Forbes* magazine, the editors asked several of America's best-known writers and scholars to do some soul-searching and try to answer this question: "Why do Americans feel so bad when they have got it so good?" Undoubtedly, we have a higher material standard of living in this country than most other people on earth. But why aren't we happier?

Peggie Noonan, former speechwriter for Ronald Reagan and George Bush, responded: "We have lost the old knowledge that happiness is overrated — that, in a way, life is overrated. Our ancestors believed in two worlds, and understood this to be the solitary, poor, nasty, brutish and short one. We are the first generations of man that actually expected to find happiness here on earth, and our search for it has caused such — unhappiness."[5]

Noonan's answer reflects the position of traditional religions. This earthly life is renounced and the emphasis is shifted from the here-and-now to the future. But are life and happiness overrated? Or is hope overrated? Postponing the good times to the great beyond may be a good tactic. For who among the living can refute it? But the prospect of living this life as a "solitary, poor, nasty, brutish and short one" is not so palatable for most of us. There has to be a better alternative.

Hope can be a problem by itself. The mainstream American culture, for example, is a culture of hope, as represented by the "American dream." To share in the American dream means to live in the future. While the American dream seems to have worked well for the baby-boom generation, the current economic situation is proving that such a dream may be a problem for their children. Many young Americans are finding their dream demolished by harsh economic realities — unemployment after college, decreasing number of job openings, declining standards of living, and massive layoffs. The great promise of unlimited progress turns out to be empty. It is now time to awaken from our dreams!

In fact, the question posed by *Forbes* magazine was answered many years ago by psychologist Erich Fromm in his book *To Have or to Be*. Fromm identified two fundamental modes of human experience: "having" and "being." In the mode of "having," the individual craves to acquire something: money, material goods, prestige, "success," etc. Modern society puts a high premium on ambition and aggressiveness. The alternative mode of experience is "being," in which one is not enslaved by cravings but "is joyous, employs one's faculties productively, and is *oned* to the world."[6] Unfortunately, many of us have lost the *art of being* in the modern world.

David Meyers, a clinical psychologist, was commissioned by *Psychology Today* to research the nature of happiness. After hundreds of interviews and questionnaires, Meyers summarized his findings as follows:

> Realize that enduring happiness doesn't come from "making it." What are you looking for? Fame? Fortune? Unlimited leisure? Imagine that I could snap my finger and give it to you. Would you now be happy? Indeed, you'd be euphoric, in the short run. But gradually you would adapt to your new circumstances and life would return to its normal mix of emotions. To recover the joy, you would now need an even higher high. The consistent finding from dozens of studies is that objective life circumstances, once we've adapted to them, bear little relation to people's happiness....
>
> Ergo, wealth is like health: Although its utter absence breeds misery (consider Somalia), having it is no guarantee of happiness. There is no need to envy the rich. Happiness is less a matter of getting what you want than wanting what you have.[7]

We cannot acquire our way to happiness because we invariably lose interest in whatever we have acquired. What is needed is the ability to "want what we have," which is precisely the art of being. Happiness is not a thing to be acquired; it is an *ability*.

For this reason, the kingdom cannot be a matter of anticipation. Rather, it is the ending of the hopeless illusion that happiness can be gained through acquisition. True happiness has to do with accepting and appreciating *what is*. To live in the kingdom is to be joyously "hopeless" and live in the moment. It begins with savoring the "small things" in life. Meyers illustrates:

> To live in the present means, for me, taking delight in the day's magic moment, from morning tea and cereal, hunched over a manuscript, to the day's last moments, snuggling and talking with my wife. Happiness isn't somewhere off in the future, but is the morning's phone conversation with someone seeking advice, in this noon's meal with a friend, in the evening's bedtime story with a child, in tonight's curling up with a good book.[8]

Jesus said, "Before Abraham was, I am." The present tense indicates a here-and-now orientation, which is critical for happiness.

In the beginning of Jesus' ministry, he proclaimed: "Repent, for the kingdom of heaven is at hand" (Matt. 4:17). Most people interpret this proclamation as a threat, translating it as: "Clean up your acts, or else...." " But this interpretation is wrong. The Greek word for repentance is *metanoia,* which means not so much being sorry as "changing your heart." If our treasure is where our heart is, then finding the kingdom means putting our heart back into what is clearly at hand. This means a full commitment to the eternal now.

It is precisely here that the practice of Zen is different from the practice of traditional religions. It is not a matter of replacing certain mundane goals with spiritual goals. *The practice of Zen has no goal at all!* Real Zen practice is simply accepting and appreciating what is. For the kingdom is not something far away that has yet to be earned. It is the present reality.

Four

Zen: The Art of Seeing

This is it.
—ZEN SAYING

I have overcome the world.
—JESUS

In the last chapter, we discussed the art of being. Mastering the art of being requires the ability to live in the moment, without formulating any hope, demand, or expectations about the future. It is a beautiful experience. The problem is that not everybody can yet do it, certainly not "all the time."

Zen is also the art of *seeing*. For those who find the art of being too difficult, Zen offers this as an alternative practice. William Shakespeare observed that "there is nothing either good or bad, but thinking makes it so." This agrees perfectly with what we said in chapter 2 above, "What Is Zen? (II)": that nature is by nature fuzzy. In chapter 21 of the *Tao Te Ching*, Lao Tzu offers the following insight:

> The nature of the Tao is fuzzy and indeterminate.
> Fuzzy and indeterminate, yet there is form.
> Indeterminate and fuzzy, yet there is substance.

"Religious" people are rarely comfortable associating the concept of fuzziness with their religion. For fuzziness is too closely related to doubt, uncertainty, and the whole "can of worms." Organized religions prefer to project an image of solidity. One of the Christian hymns that I sang as a child is titled "Rock of Ages." But the Tao is fuzzy and indeterminate. To see this, all we have to do is to pay attention to the way we interact with ordinary things.

Data about the external world have no meaning to us until they are processed, filtered, organized, and interpreted by our mind. Reality, therefore, is a function of its observer. When a red apple is presented to a man and a dog, the man will see the redness but the dog will not because it is color-blind. Color is the result of an extraneous condition (the existence of color sensors in the observer) and not an intrinsic property of the apple.

Sound is also a function of its observer. What is the "sound" of a falling tree if there is no one around to hear it? In the absence of a listener, the tree will still fall, but its "sound" will be indeterminate. Sound is not an inherent property of a falling tree. "Loudness" is equally fuzzy; it is a function of how sensitive our ears are. As we all know, hearing acuteness varies widely within the animal kingdom. It is not difficult to imagine that for some animal with supersensitive hearing organs, the humming of a mosquito can sound like an airplane and the chewing of a little caterpillar on a leaf can sound like a pack of hungry tigers having their meals. It is all relative.

Thus, none of the "ordinary" sights, sounds, tastes, and smells that we know of are really that ordinary. When we realize that none of them are intrinsic properties of the "thing-in-itself," we might start to wonder what "reality" is like. What is "reality" if what is perceived depends on who the perceiver is? Indeed, reality is "fuzzy" because we all seem to live in our idiosyncratic universes, looking at the world through our personal lenses.

While "religious" people treat fuzziness as a liability, Zen people treat it as an asset. For this fuzziness of nature, combined with the creativity innate in the human mind, translates into opportunities for our liberation. If the world is indeterminate, then we can use our creativity to interpret it in a way that fosters inner peace and enables spiritual growth. As we shall see, enlightenment is largely a matter of *creative visualization.*

As a teenager I was impressed by graphic art works that generate visual illusions or lend themselves to multiple interpretations. A well-known example is the "Mistress or Wife?" drawing produced by American psychologist E. G. Boring. Depending on how we focus our attention, we may either see a beautiful young woman or an old hag. The "Mistress or Wife?" drawing illustrates how our mind can operate on the same set of visual data to create two contradictory, but equally valid, images. It is a beautiful way to visualize the concept of *paradox,* the coexistence of opposites.

MISTRESS OR WIFE?

I don't want to sound flippant about it, but *satori* (enlightenment) is essentially one of these mental flips on our picture of reality. Of course, there are also important differences between the mental flip in *satori* and that in visual art. The former is existential and spontaneous whereas the latter is visual and can be self-initiated. An in-depth discussion of the *satori* experience will be provided in the next chapter.

Spiritual awakening comes when we develop a radically new perspective on life. Zen is primarily concerned with creative visualization, which means changing our old habits of seeing the world. Among the modern artists, M. C. Escher and René Magritte are two of the most prominent pioneers of visual Zen. Their works represent an open invitation to explore the richness of "alternative realities." Escher, in particular, loves to experiment with visual paradoxes, illusions, and double meaning. Most of his works are pictures that can be interpreted in many different, yet equally valid, ways. They are ideal for dissolving our mental rigidity.

It is important to realize that fuzziness and paradoxes appear not only in theories and art work. They also have tremendous applicability in real life. I learned the art of flipping the hard way. I used to have a difficult boss. He was authoritarian and unreasonable in his demands. Working for him was an ordeal. The situation was so unpleasant that I contemplated quitting my job on several occasions. It did not turn around until I learned about the secret of the "reverse bodhisattva."

In the Buddhist Mahayanist sutras, bodhisattvas are portrayed as enlightened beings who possess great powers. They are also very compassionate: they have vowed to dedicate their lives to helping others. But while most bodhisattvas are like angels, there is a special class of them called "reverse bodhisattvas." Although equally compassionate at heart, the "reverse bodhisattvas" have terrible appearances and their mission is to enlighten others through creating difficulties, challenges, and hardships. Once I learned about this special class of bodhisattvas, I immediately applied what I had learned to the situation at hand; I "flipped" my boss into a bodhisattva and visualized him as a compassionate being who was inflicting hardships on me for my own good. I started to take the difficulties he created for me as spiritual practices designed to help me reach new heights and enhance my spiritual growth.

Of course, I did not tell my boss that I had flipped him. But the strategy worked. I was able to relax myself much more and take difficulties in a constructive manner. That was not all; my boss also left very shortly afterward. I could not figure out whether it was because he could not take my new attitude, but it doesn't matter.

To a certain degree, we determine whether we want to be happy or sad, because it is up to us to decide how to interpret the world. The same reality can be viewed as either heaven or hell. As the French essayist Montaigne observed: "A man is not hurt so much by what happened as by his opinion of what happened."

This is precisely why we said in the last chapter that the kingdom is in the here-and-now. Reality is neither good or bad; it is a matter of how we choose to perceive it. For someone who has mastered the art of seeing, the world is *always* perfect. External reality does not have to change in order to make us happy. The secret lies in changing our perception of it. Happiness is a matter of *inner alchemy*, a transformation of the way we see the world.

Dale Carnegie, the popular American psychologist, illustrated the principles of inner alchemy through a real-life story provided by a woman named Thelma Thompson. Thelma related to us how she managed to turn a minus into a plus:

> During the war, my husband was stationed at an Army training camp near the Mojave Desert in California. I went to live there in order to be near him. My husband was ordered out on maneuvers in the Mojave Desert, and I was left in a tiny shack alone. The heat was unbearable — 125 degrees in the shade of a cactus. Not a soul to talk to. The wind blew incessantly, and all the food I ate, and the very air I breathed, were filled with sand, sand, sand!
>
> I was so utterly wretched, so sorry for myself, that I wrote to my parents. I told them I was giving up and coming back home. I said I couldn't stand it one minute longer. I would rather be in jail! My father answered my letter with just two lines — two lines which will always sing in my memory — two lines that completely altered my life:
>
> > Two men looked out from prison bars,
> > One saw the mud, the other saw the stars.[1]

Inspired by her father, Thelma turned her living hell into a living paradise by taking the initiative to make friends with the natives of the desert, developing a genuine interest in their lives and culture. She also discovered a new world of wonder by learning about prairie dogs, watching for the desert sunset, and hunting for seashells that had been left there millions of years ago when the sands of the desert had been an ocean floor. Not only was Thelma able to turn her own situation around; she also became a teacher of "ordinary magic." She told us of her discoveries and insights:

> What brought about the astonishing change in me? The Mojave Desert hadn't changed. But I had. I had changed my attitude of mind. And by doing so, I transformed a wretched experience into the most exciting adventure of my life.... I had looked out of my self-created prison and found the stars.[2]

Dale Carnegie concluded that what Thelma discovered was a truth that the Greeks taught five hundred years before Christ was born: "The best things are the most difficult." This also happens to be a teaching of Zen.

Master Jesus, also a "flipper," taught the art of internal alchemy extensively throughout the Gospels. The reason that most of us are not aware of this is because he used a different terminology: "being born anew." The phrase, while a familiar one in this country, has unfortunately been much vulgarized. Many people describe themselves as "born-again Christians." The American Heritage Dictionary defines a born-again person as someone who "has made a conversion or renewed a commitment to Jesus Christ as personal savior." Taking this as the definition, certain Christian groups have divided the human race into two categories: those who are "born again" and those who are not. Their understanding is that only those "born again" are entitled to eternal life while those who are not are condemned to eternal suffering.

Jesus did not see the matter this way. For him, whether someone is "born anew" or not is a matter of spiritual awakening and not a matter of religious belief. The original passage that introduces the concept can be found in St. John:

> Now there was a man of the Pharisees, named Nicodemus, a ruler of the Jews. This man came to Jesus by night and said to him, "Rabbi, we know that you are a teacher come from God; for no one can do these signs that you do, unless God is with him." Jesus answered him, "Truly, truly, I say to you, unless one is born of water and the Spirit, he cannot enter the kingdom of God. That which is born of flesh is flesh, and that which is born of the Spirit is spirit. Do not marvel that I said to you, 'You must be born anew.' The wind blows where it wills, and you hear the sound of it, but you do not know whence it comes or whither it goes; so it is with every one who is born of the Spirit."
>
> Nicodemus said to him, "How can this be?" Jesus answered him, "Are you a teacher of Israel, and yet you do not understand this? Truly, truly, I say to you, we speak of what we know, and bear witness to what we have seen; but you do not receive our testimony. If I have told you earthly things and you do not believe, how can you believe if I tell you heavenly things? No one has ascended into heaven but he who descended from heaven, the Son of man. And as Moses lifted up the serpent in the wilderness, so must the Son of man be lifted up, that whoever believes in him may have eternal life." (John 3:1–15)

"Being born anew" means spiritual awakening. Jesus compares the enlightenment experience to the wind that "blows where it wills, and you hear the sound of it, but you do not know whence it comes or whither it goes." Baptism, for Jesus, is not a religious ceremony but a spontaneous event; it cannot be controlled or predicted. Just like the wind, it has to come by itself. The parallel between Jesus' version of spiritual awakening and Zen's can be seen in the following quotation from Zen scholar D. T. Suzuki:

Satori comes upon a man unawares, when he feels that he has exhausted his whole being. Religiously, it is a new birth; intellectually, it is the acquisition of a new viewpoint. The world now appears as if dressed in a new garment, which seems to cover up all the unsightliness of dualism, which is called delusion in Buddhist phraseology.[3]

Nicodemus, a representative of the religious establishment of Jesus' time, opened his discussion with Jesus by commenting that "no one can do these signs that you do." This opening statement marks the main difference between Jesus' vision of the kingdom and that of the traditional mind. The traditional mind sees the kingdom as an *external* event in history, preceded by various supernatural signs. But spiritual awakening requires a much deeper kind of seeing, which is not possible without the opening of one's spiritual eye. Jesus mentioned specifically that the kingdom of God is not coming with signs to see and that it is in our midst (Luke 17:20).

Jesus' usage of the verb "see" in this context has a very deep and special meaning. For herein lies the entire secret of the kingdom: that it has already arrived, and indeed it is in the here-and-now. *This is it!* Therefore, all one has to do is to *see* its beauty. As you recall, in my dealing with my old boss, I did not have to change him physically. All I had to do was to visualize him differently. The biggest mistake that people make about the kingdom is to believe that it is something that has yet to come. For "baptism by the Spirit" is, by itself, the realization of the kingdom. As John Marsh observes, "Spiritual begetting enables a man to see the presence of eternity in time, the end in the historical, the divine itself in the human flesh of Christ."[4] One is instantaneously born into the new world!

The closest Buddhist equivalent to the kingdom of God is nirvana. Buddha referred to nirvana as the *Unconditioned,* the *Ungrown,* and the *Unborn.* As Buddhist scholar Edward Conze has pointed out, "When we compare the attributes of the Godhead as they are understood by the more mystical tradition of Christian thought with those of Nirvana, we find no difference at all."[5] But just like many Christians have mistaken the kingdom as a future reward to be earned through merit, many Buddhists think of nirvana as a matter of achievement, to be realized by the spiritual practitioner after years and years of hard work. To correct this common misconception, Buddhist teacher Walpola Rahula offers us the following insight:

It is incorrect to think that Nirvana is the natural result of the ex-
tinction of craving. *Nirvana is not the result of anything.* If it were
a result, it would be an effect produced by a cause. It would be
samkhata, "produced" and "conditioned." Nirvana is neither cause
nor effect. . . . It is not produced like a mystic, spiritual, mental state,
such as *dhyana* or *samadhi.* TRUTH IS. NIRVANA IS. The only thing
you can do is to see it, to realize it. There is a path leading to the realization of Nirvana. But Nirvana is not the result of this path. You can
go to the mountain along a path, but the mountain is not the result.[6]

For Jesus, the kingdom is the present reality. This is where he
broke with the Old Testament tradition. The traditional mentality
says, "Let's wait for it." But Jesus was effectively saying, "Look! It
has already arrived!" The dualistic two-world view where the present
world and the kingdom are seen as separate is replaced by a holistic
one-world view where *this* world is the kingdom. However, in order
to really see this, one needs the gift of the Spirit. Jesus elaborates:
"Unless one is born of water and the Spirit, he cannot enter the kingdom of God." Here a little historical background may help. Jesus'
predecessor, John the Baptist, baptized people with water, which is
a symbol for purification. But purification alone is not adequate for
spiritual awakening. There is a missing element: *spirit.*

In the Christian theology of the Trinity, the Spirit is the third
person of God. While the Father is the creator of the universe and
the Son is God incarnate (the point where infinity meets with the
finite world), the Spirit is the bringer of truth. Jesus told his disciples that "when the Spirit of truth comes, he will guide you into
all truth" (John 16:13). Elsewhere he also referred to the Spirit as
the Counselor (John 14:16). Spirit and truth always go together. We
may, therefore, think of the Spirit as the personification of wisdom.
Nicodemus could not see truth because his wisdom had not yet been
awakened.

The story of Nicodemus has multiple layers of spiritual meaning.
On one hand, it seems that Nicodemus's question stems from his personal concern about eternal life. On the other hand, Nicodemus is
also a spokesman for the religious establishment. The traditional belief is that the kingdom of God will not be realized until the closing
of this age, marked by the arrival of the Messiah. In this context,
Nicodemus's question may be interpreted in this way: "How can the
kingdom be the present reality? Aren't we supposed to wait?" In response to this, Jesus answered that "as Moses lifted up the serpent

in the wilderness, so must the 'Son of man' be lifted up, and that whoever believes in him may have eternal life."

Many Christians do not see anything profound in this reply of Jesus because they are so accustomed to the traditional view of treating Jesus as a deity. To them, the "lifting up of the Son of man" simply means the worship of Jesus as crucified savior (lifted upon the cross) and as the one and only Son of God. Thus, the statement can be translated into something like: "Believe in Jesus and earn eternal life." But the problem with this interpretation is that if this is really what Jesus meant, then why couldn't he be more direct and say: "Worship me and I will reward you with eternal life"? Why did Jesus have to speak of the "Son of man" as a *third person* at all?

In fact, this statement of Jesus can be interpreted in a much deeper manner. Just as we can switch back and forth between the young woman image and the old hag image in Figure 1, we can also flip the traditional interpretation into a Zen interpretation for this story of Nicodemus. My own interpretation of this is that Jesus was giving Nicodemus a koan to meditate on: the koan of the Son of man. According to Jewish tradition, the term "son of man" is not the exclusive title of the Messiah; instead, it can be used to refer to any man. Thus, the "Son of man" may be taken as a symbol for humanity as a whole.

Taking "the Son of man" as a generic term, we can then see that Jesus was asking Nicodemus to focus on the human condition. To help Nicodemus along, Jesus even dropped him a hint by drawing an analogy between the "Son of man" and the fiery serpent mentioned in the Old Testament. But what exactly is the spiritual insight here? Again, I advise you to try resolving the puzzle yourself before you look at the answer provided below.

The allusion to the Old Testament can be found in the Book of Numbers, where God said to Moses: "Make a fiery serpent, and set it on a pole; and every one who is bitten, when he sees it, shall live" (Num. 21:8). "See" is the magic word here. The Lord said that life is made possible by the act of seeing; seeing heals. Apparently, Jesus asked the Jews to lift up the "Son of man" for the same reason: so that people could direct their attention to it and be healed.

Note that the great poet Jesus is at work again here. In fact, this whole story about Nicodemus is pregnant with symbolism. Jesus drew a parallel between the fiery serpent and the "Son of man." The fiery serpent stands for something that bites us from time to time and inflicts sorrow — a rather fitting metaphor for fate. For me, the term "fate" has no superstitious or supernatural connotation at all. It is simply a poetic expression of human limitations and a symbol for the summation of all uncontrollable and unpredictable factors in our lives.

It is no coincidence that we have a common expression that "life is a bitch," — for both the serpent and the bitch bite. The "Son of man," on the other hand, is the other side of the same existential reality. It is a symbol (or an "archetype" in Jungian terms) for the human condition. For as mortals, we are often vulnerable, full of anxieties, wounds, sufferings, and limitations. The central message of Jesus is this: we can alleviate our suffering by becoming aware of our existential situation as human beings. The big question is how this is possible.

To learn the secret of liberation, we have to become familiar with the Zen art of *finding the answer in the question itself.* Albert Camus illustrates this art in "The Myth of Sisyphus."According to the myth, Sisyphus is an absurd hero whose scorn of the gods, hatred of death, and passion for life won him an unspeakable penalty in which he was condemned to an absolutely futile task — that of rolling a rock to the top of a mountain, only to watch it fall down the mountain again. His dreadful fate was to have to repeat this over and over, with no end in sight. What is particularly interesting is not the myth itself but Camus's insightful commentaries that make connection between consciousness, suffering, and liberation:

> Where would his torture be, indeed, if at every step the hope of suc-
> ceeding upheld him? The workman of today works every day in his
> life at the same tasks, and this fate is no less absurd. But it is tragic
> only at the rare moments when it becomes conscious. Sisyphus, the
> proletariat of the gods, powerless and rebellious, knows the whole
> extent of his wretched condition: it is what he thinks of during his
> descent. The lucidity that was to constitute his torture at the same
> time crowns his victory. There is no fate that cannot be surmounted
> by scorn.[7]

Sisyphus is crushed by fate. He is condemned to an endless cycle of suffering and temporary relief. Does this sound a bit like you and me? For who can escape from the tyranny of the fiery serpent, which attacks us from time to time with its poisons — disappointments, de-feats, sickness? We are forever on an emotional roller-coaster. No matter how "happy" we are in a particular moment, sorrow is bound to return. From this perspective, the human condition is indeed hopeless. But if the human condition is the problem, it is also within it that we can find the solution. Camus showed us how:

> Where the call of happiness becomes too insistent, it happens that melancholy rises in man's heart: this is the rock's victory.... These are the nights of Gethsemane. But crushing truths perish from being acknowledged.[8]

The key is acknowledgement. The fiery serpent is like the visual paradox we looked at in the beginning of this chapter. It loses its teeth once we learn to accept it as it is. The acknowledgement of truth, even if it is a tragic one, always has a liberating effect. Friedrich Nietzsche remarked that the ability to appreciate tragedy is a sign of strength rather than weakness and that the flowering of Greek tragedies occurred during the Greek people's most prosperous and vigorous period. Commenting on his first book *The Birth of Tragedy,* Nietzsche says that "the Greeks are not pessimists, their tragedies are proofs — this is where Schopenhauer has erred." Paradoxically, it is only when we become aware of the tragic elements of our lives and face them squarely that we can transform them into something beautiful.

In the same spirit, Jesus asks us to lift up the "Son of man," to come to terms with the nasty little facts of life and affirm our humanity in spite of its difficulties. Note that Jesus told Nicodemus that "no one has ascended into heaven but he who descended from heaven, the Son of man." This statement does not have to be interpreted in a supernatural manner. In the context of Zen, it means that we cannot be liberated ("ascend into heaven") without first recognizing the helplessness of our situation ("descend from heaven"). The kingdom should not be conceived in otherworldly terms, for according to Master Jesus' inverse logic, ascent and descent are the same thing. If we want to reach heaven, we have to go through hell!

Difficulties are a fact of life. Many of us create unnecessary suffering for ourselves because we expect life to be easy and fail to see our own limitations as mortals. Thus, we try to do the impossible, control the uncontrollable, and predict the unpredictable. We also have the illusion that if we try hard enough, we can secure a problem-free life. Our suffering is the combined result of our ignorance and our inner violence.

Spiritual liberation is not a matter of achievement or hard work.

It is a matter of insight. As Camus remarked, "The crushing truths perish from being acknowledged." Confucius said, "At fifty, I knew the decrees of Heaven (Tien ming). At sixty, I heard them with docile ears" (Analects 2:4). The "decrees of Heaven" is the Confucian term for fate (i.e., something that we cannot control or avoid). Knowing what is humanly possible and what is not certainly requires great wisdom; it took Confucius fifty years to know what fate is. But even more difficult is to sincerely accept fate — without any fighting, whining, or screaming. It was not until he was sixty that Confucius came to fully embrace God's will. Until we have learned to do the same, we cannot really have inner peace.

The core of enlightenment is the simple recognition that we are not omnipotent, that there are many things in life that we cannot control or avoid: aging, illness, accidents, job insecurity, human foibles. Although these are often problems that we would rather not face, a sincere acceptance of them paves the way to real liberation.

The realization of "powerlessness" is itself a very powerful spiritual experience. As J. Krishnamurti observed, this realization — "I cannot do" — is intelligence. Consciousness is a double-edged sword. On the one hand, it is the cause of our suffering. Human beings, being the most conscious within the animal kingdom, also tend to suffer the most. On the other hand, consciousness is the seed of our salvation. The human condition may look tragic, but it flips when we direct our attention to it. M. Scott Peck brings a new appreciation to one of the Four Noble Truths taught by Buddha:

> Life is difficult. This is a great truth, one of the greatest truths. It is a great truth because once we truly see this truth, we transcend it. Once we truly know that life is difficult — once we truly understand and accept it — then life is no longer difficult. Because once it is accepted, the fact that life is difficult no longer matters.[9]

Awareness transforms! As long as we are busy fighting life or trying to escape from it, we cannot really look at it clearly, and the fiery serpent will appear to be as oppressive as ever. We will then remain its victim. But the serpent cannot bear the power of our attention. Jesus said that attention heals. Indeed, the word "heal" shares the same root as the word "whole." Healing is *making whole*. Healing is not possible without first developing a holistic vision of the world. Camus taught us how we can "lift up the Son of man" and be made whole:

All Sisyphus' silent joy is contained therein. His fate belongs to him. His rock is his thing. Likewise, the absurd man, when he contemplates his torments, silences all the idols. In the universe suddenly restored to its silence, the myriad wondering little voices of the earth rise up. Unconscious, secret calls, invitation from all the faces, they are the necessary reverse and price of victory. There is no sun without shadow, and it is essential to know the night.[10]

This is the main point: that we are not separate from our fate. Fate should not be regarded as an external enemy with whom we fight. As the common saying goes, it is the environment that makes the person. If we see that our entire life is shaped by fate, then we will understand that it is absurd to fight it, for we are it. There is no separate "me" that can be distinguished from this mysterious force called Fate. Our liberation as existential human beings depends on our seeing that we and our fate are one. Sisyphus realized that "his fate belongs to him. His rock is his thing." This is holistic vision. When the whole is seen, where is the fight?

Therefore, seeing is the only truth. For seeing makes whole. The realization of helplessness, far from being a curse, is indeed a blessing in disguise. This is absurd wisdom. Just a flash of insight, and a profound sense of pessimism is transformed into a profound joy. Camus has experienced enlightenment.

Paradoxically, big problems have a way of turning into big opportunities. Pablo Picasso once remarked that "computers are useless. They can only give you answers." What Picasso was really complaining about is the fact that computers do not know how to turn problems into opportunities. Like left-brain thinkers, computers cannot entertain the intrinsic fuzziness of life's situations and generate new options based on the recognition of multiple possibilities. The best commentary to Picasso's "computers are useless" koan is provided by another genius of our time, Albert Einstein:

> The formulation of a problem is often more essential than its solution, which may be merely a matter of mathematical or experimental skills. To raise new questions, new possibilities, to regard old questions from a new angle, requires creative imagination and makes real advances in science.[11]

Zen is the art of creative visualization, which involves a complete reformulation of old problems. Zen says that "this is it." It means that this troubled world, this world of imperfection, lamentation, sorrow, and defilement is indeed nirvana if we learn to view it from a new light. To the logical and traditional mind, this is simply un-thinkable. Traditional people ask, "How can this be it? Look at all the hatred, anger, envy, greed, and lust in the human soul. And con-sider the suffering that is going on in every single corner of the earth. Where is the joy? Where is the fulfillment?" So they look for a better day. They have already been waiting for a long time. And they will still be waiting...until they have learned the art of seeing.

Enlightenment puts an end to all waiting. This world, *as it is,* is nirvana. Our problems are our opportunities. What is our biggest problem? For most people, it is the human condition. As mortals, we have tremendous limitations. We have no way to avoid emotional disturbances, human foibles, sickness, and death. But the solution is not to be sought outside this earthly life. The key is to focus on life-as-it-is-now, no matter how unpalatable it may seem. Jesus told Nicodemus, "If I have told you earthly things and you do not be-lieve, how can you believe if I tell you heavenly things?" The problem with Nicodemus is that he asked about spiritual birth without first understanding ordinary birth.

Where do we come from? This basic question cannot be answered without first answering an even more basic question: Who am I? Am I this body that is bound to decay and die? Am I my thoughts and emotions that are so whimsical? Human beings are the most con-scious beings in the animal kingdom, but what is consciousness? Is this consciousness that we call "self" simply a catchall term for our idiosyncratic collection of thoughts, memories, values, and tastes? Where did we acquire our beliefs, ideologies, values, and tastes in the first place? The more we ask these questions, the more we realize that the "self" that we cherish so much is incredibly elusive. In fact, it is no less elusive than the wind: we do not know "whence it comes or whither it goes." But if the "self" is nowhere to be found, where is the problem? As Ramana Maharshi comments, "The enquiry 'Who am I?' is the only method of putting an end to all misery and ushering in supreme Beatitude."

The question "Who am I?" may not have an answer, but the rais-ing of the question has a healing effect by itself. Perhaps the question is its own answer.

Spiritual liberation is not a matter of intellectually solving life's problems. It is a matter of clearly seeing these unresolved and unre-solvable paradoxes of life, not to be baffled by life, but to be taken by its poignant beauty. John Marsh observes that "it would not be an overstatement to say that in the synoptic gospels Jesus' path takes him through suffering and death to glory, whereas in the fourth gospel it leads him to something which is suffering, death and glory simultaneously....Passion and action are spoken by the same word; defeat and victory, suffering and glory are particularly together."[12]

In the same way the Cross is, at once, a symbol of suffering, an expression of self-renunciation, and a sign of ultimate salvation. Perhaps the solution is always to be found in the problem itself, and the very seeing of this is liberation.

— Five —

The Looking-Glass Universe

Buddhism seeks not to overcome pain but to become one with it so that the pain is no longer a stranger, an enemy.
— BONNIE MYOTAI TREACE

The Son of God suffered unto the death, not that men might not suffer, but that their suffering might be like His.
— GEORGE MACDONALD

Entering the Zen world is like Alice going into her Wonderland: we often find that things are upside-down relative to our everyday world. In the old days, Zen masters and Tao practitioners were often considered as crazy people or social outcasts. We have already explored the humor, poetry, and art of Jesus. In this chapter, we are going to venture into his topsy-turvy world.

Jesus is one of the most enigmatic figures in human history. When we interpret Jesus and his teachings, we are bound to run into a difficult question: What to make of Jesus? Like many honest and intelligent Christians, I have struggled with this question for a long time. Was Jesus of Nazareth the Son of God, as many of his followers have claimed, or was he a mortal like you and me? And are these two characterizations mutually exclusive?

For many people who are brought up as Christians (which includes myself), the deity of Jesus is accepted as a matter of fact. In the defense of Jesus' special divinity, many modern-day apologists resort to what I call "the tactic of pigeonholing." First, they appeal to the public's good-will toward Jesus. The spotlight is thrown on Jesus' personal integrity. Second, they try to make a case that Jesus made many explicit statements that would seem egocentric or megalomanic if he were not the Son of God. Third, they argue that to attribute these statements to the lunacy or dishonesty of Jesus would be incongruent with his commonly accepted integrity. C. S. Lewis, for example, made an argument along this line:

> That [Christian] hypothesis is that God has come down into the created universe, down to manhood.... The alternative hypothesis is not legend, nor exaggeration, nor the apparition of a ghost. It is either lunacy or lies. Unless one can take the second alternative (and I can't) one turns to the Christian theory.[1]

So the apologists try to force us to choose between accepting Jesus as deity and branding him as a liar or a madman. Given what we know about Jesus' character, the latter alternatives obviously look unattractive.

The big question is this: Are these characterizations of Jesus as deity, liar, or lunatic the only available alternatives? Have the apologists simplified the matter too much? It seems to me that in their rush to defend Jesus' deity, the apologists have conveniently overlooked the fact that Jesus had openly denied any monopoly on the "son of God" title or any claim to special divinity. The evidence suggests that Jesus has used the term as a *generic* one. In fact, according to John (10:34–36), Jesus took pains to explain to others the generic meaning of the term, citing biblical authority from the Psalms:

> I say, "You are gods,
> sons of the Most High, all of you;
> Nevertheless, you shall die like men,
> and fall like any prince." (Ps. 82:6–7)

But Jesus was also well aware that the term "Son of God" can also be used to denote a very special and privileged status — that of the Messiah. When people used the term in this special way and asked Jesus whether he identified himself with it, he typically gave an ambiguous answer. The following is Luke's account of the trial of Jesus in which Jesus was asked to reveal his true identity:

> When day came, the assembly of the elders of the people gathered together, both chief priests and scribes; and they led him away to their council, and they said, "If you are Christ, tell us." But he said to them, "If I tell you, you will not believe; and if I ask you, you will not answer. But from now on the Son of man shall be seated at the right hand of the power of God." And they all said, "Are you the Son of God, then?" And he said to them, "You say that I am." (Luke 22:66–70)

Note that Jesus' answer was "You say that I am." Certainly, this is different from the straight answer of "I am." Even a second grade student can tell the difference. "You say that I am" is obviously an ambiguous answer. But the Jewish authorities apparently took it as a "yes," and this constituted a valid charge against Jesus. Bible scholar G. B. Caird gave the following insightful interpretation of the event:

> "Are you the Messiah?" At first Jesus declined to answer; "Messiah" is an ambiguous term, and he recognizes that the court is in no mood to discuss definitions. . . . Finally, however, Jesus replies to the question with a veiled answer, which the interrogators take as assent.[2]

I find much of the so-called biblical evidence of Jesus' special divinity to be misinterpretations like the one just mentioned. Another example is Jesus' proclamation that "I and the Father are one." While many people have taken this as further evidence for Jesus' special divinity, it is equally valid to interpret it as a soulful expression of Jesus' inner harmony and a poetic metaphor for the spiritual state in which one feels completely at ease with All There Is.

Therefore, to view Jesus as a deity, to view him as a liar, or to view him as a lunatic are not the only options available. There is a fourth alternative: to view him as an enlightened teacher (rabbi, Zen master) who taught in a mystical, paradoxical language.

C. S. Lewis compared the task of interpreting Jesus with a situation where we are holding only parts of a novel and are trying to figure out the entire story. If someone suddenly comes along and claims to have discovered the missing part of the work, how shall we regard that "discovery"? Lewis suggested that we apply the following principle for quality control:

> Our business would be to see whether the new passage, if admitted to the central place which the discoverer claimed for it, did actually illuminate all the parts we had already seen and "pull them together." Nor should we be likely to go very wrong. The new passage, if spurious, however attractive it looked at the first glance, would become harder and harder to reconcile with the rest of the work the longer we considered the matter. But if it were genuine, then at every fresh hearing of the music or every fresh reading of the book, we should find it settling down, making itself more at home, and eliciting significance from all sorts of details in the whole work which we hitherto neglected. Even though the new central chapter or main theme contained great difficulties in itself, we should still think it genuine provided that it continually removed difficulties elsewhere.[3]

The Zen perspective on Jesus might just be this missing piece in the search for the historical Jesus. As we have already seen, the Zen perspective has been highly successful in making sense out of many of Jesus' dark sayings. And we shall see that it will continue to help us resolve many other mysteries surrounding Jesus, including his defeat of death. The Zen perspective not only satisfies Lewis's criterion of coherence; it also provides many illuminating new insights that can serve as the basis for the liberation of our own souls.

Let us now see how the Zen perspective can account for the central theme of Christianity: the resurrection story. That Jesus has defeated death is perhaps the most important Christian message. St. Paul remarked that "if Christ has not been raised, your faith is futile" (1 Cor 15:17). While the physical resurrection of Jesus' body is still a matter of debate, many agree that a dramatic change did occur in the behavior of Jesus' disciples not long after his death. The disciples seemed to be able to endure all kinds of hardships, persecutions, and sufferings with amazing equanimity. Peter's transformation from a deserter to a witness and a martyr is a case in point.

The Easter story is of great importance because it represents humankind's triumph over death. But to account for this triumph in the context of Zen takes some work; we must remember that the Zen perspective is a nonsupernatual one. While Zen does not rule out the occurrence of supernatural events, it does put the emphasis on "ordinary magic." But how can we explain the behavioral changes and the bravery of Jesus' disciples under the scenario that Jesus had not physically risen from the dead?

To make sense out of this, we have to have a solid understanding of Jesus' *looking-glass universe*. We can catch a good glimpse of it in the following excerpt from the Gospel of John:

> "A little while, and you will see me no more; again a little while, and you will see me." Some of his disciples said, "What is this that he says to us, 'A little while, and you will see me, and again a little while and you will see me no more'; and, 'because I go to the Father'?" They said, "What does he mean by 'a little while'? We do not know what he means."
>
> Jesus knew that they wanted to ask him; so he said to them, "Is this what you are asking yourselves, what I mean by saying, 'A little while, and you will not see me, and again a little while, you will see me'? Truly, truly, I say to you, you will weep and lament, but the world will rejoice; you will be sorrowful, *but your sorrow will turn into joy.* When a woman is in travail she has sorrow, because her

hour has come; but when she is delivered of the child, she no longer remembers the anguish, for joy that a child is born into the world. So you have sorrow now, but I will see you again and your heart will rejoice, and no one will take your joy from you. In that day you will ask nothing of me. Truly, truly, I say to you, if you ask anything of the Father, he will give it to you in my name. Hitherto, you have asked nothing in my name; ask, and you will receive, that your joy may be full.

"I have said this to you in figures; the hour is coming when I shall no longer speak to you in figures but tell you plainly of the Father. In that day you will ask in my name; and I do not say to you that I shall pray the Father for you; for the Father himself loves you, because you have loved me and have believed that I came from the Father. I came from the Father and have come into the world; again, I am leaving the world and going to the Father."

His disciples said, "Ah, now you are speaking plainly, not in any figure! Now we know that you know all things, and need none to question you; by this we believe that you came from God." Jesus answered them, "Do you believe? The hour is coming, indeed it has come, when you will be scattered, every man to his home, and will leave me alone; yet I am not alone, for the Father is with me. I have said this to you, that in me you may have peace. In the world you have tribulation; but be of good cheer, *I have overcome the world.*" (John 16:16–33)

Note that Jesus was hinting at his own death. Given this ominous pretext, it is all the more remarkable that Jesus ended this particular teaching on a very positive note: "in the world you have tribulations; but be of good cheer, I have overcome the world." Here lies the irony: Jesus said that he had overcome the world precisely at the moment when he knew that his death was imminent. He also predicted the radical transformation that was to take place in his disciples. For he told them that "your sorrow will turn into joy."

To trigger a student's enlightenment, it is usual for a Zen teacher to assign koans as "homework." As mentioned before, koans are meditation objects. Some koans are classics and are handed down from generation to generation. "Death" is a classic koan. It is also a very potent one because of its existential significance. Most of us do not feel comfortable contemplating the topic of death, either our own death or death of our loved ones. But it is precisely because the koan is so anxiety-provoking that it has the potential to induce spiritual awakening.

The basic mystery in this quotation from John is this: What did

Jesus mean when he said "I have overcome the world"? This is what I refer to as the "death koan of Jesus." It is perhaps the most important koan in his entire teaching. As we shall see later, if we really understand the secret of this koan, we will be on our way to join Jesus in the "Deathless Zone."

The death koan helps to focus our existential anxiety and highlights our fragility as humans. Intellectually, we all know that we cannot avoid death. But for most people, there is usually a wide discrepancy between intellectual reality and psychological reality. Psychologically, we tend to deny death. If this were not so, then we would not be shocked at all if our doctor were to tell us that we had contracted some terrible disease and would die within a few months. Recognizing the reality of death psychologically and not just intellectually is an important part of spiritual awakening.

To shed some light on Jesus' koan of death, let us first work on another famous Zen koan which we will henceforth refer to as the "Tale of the Unfortunate Traveler":

> A man traveling across a field encountered a tiger. He fled, but the tiger ran after him. Coming to a precipice, he caught hold of a root of a wild vine and swung himself down over the edge. The tiger sniffed at him from above. Trembling, the man looked down to where, far below, another tiger was waiting to eat him. Only the vine sustained him.
>
> Two mice, one white and one black, little by little started to gnaw away the vine. The man saw a luscious strawberry near him. Grasping the vine with one hand, he plucked the strawberry with the other. How sweet it tasted!

See any similarity between this tale and Jesus' koan of death? What is the key insight?

To begin with, doesn't the traveling man look a little bit like you and me? Aren't we chased by death as the man was chased by the tiger? And aren't the two mice, one black and one white, a great symbol for the cycle of night and day? There is no doubt that the story is a poetic expression for the existential anxiety of being a human being. Just like the traveling man, our lives hang by a thin line. Living in a world of uncertainty, we do not know exactly when our end will come. All we know is that death is a certainty. In fact, we walk closer to it every day. Under this circumstance, what would you do?

We can further simplify this koan of the unfortunate traveler into one question: "When you can do nothing, what can you do?" The truth is that the unfortunate traveler had no choice. The only logical thing for him to do is to enjoy the moment, no matter how transient it is. Why worry about death if we know clearly that it is unavoidable? Why make life more miserable? This is the most amazing, yet most obvious and logical answer: that in the certainty of death, one should get as much out of life as possible. Paradoxically, it is the absence of choice in this matter that allows us to have more inner freedom. Here is the surprise answer to the Zen koan of "When you can do nothing, what can you do?": *nothing and everything!* Precisely this is absurd wisdom.

So we finally discover the secret to Jesus' jubilation: death is a blessing in disguise! Contrary to what the common mind may think, a genuine acceptance of death as a reality (i.e., true hopelessness) leads to liberation and peace. As Albert Camus has so astutely observed, "Death, too, has patrician hands which, while crushing, also liberate."

After all, Jesus is not unlike the absurd hero in Camus's novel *The Stranger,* who in accepting the fact that he was a condemned man with a limited number of days remaining, suddenly found life becoming more abundant to him. Indeed, happiness and the absurd cannot be separated. Absurd wisdom says that nothing is as soothing, as hope-filled, as total hopelessness. Shortly before his execution, Meursault, the condemned man in Camus's story, recalled this about his mother's last days:

> And now, it seemed to me, I understand why at her life's end she had taken on a "fiancé"; why she'd played at making a fresh start.... With death so near, Mother must have felt like someone on the brink of freedom, ready to start life all over again. No one, no one in the world had any right to weep for her.[4]

You may think that the idea of death as liberator is novel, but many medical professionals who work with terminally ill patients have witnessed this truth. Dr. Rachel Naomi Remen suffers from Crohn's disease (a chronic illness) and has undergone several major surgeries. She is the medical director of the Commonweal Cancer Help Program in Bolinas, California. She shares with us this insight:

> Most serious diseases call into question the way you live and what's important. There is a whole reshifting of values. Someone once described it to me as a "wake-up call." ...I think that's what cancers do to people: "The ears of my ears awake and the eyes of my eyes opened...." We are not a special group of people here, we're just

human beings, frightened, lonely, hurting, and able to grow in response to crisis. That's what's available if you're willing to allow yourself to be human.[5]

Perhaps encroaching death does have a healing effect. One cancer patient remarked how her illness put her life in order:

> I consider my cancer to be such a blessing because through it we have learned so much about how to handle our lives, how to speak out our feelings to each other, how to throw away the junk forever and have more contentment in our lives.[6]

Death is treated like a taboo in our culture, and all medical efforts are directed toward fighting this law of nature. But perhaps there is a beautiful side to death. *Wabi-sabi* is a culture of Japanese aesthetics that has close ties with *chado* (the Japanese art of tea) and Zen. According to Leonard Koren, *wabi-sabi* is "a beauty of things imperfect, impermanent, and incomplete. It is a beauty of things modest and humble. It is a beauty of things unconventional."[7] Perhaps death is God's *wabi-sabi*. A fifty-year-old woman who had a double mastectomy sees death as a teacher of Zen and beauty. She exclaimed how death has *enlivened* her life:

> it wasn't until I got cancer that I really started to pay attention to the preciousness of each breath, to the moment of each thought, till I saw that this moment is all. All my other teachers gave me ideas. This caused me to directly experience my life. When I got cancer, it was up to me to get born before I died.[8]

Death is both the root of our existential anxiety and its ultimate cure. Lest you think that this is some kind of crazy logic thought up by existentialist philosophers, I must point out that C. S. Lewis came to a similar conclusion:

> On the one hand Death is the triumph of Satan, the punishment of the fall, and the last enemy.... On the other hand, only he who loses his life will save it. We are baptized into the death of Christ, and it is the remedy for the Fall. Death is, in fact, what some modern people call "ambivalent." It is Satan's great weapon and also God's great weapon: it is holy and unholy; our supreme disgrace and our only hope; the thing Christ came to conquer and the means by which He conquered.[9]

This is the true miracle: Jesus has defeated death by accepting it. The reason that most of us are so oppressed by death is that, subconsciously, we cannot accept it as a reality. We are still secretly hopeful it won't come, and this is the root of our existential anxiety. In our vain attempt to run away from our anxiety, we pursue all kinds of "happiness": money, sensual pleasure, power, status. However, as long as we have not honestly accepted death as a personal reality, these excursions into "happiness" are just temporary painkillers. The demon of death keeps coming back, asking for acceptance.

By the time that Jesus declared that "I have overcome the world," he could see no earthly future; the future was death. He could almost see himself being delivered into the hands of his executioners. He became truly hopeless (poetically, this means that he "surrendered his will to God's"). But the beauty of it all is how this utterly hopeless situation has a way to turn around and become the kingdom once he accepted his fate and let go. (Remember those mental flips we introduced in the last chapter?) In acknowledging the inevitability of death, Jesus gained inner freedom. Nothing in the world could cause him any anxiety anymore. Truly, he had overcome the world! Surrender means victory in the paradoxical world of the enlightened.

The way to spiritual liberation is to accept the ultimate existential choicelessness — death. I suggest that this is the truth that Jesus' disciples finally discovered, and it accounts for their dramatic behavioral change. Acceptance is one of the bases for "ordinary magic." C. S. Lewis offers this insight:

> But to convert this penal death into the means of eternal life — to add to its negative and preventive function a positive and saving function — it was further necessary that death should be accepted. Humanity must embrace death freely, submit to it with total humility, drink it to its dregs, and so convert it into that mystical death which is the secret of life.[10]

Similarly, inverse laws can be used to tackle the problem of insecurity. In the Sermon on the Mount, Jesus asked his disciples not to be anxious about their lives (Matt. 6:25). As an antidote for anxiety, Jesus asked them to "seek first his [God's] kingdom and his righteousness." In a different context, he explains what this entails:

> Truly, truly, I say to you, unless a grain of wheat falls into the earth and dies, it remains alone; but if it dies, it bears much fruit. He who loves his life loses it, and he who hates his life in this world will keep it for eternal life. (John 12:24–25)

The insight is now clear. As Alan Watts has pointed out, insecurity is the result of trying to be secure. Those who are neurotic about their security ("those who love their life") cannot truly live since they have become slaves to their fear. Conversely those who accept insecurity as a fact of life ("those who hate their life in this world") can put away their worries and live as free persons. The ultimate expression of acceptance of reality is to renounce the self, just as the little seed does. Ironically, when one comes to embrace insecurity, true peace of mind is gained. Inverse law says that if we are to truly live, we must not be attached to life. Jesus teaches this principle in the Parable of the Harsh Master:

> For it will be as when a man going on a journey called his servants and entrusted to them his property; to one he gave five talents, to another two, to another one, to each according to his ability. Then, he went away. He who had received the five talents went at once and traded with them; and he made five talents more. So also, he who had the two talents made two talents more. But he who had received the one talent went and dug in the ground and hid his master's money.
>
> Now, after a long time, the master of those servants came and settled accounts with them. And he who had received the five talents came forward, bringing five talents more, saying, "Master, you delivered to me five talents; here I have made five talents more." His master said to him, "Well done, good and faithful servant; you have been faithful over a little, I will set you over much; enter into the joy of your master." And he also who had the two talents came forward, saying, "Master, you delivered to me two talents; here I have made two talents more." His master said to him, "Well done, good and faithful servant; you have been faithful over a little, I will set you over much; enter into the joy of your master." He also who had received the one talent came forward, saying, "Master, I knew you to be a hard man, reaping where you did not sow, and gathering where you did not winnow; *so I was afraid,* and I went and hid your talent in the ground. Here you have what is yours."
>
> But his master answered him, "You wicked and slothful servant! You know that I reap where I have not sowed, and gather where I have not winnowed. Then, you ought to have invested my money with the bankers, and at my coming I should have received what was my own with interest. So take the talent from him, and give it to him who has ten talents. For to every one who has will more be given, and he will have abundance; but from him who has not, even what he has will be taken away. And cast the worthless servant into the outer darkness; there men will weep and gnash their teeth." (Matt. 25:14–30)

The third servant was punished not so much for his sloth as for his poor judgment and conservatism. Indeed, the conservative servant had correctly seen that life is full of risks, but he drew the wrong conclusion. Seeing the risk of losing, he was reluctant to make any investment. The correct logic is that since life is full of hazards regardless of what we do, we should be more adventurous with our capital. As the popular lyric goes, "It's the heart afraid of breaking which never learns to love." Again, inverse laws apply here.

It is quite obvious that the harsh master is another metaphor for life, similar to the fiery serpent that we discussed in the last chapter. For life is indeed difficult and full of hazards. Not only that, it is also bound to end at some point; the Grim Reaper must come. But this does not mean that we should live timidly. If risks are unavoidable in any case, it is only logical that we become more courageous and take calculated risks. Instead of withdrawing from life like the conservative servant, we should live life to its fullest. Jesus concluded that "to everyone who has will more be given ... but from him who has not, even what he has will be taken away." This means that the more we embrace uncertainty, the more abundant our life will be. Jesus' insight resonates with Nietzsche's motto: "The secret of the greatest fruitfulness and the greatest enjoyment of existence is: to live dangerously!"

"Living dangerously" does not mean taking foolish risks. Rather, it means accepting insecurity as a fact of life and living in peace instead of in neurosis. And "living dangerously" was what some of the early Christians did.

By now, it should be obvious that Jesus did not have a rosy view of the world at all. Indeed, the world is quite lamentable: Death is certain. Life is fragile. Dangers abound. Human beings are full of limitations. None of these are desirable conditions. In this sense, we are all condemned to some kind of "existential choicelessness."

But being aware of the inevitability of problems, illness, danger, and eventually death, we will not strive to do the impossible. As we learn to "leave things to God" and let go of our unnecessary and counterproductive fight or fear, we can finally relax and enjoy the moment. Paradoxically, awareness to our existential choicelessness brings a deep sense of inner freedom. It is what liberates! Philosopher Friedrich Engels observed that "freedom is the recognition of necessity." Thus, we have one of the most profound of the inverse laws: life is miserable, yet life is great! Perhaps it is precisely because life is so often miserable that it is great.

It is difficult to look at this looking-glass universe without being taken by its amazing beauty. How can things be so "right" when they appear to be so "wrong"? A Zen master once observed that "all things are in nirvana from the very beginning." Alan Watts provides an excellent description of the *satori* experience:

> To the individual thus enlightened it appears as a vivid and over-whelming certainty that the universe precisely as it is at this moment, as a whole and in every one of its parts, is so completely right as to need no explanation or justification beyond what it simply is. Exis-tence not only ceases to be a problem; the mind is so wonder-struck at the self-evident and self-sufficient fitness of things as they are, includ-ing what would ordinarily be thought the very worst, that it cannot find any word strong enough to express the perfection and beauty of the experience.[11]

Enlightenment is not an achievement; it is just the seeing of reality as it is. In fact, nirvana is simply what *is*. We have been staring at it all our lives, and yet so few of us get it. The fact is that life is at the same time lamentable and beautiful. When we realize this humorous and absurd beauty of life, what can we do but to burst into laughter? I can only imagine Jesus laughing on the cross.

To sum up: acceptance is a key of spirituality. Acceptance of our existential choicelessness (the understanding that there are many things in life that we simply cannot control) leads to inner freedom. The embracing of insecurity as a fact of life leads to inner peace. The sincere acceptance of death as being inevitable makes life more abun-dant to us. These are the Zen wisdom teachings of Jesus taught and they operate according to an inverse logic.

One of the most profound truths that Mahayana Buddhism teaches is that nirvana is samsara (the troubled world). Hui Neng, the famous sixth patriarch of Zen, observed that to seek nirvana outside samsara is plain stupidity. The same truth is expressed most beautifully in the Christian image of the Incarnation: God descends to reascend. There can be no ascension without descent. We must realize that Zen and Christianity are not telling two different stories but one story. The only difference is in the language.

— Six —

The Usual Hell

Repent! The kingdom of God is at hand.

— JESUS

*Paradise is nearer you than the thongs of your sandal;
and the Fire likewise.*

— MUHAMMAD

While it is widely acknowledged that hell is a grim place, the human mind has nevertheless come up with a kaleidoscope of colorful and entertaining tales about it. So let's talk about fire, worms, monsters, and the secrets of hell. But don't despair, for this story has a surprising ending.

One of the famous tourist sites in Hong Kong is the Fu and Po Mansion. Inside it there are many vivid scenes from Chinese folklore, including several drawings about the eighteen levels of hell. Going through them is a hair-raising experience. The pictures show all the gory details: people being skinned alive, the torture of boiling oil...I have always wondered why there aren't corresponding graphic details about the joys of heaven. The fact is that heaven, if portrayed at all, is usually glossed over as a place of bland bliss. There is no corresponding sense of realism. Alan Watts noticed a similar pattern in Christian imagery:

> Christian imagery is very vague about the glories of heaven and amazingly specific about the agonies of hell. Pictures of people in heaven are invariably demure and dull, whereas hell is a writhing orgy.[1]

In his book *The Great Divorce,* C. S. Lewis wrote about a group of people in hell who were given the opportunity to have a tour of heaven. Although they found heaven to be a delightful place, they nevertheless chose to return to hell. Heaven is the loser in a popularity contest. The reason: there is no "fun" in heaven; those potential emigrants could not stand the boredom there. While love and equality are emphasized in heaven, competition and ego are the buzzwords in hell. Hell seems to be a more interesting place for most people because it offers an opportunity for gratification of the ego. Lewis described hell as follows:

> Hell is a state where everyone is perpetually concerned with his own dignity and advancement, where everyone has a grievance, and where everyone lives the deadly serious passions of envy, self-importance, and resentment.[2]

Hell is "serious" business. It is about personal dignity, self-advancement, self-importance, and ego gratification. Heaven is no competition for hell because it has no such "goodies" to offer. The fact is that most people subconsciously have an infatuation with hell. Perhaps this is why our world is so miserable.

The main point is this: those who are in hell *choose* to be there. Lewis offers this diagnosis of their residence preference:

> I willingly believe that the damned are, in one sense, successful, rebels to the end; that the doors of hell are locked on the *inside*. I do not mean that the ghosts may not wish to come out of hell in the vague fashion wherein an envious man "wishes" to be happy: but they certainly do not will even the first preliminary stages of that self-abandonment through which alone the soul can reach any good. They enjoy forever the horrible freedom they have demanded.[3]

Jean Paul Sartre told a story in which three people died and descended to hell. To their surprise, they found no instrument of torture in the underworld. It was only later that they found out that they were supposed to be each other's hell. To Sartre, hell is other people.

But while these are all witty tales, they fall short of telling us the ultimate secret: that hell is already here!

The first secret about hell is that it is in the here-and-now. This is not a joke. It may not be immediately obvious, but once we have finished our discussion about the kingdom of God, there is very little remaining to be said about hell. For hell is simply the *complement* of heaven. In other words, it is whatever is outside the kingdom. Christians traditionally conceive of heaven and hell as mutually exclusive states of reality. While there are flaws in this dichotomous view, it does help simplify our conceptualization.

Both heaven and hell can be found in the present. Both Jesus and John the Baptist have used the phrase "the kingdom of God is at hand" to indicate that these two polarities are internal realities. But of all spiritual teachers, the prophet Muhammad is the most explicit about this. For he declared that "Paradise is nearer you than the thongs of your sandal; and the Fire likewise."

Certainly, nothing is closer to us than our own mind! Whether we experience heaven or hell is a matter of our attitude and values. C. S. Lewis considers self-abandonment (surrender to God) as the critical factor. In the Zen language, this is called gentleness toward life. As you may recall, Thelma Thompson was able to transform a living hell into a wonderland by simply adopting a positive attitude to what is. There is also a beautiful tale about two salesmen who are given the assignment of selling shoes to an uncivilized people. One agonized over the fact that this was a tough sale since the people had never worn shoes before. The other, however, rejoiced over this exciting opportunity, — for a shoeless people holds the promise of millions of sales!

The second secret about hell is that, contrary to the common understanding, it is not a place of perpetual suffering. The notion of an everlasting hell is a terrible one. As C. S. Lewis has pointed out, the hell doctrine "is one of the chief grounds on which Christianity is attacked as barbarous and the goodness of God impugned."[4]

Needless to say, the notion of permanent condemnation is totally incompatible with the reality of God's infinite love. It is blasphemy, period. C. S. Lewis's tale of hell with open doors strikes me as being more credible. M. Scott Peck expressed a similar opinion:

> My vision of Hell is distinctly like that of Lewis. The gates of Hell are wide open. People can walk out of Hell, and the reason they are in Hell is that they choose not to.... I simply cannot accept the view of Hell in which God punishes people without hope and destroys souls without a chance of redemption. She/He wouldn't go to the trouble of creating souls, with all their complexity, just to fry them in the end.[5]

Jesus talked about eternal life, but he never talked about eternal death. It seems that the myth of permanent hell is the joint product of a vengeful mind-set and a general handicap in poetic and literary ability. Crucial is the differentiation between eternity and perpetuity. As we observed in chapter 3 above, that eternity is the disappearance of psychological time and not the indefinite extension of physical time. Paul Tillich made a similar observation:

It is necessary, however, to distinguish between eternal and ever-lasting. Eternity as a quality of divine life cannot be attributed to a being which is condemned and separated from divine life. Where the divine love ends, being ends; condemnation can only mean that the creature is left to the nonbeing it has chosen.... If, however, one speaks of everlasting or endless condemnation, one affirms a temporal duration which is not temporal. Such a concept is contradictory by nature.[6]

Thus, the crux of the problem lies in the popular notion of eternity as elongated time. But perhaps our conventional concept of heaven and hell as coexisting in an indefinite extension of linear time is faulty. Commenting on the geometry of hell, C. S. Lewis observes: "that the lost soul is eternally fixed in its diabolical attitude we cannot doubt: but whether this eternal fixity implies endless duration — or duration at all — we cannot say."[7] We have already seen that the kingdom exists in the moment. If hell is whatever is outside the kingdom, it is logical to conclude that it too exists in the eternal now.

The third secret about hell is that it is a result of our thought. The devil king, the great Satan, does not want us to know this, but hell has a very humble origin. It begins with a seemingly innocuous thought: "I want to have the same pleasure tomorrow." Out of this little thought, all hell breaks loose. Fear arises. In our attempt to secure our pleasure, we try to take possession of our objects of desire. And we try our damnedest to eliminate those who are jeopardizing our chance of getting that pleasure tomorrow. Thus, a whole cycle of fear, hatred, and violence begins. This is the origin of slander, backstabbing, office politics, robbery, and murder.

Thus, hell is a result of not living in the moment. C. S. Lewis offered this insight in a fictional conversation between two devils:

> Our business is to get them [humans] away from the eternal and from the Present.... It is better to make them live in the Future. Biological necessity makes all their passions point in that direction already, so that thought about the Future inflames hope and fear. Also, it is unknown to them, so that in making them think about it we make them think of unrealities. In a word, the Future is, of all things, the thing least like eternity.... Hence nearly all vices are rooted in the Future. Gratitude looks to the Past and love to the Present; fear, avarice, lust and ambition look ahead.[8]

When we fix our attention on the future, our anxiety will be endless. Jesus portrays hell as the place "where their worm does not die, and the fire is not quenched" (Mark 9:48). His metaphors seem to come directly from the prophet Isaiah:

> And they shall go forth and look on the dead bodies of the men that have rebelled against me [God]; for their worm shall not die, their fire shall not be quenched, and they shall be an abhorrence to all living beings. (Isa. 66:24)

The symbolic nature of these descriptions is even more obvious from this passage from the Old Testament. The fire and the worm are not external instruments of torture to be found in hell. The prophet Isaiah used the terms "their fire" and "their worm" to convey the message that the source of suffering is *internal*. The fire in hell, unlike other kinds of fire, shall not be quenched because it burns from within. Unless we have a way to get deep inside the psyche to the source of that fire, we have no way to put it out.

Similarly, the "worm" is an apt metaphor, for a worm eats from within. It does not die because it derives its nutrients from our inner world. The "dead" mentioned here means the spiritually dead, who are constantly tormented by their own greed, lust, anger, and jealousy and who have no peace. They are a tragedy to those who are spiritually alive. For the former live like zombies, tortured by inner suffering and yet totally unaware of the kingdom within.

Buddha also used the imagery of fire to describe the human situation. In the famous Fire Sermon, he told his disciples that the eye, the ear, the nose, the tongue, the body, and the mind (the Buddhist notion of six senses) are all burning — with the fire of greed, lust, hate, and delusion.

Jesus, being a Zen teacher, has no taste for the macabre and the grotesque. We must remember that the "fire" and the "worm" are creations of our mind.

The fourth secret about hell is that it is an outcome of unawareness. The other name for hell is the "outer darkness." An example of this usage is found in the Parable of the Great Banquet:

> And again Jesus spoke to them in parables, saying, "The kingdom of heaven may be compared to a king who gave a marriage feast for his son, and sent his servants to call those who were invited to the marriage feast; but they would not come. Again he sent other servants, saying, 'Tell those who are invited, Behold, I have made ready my dinner, my oxen and my fat calves are killed, and everything is ready; come to the marriage feast.' But they made light of it and went off, one to his farm, another to his business, while the rest seized his

servants, treated them shamefully, and killed them. The king was angry, and he sent his troops and destroyed those murderers and burned their city. Then he said to his servants, 'The wedding is ready, but those invited were not worthy. Go therefore to the thoroughfares, and invite to the marriage feast as many as you find.' And those servants went out into the streets and gathered all whom they found, both bad and good; so the wedding hall was filled with guests.

But when the king came in to look at the guests, he saw there a man who had no wedding garment; and he said to him, 'Friend, how did you get in here without a wedding garment?' And he was speechless. Then the king said to the attendants, 'Bind him hand and foot, and cast him into the *outer darkness;* there men will weep and gnash their teeth.' For many are called, but few are chosen." (Matt. 22:1–14)

Going to a wedding banquet without a proper garment is a sure sign of absent-mindedness. To take this story literally is misleading: one does not get arrested for sleep-walking. But absent-minded people are not sensitive to reality. Lacking mindfulness, it is highly unlikely that they will ever see the truth that liberates. Thus, the "outer darkness" is the "Land of the Half-asleep" where those who are spiritually dead are imprisoned.

Attentiveness is critical for entry into the kingdom because it lays the basis for spiritual awakening. A similar lesson is taught in the Parable of the Ten Maidens:

Then the kingdom of heaven shall be compared to ten maidens who took their lamps and went to meet the bridegroom. Five of them were foolish, and five were wise. For when the foolish took their lamps, they took no oil with them; but the wise took flasks of oil with their lamps. As the bridegroom was delayed, they all slumbered and slept. But at midnight there was a cry, "Behold, the bridegroom! Come out to meet him." Then, all those maidens rose and trimmed their lamps. And the foolish said to the wise, "Give us some of your oil, for our lamps are going out." But the wise replied, "Perhaps there will not be enough for us and for you; go rather to the dealers and buy for yourselves." And while they went to buy, the bridegroom came, and those who were ready went in with him to the marriage feast; and the door was shut. Afterward the other maidens came also, saying, "Lord, lord, open to us." But he replied, "Truly, I say to you, I do not know you." Watch therefore, for you know neither the day nor the hour. (Matt. 25:1–13)

The lamp is a commonly used symbol for mindfulness. The story illustrates the important point that the opportunity for enlightenment comes unexpectedly. Many people miss the opportunity for enlightenment because they are not alert. In the Parable of the Great Banquet, many of those who failed to share the joy of the feast were ordinary people who were simply too busy with their future-oriented life. As the invitation came, they ignored it and went off to tend their everyday business. Like most people, they felt that it is more important to make a living than to go to a feast and make merry. In a word, they are too "serious."

The fifth secret about hell is that it is the normal state for most people. Hell is not the consequence of a crime. In fact, most of the people in hell are innocent. The Parable of the Ten Maidens bears out this point clearly. The only "sin" that the foolish maidens committed was their lack of attention to details: they forgot to bring oil to refill their lamps. To consider them as criminals who deserve punishment is ludicrous. The "outer darkness" is not a physical dungeon; it is Jesus' poetic way of portraying the human tragedy of missing out on the joy of heaven due simply to absent-mindedness or a misplaced sense of priorities.

Now we can understand why we are a lot more conversant about hell than about heaven. Hell is our usual habitat! It is the state of mind where most of us find ourselves. As Jesus himself attests, "Many are called, but few are chosen" (Matt. 22:14) How many of us are fully awake?

The sixth secret about hell is that it is not a punishment. Our suffering in hell is due to our own lack of mindfulness and not due to the wrath of a vengeful God. This is best illustrated by the Parable of the Prodigal Son:

There was a man who had two sons; and the younger of them said to his father, "Father, give me the share of property that falls to me." And he divided his living between them. Not many days later, the younger son gathered all he had and took his journey to a far country, and there he squandered his property in loose living.

And when he had spent everything, a great famine arose in that country, and he began to be in want. So, he went and joined himself to one of the citizens of that country, who sent him into his fields to feed swine. And he would gladly have fed on pods that the swine ate; and no one gave him anything. But when he came to himself, he said, "How many of my father's hired servants have bread enough and to spare, but I perish here with hunger! I will arise and go to my father, and I will say to him, 'Father, I have sinned against heaven and before you; I am no longer worthy to be called your son; treat me as one of your hired servants.' "

And he rose and came to his father. But when he was yet at a distance, his father saw him and had compassion, and ran and embraced him and kissed him. And the son said to him, "Father, I have sinned against heaven and before you; I am no longer worthy to be called your son." But the father said to his servants, "Bring quickly the best robe, and put it on him; and put a ring on his hand, and shoes on his feet; and bring the fatted calf and kill it, and let us eat and make merry; for this my son was dead, and is alive again; he was lost, and is found." And they began to make merry. (Luke 15:11–24)

The "far country" mentioned here is the same as the "outer darkness"; it is the Unconscious Zone. Note that the prodigal son went to the "far country" on his own initiative. And he would have stayed there if not for the redeeming flash of insight in which he "came to himself." And when he did try to go home, his father did not have any hesitation in welcoming him back. He did not say, "Wait a minute, young man. Let us first settle our account." Neither did he ask his son any embarrassing questions. The father held no grudge at all. In fact, he *ran* to greet his delinquent son even while he was still at a distance, before the son opened his mouth to apologize.

No, hell is not a result of God's punishment; it is the result of our unwillingness to accept God's love in the present moment. The theologian Paul Tillich offers the following insight:

> It is true that finite freedom cannot be forced into unity with God because it is a unity of love. A finite being can be separated from God; it can indefinitely resist reunion; it can be thrown into self-destruction and utter despair; but even this is the work of divine love, as the inscription which Dante saw written over the entrance of hell so well shows (Canto III). Hell has being only in so far as it stands in the unity of the divine love. It is not the limit of the divine love. The only preliminary limit is the resistance of the finite creature.[9]

In this sense, hell is our own handiwork. Orthodox Christian theology states that hell is a reflection of our freedom: our freedom to choose either union with or separation from God. Hell exists because God cannot force us to unite with him. The essence of love is freedom. What can be forced is rape and not love! Hell is not a punishment; it is a mirror image of our inability to love.

Christians talk about love, while Zen people talk about wisdom (*prajna*). Is there any connection between the two? It seems that the bridge between these two worlds lies in the Greek word *epiginōskō*, which denotes a deep knowledge that perfectly unites the subject with the object. *Epiginōskō* is not ordinary knowledge, for it goes beyond the intellectual. It is also revealing to go back to the archaic meaning of the English word "knowledge," which stands for sexual intercourse and erotic love. Paul Tillich observes that the word "can designate both knowledge and sensual love.... Both meanings express an act of union, an overcoming of the cleavage between beings."[10]

In this regard, the difference between Zen and Christianity is just a difference in vocabulary. For knowledge is love. To love God is to know God, and to know God is to love God. Tillich says: "Full knowledge does not admit a difference between itself and love, or between theory and practice."[11] St. John talks about this special knowledge:

> The true light that enlightens every man was coming into the world. He was in the world, and the world was made through him, yet the world knew him not. He came to his own home, and his own people receive him not. But to all who receive him, who believed in his name, he gave power to become children of God. (John 1:9–12)

John says that the True Light was coming into the world, yet the world knew him not. Sin is an expression of ignorance. This is actually quite obvious. For if we do know what is truly good for us, there is no reason why we would not do it. Why should we deliberately harm ourselves? Jesus' portrayal of hell as "outer darkness" is most appropriate. We are imprisoned and tortured by our own ignorance.

Zen people almost never talk about hell or sin. For the real problem is ignorance, especially ignorance about our true identity. Hui Neng, the sixth patriarch of Zen, says that all he ever teaches is "seeing into one's self-nature." Here the advice of "Know thyself!" takes on a new meaning.

Buddha told a slightly different version of the Parable of the Prodigal Son in the Lotus Sutra. He put a heavier emphasis on the role of ignorance in the plight of man. The story goes that the son left home when he was just a young boy. He wandered from place to place for fifty years, living in abject poverty although his father was a very rich man whose wealth could rival a king's. One day the prodigal son wandered inadvertently back to the city where his father lived. *But he had been away for so long that he could not even recognize his own father!* The father understood that the son would not believe it even if he told him the fact then. So he made arrangements so that the son could work as a janitor in his house, believing that he was just a servant to his father. This went on for another twenty years before the father judged that the time was right to tell his son the truth. It was only then that the son reclaimed his inheritance.

What is more effective: to lock up someone whenever he steals something or to make him realize that he is actually an heir who is sitting on billions of dollars? Knowing oneself is what we will discuss next.

The seventh secret about hell is that it is a consequence of not believing in the Son of God. St. John told us about the relationship between belief and salvation:

> For God sent the Son into the world, not to condemn the world, but that the world might be saved through him. He who believes in him is not condemned; he who does not believe is condemned already, because he has not believed in the name of the only Son of God. And this is the judgement, that the light has come into the world, and men love darkness rather than light, because their deeds were evil. For every one who does evil hates the light, and does not come to the light, lest his deeds should be exposed. But he who does what is true comes to the light, that it may be clearly seen that his deeds have been wrought in God. (John 3:17–21)

We condemn ourselves by "not believing in the name of the only Son of God." Fundamentalists often quote this statement as the reason why we should "accept Jesus Christ as our personal savior." The only problem, however, is that they often do not understand what this term "Son of God" means. Tillich writes:

> Literalists often ask whether one believes that "Jesus was the Son of God." Those who ask this question think that they know what the term "Son of God" means and that the only problem is whether this known designation can be attributed to the man Jesus of Nazareth. If the question is asked in this way, it cannot be answered, because either an affirmative or a negative answer would be wrong. The only way to answer the question is to ask another one, namely, What do you mean if you use the term "Son of God"? If one receives a literalist answer to this question, one must reject it as superstitious. If one receives an answer which affirms the symbolic character of the term "Son of God," the meaning of the symbol can be discussed.[12]

For Tillich, the "Son of God" is not a person but a symbol. This symbol, sometimes also referred to as the Incarnation, is indeed at the heart of the Christian doctrine. The crux of the problem is that the symbol is a paradoxical one: the Son of God is neither purely divine, nor purely human, nor hybrid (half-divine and half-human), but both fully divine and fully human. For someone who has little experience working with paradoxes, this is extremely difficult to conceive.

The failure to appreciate this grand paradox has led to a plethora of heresies. The best definition of a heresy that I have seen is coined by author M. Scott Peck, who says that "heresy most commonly arises when we run with just one side of a paradox." An example of heresy is to say that Jesus was totally divine and had no human limitation. This heresy has done Christianity a great disservice by putting distance between Jesus and us. Peck explains how this happens:

> Christians guilty of this heresy have had enough religious training to know the paradoxical reality of Jesus being both human and divine, but put ninety-nine percent of their money on His divinity, and only one percent on his humanity. This leads to the excuse that we can't really be expected to behave like Jesus because it places us way down here, ninety-nine percent human, and Him way up there, beyond identification or imitation.[13]

This is the common problem of deifying a religious leader. We tend to elevate him out of existence or relevance. Frankly, there are many of us who think of Jesus as almost a fairy, a being with great supernatural power who can will anything to happen and is not subject to the normal physical, psychological, and spiritual constraints that a human being has to face. According to Tillich, "much harm has been done in Christianity by a literalistic understanding of the symbol Son of God."[14] By excessive deification, we have made a travesty out of one of the truest and most powerful symbols in Christianity.

To me, the "Son of God" is one of Jesus' greatest koans, a koan not presented to us in words but in the totality of Jesus' life. The challenge, however, is to interpret this great koan in such a way that we don't debase or trivialize it.

I admit that there is no easy solution. My own approach is to treat it as a symbol for the paradoxical nature of the human being: on the one hand, it embodies God's divinity, fully endowed with life, consciousness, and the potential for enlightenment; on the other hand, being part of the finite world, it is seriously constrained by all kinds of weaknesses and limitations. To believe in the Son of God does not mean to believe in the exclusive divinity of Jesus. Rather, it means to see the hidden value of the imperfection so evident in the human condition. It is to see "perfection in imperfection." To transcend the difficulties inherent in the life of a mortal, we have to learn to treat them as part of our spiritual path. So instead of seeing them as obstacles, we can use them to accelerate our personal growth. The apostle Paul explains this paradox as follows:

> And to keep me from being too elated by the abundance of revelations, a thorn was given me in the flesh, a messenger of Satan, to harass me, to keep me from being too elated. Three times I besought the Lord about this that it should leave me; but he said to me, "My grace is sufficient for you, for my power is made perfect in weakness." I will all the more gladly boast of my weaknesses, that the power of Christ may rest upon me. For the sake of Christ, then, I am content with weaknesses, insults, hardships, persecution, and calamities; *for when I am weak, then I am strong.* (2 Cor 12:7–10)

To believe in the name of the Son of God is to believe in our *inner divinity,* regardless of the circumstances. It is the opposite of self-loathing. Zen masters refer to this inner divinity by a different name: Buddha-nature. This Buddha-nature is our seed of enlightenment. It is present in all sentient beings without discrimination.

Self-loathing is a much wider problem than is commonly recognized. The fact is that very few of us can really accept ourselves as we are. Although selfishness is rampant, it doesn't mean that we can therefore love ourselves. To equate selfishness with self-love is a grave mistake, for love has to be unconditional. Evidence of our lack of self-love is abundant. How often do we curse ourselves even for the slightest mistakes and say "You idiot," "You screwed it up," "You can never do anything right"? The secret is that we condemn ourselves to hell through our self-loathing.

For Paul self-loathing has taken on inordinate proportions. Listen to him: "Nothing good dwells in me, that is my flesh. I can will what is right but I cannot do it" (Rom. 7:18). He was constantly being tortured by his inner conflict: "I pummel my body and subdue it, lest after preaching to others I myself should be disqualified" (1 Cor. 9:27).

Spiritual teacher and author Marianne Williamson points out the relationship between self-loathing and violence:

> Emotional energy has got to go somewhere, and self-loathing is a powerful emotion. Turned inward, it becomes our personal hells:

addiction, obsession, compulsion, depression, violent relationships, illness. Projected outward, it becomes our collective hells: violence, war, crime, oppression.[15]

I learned about the importance of self-acceptance while reading bedtime stories to my children. One book I read is called *There Is a Boy in the Girls' Bathroom*. It tells the story about a boy named Bradley, who was a bully and troublemaker. Bradley had no friends. Everyone considered him a monster and would not want to sit near him. The situation did not turn around until Bradley met the new school counselor, Carla, who was able to accept him as he was. During one of the counseling sessions, Bradley and Carla had a discussion about "monsters from outer space." Bradley asked Carla whether she believed in the existence of such creatures. Carla answered that while she believed that there are a myriad of creatures in the universe, she did not think that any one of them were monsters:

> [Bradley asked,] "Not even one?"
> "No," said Carla. "I think everyone has "good" inside him. Everyone can feel happiness and sadness and loneliness. But sometimes people think someone's a monster. But that is only because they can't see the "good" that is there inside him. And then a terrible thing happens."
> "They kill him?"
> "No, even worse. They call him a monster, and other people start calling him a monster, and everyone treats him like a monster, and then after a while, he starts believing it himself. He thinks he's a monster too. So he acts like one. But he still isn't a monster. He still has lots of good, buried deep inside him."[16]

Bradley spent the rest of the session drawing a "monster from outer space." He drew one with three arms and six hands, but had some difficulty fitting eight fingers onto each hand. Then the conversation resumed:

> He looked up. "Carla?"
> "Yes, Bradley."
> "Can you see inside monsters?" he asked. "Can you see the 'good'?"
> "That's all I see."
> He returned to his picture. He drew a black eye in the middle of the creature's face. He drew a red heart inside the creature's chest to show all the "good" that was there.

"Well, how does a monster stop being a monster?" he asked. "I mean, if everyone sees only a monster, and they keep treating him like a monster, how does he stop being a monster?"

"It isn't easy," Carla said. "I think, first, he has to realize for himself that he isn't a monster. That, I think, is the first step. Until he knows he isn't a monster, how is everybody else supposed to know?"[17]

To believe in the name of the Son of God is to realize that we are not monsters but sentient beings with a heart. The first step to spirituality is to believe in the Christ-in-us.

The eighth secret of hell is that it is part of the kingdom. In the beginning of this chapter, I said that hell is the complement of the kingdom. That gives us the impression that hell and the kingdom are distinctly apart. This is not true. Returning to the Parable of the Prodigal Son, does it strike you as strange that the father did not try to stop his son from leaving home and he did not punish him when he returned?

One explanation for this is that the father secretly condoned the son's "little excursion" — out of love. When we are young, we tend to be adventurous and eager for new excitement. Surely, being inexperienced, we are bound to make mistakes and get hurt sometimes. And the prodigal son did suffer for his recklessness. There was a point in his life when he was starving and would even eat what the swine ate. But while mistakes hurt, they also educate. It would have been a big mistake indeed if the father had forced the son to stay home, thus depriving his son of the opportunity to grow.

The ninth secret of hell, perhaps the most important one, is that it is a game invented by a hide-and-seek God. The understanding of this is critical for resolving the "problem of evil" in Christian theology: if God is the creator of everything and God is omnipotent, why does God allow the existence of evil and suffering?

To answer this question, we have to get into the secret of secrets. Alan Watts calls it "inside information." This "inside information" is deeply embedded in the religious literatures of the world, but it is usually highly coded and camouflaged, thus inaccessible to ordinary people. The superficial mind cannot quite grasp its profundity and the traditional mind finds it subversive. But if we are really interested in knowing the meaning of life, we have no choice but to break this taboo: *the taboo against knowing who we really are.*

Suppose you are an enlightened grandfather or grandmother, and you would like to pass on to your grandchildren certain wisdom that can help them through their own journeys of life, what would you tell them? Alan Watts suggests that we create a myth that is not supposed to be exactly true but is used as a poetic tool by which we make sense out of life. How shall we begin? Borrowing heavily from the mythologies of the world and from Watts, I create this version of "secret knowledge":

> In the beginning, there was nothing but God. God was like a child — creative, playful, fun-loving, and full of life. There was nothing that God could not do. Whatever he willed became reality. God had only one "problem": he had no one to play with.
>
> To pull himself out of his loneliness and boredom, God came up with an ingenious solution: he begot his own playmates. He split himself up into many pieces, which became you and I and everybody else. On the surface, we are all different and separate beings; but underlying the superficial multiplicity, we are one single reality: God.
>
> Having split himself up into many pieces, God was ready for his game. But before he could have any fun, there was one more thing he had to do: forget about himself! He had to hide his own identity. So he induced his own amnesia and lost himself into the world. Taking up different forms just like a child in play, he got into all kinds of adventures; some of these are like sweet dreams, but others are like the worst of nightmares. In fact, they can be downright violent and frightful. This way, the world goes on and on. We have the cosmic dance of *yin* and *yang,* goodness and evil, war and peace, love and hate, joy and horror, tears and laughter. But happy or sad, these are all *lila* (God's play). It is God's way of entertaining himself.
>
> So this is the human condition; we are all *Deity-in-amnesia.* We look so helpless, so much a prey to Fate. But deep inside, we are God hiding his omnipotence in order to generate challenges to exercise his creativity. Forgetting our true identity, we may weep or "gnash our teeth" in our self-created hell. But in the very center of our beings, there remains a primordial memory, waiting to be awakened.

Complaining about suffering and other problems of life, therefore, makes no sense at all in the grand scheme of things. Who is the sufferer and who can we complain to, if we are all One? Remember, we are the God-turned-prodigal-son, enjoying himself in blissful self-abandonment! There is no one to complain to, and there is nothing to complain about because we are it. This is precisely why Jesus exclaimed: "I am the Way, and the Truth, and the Life." Lest we misinterpret this statement, he also said that he is the hungry one in the street, the naked one without clothes, the sick one in bed, the prisoner in jail. For each one of us is like a mirror reflecting the same reality. As J. Krishnamurti said, "You are the world."

In the midst of a political uprising, a Japanese general sought advice from a Zen master. "Is there a way to win without fighting?" the general asked. The master replied:

> The world is a dream; only that the dreamer is not aware of it. When we fight with others, that fight is an illusion; when we awaken, where is the enemy? Thus, when we treat the world as real, it is because we are dreaming without knowing it. As such, we are happy when we win, but sad when we lose. But if we are just fighting in a dualistic dream, what sense does it make to be happy or sad? The fight in the dream has to be stopped — detach yourself from the illusions of winning, losing, and striving!

But most of us find it difficult to awaken. Even that may not be so bad. Alan Watts told us the reason:

> Now when God plays hide and pretends that he is you and I, he does it so well that it takes him a long time to remember where and how he hid himself. But that's the whole fun of it — just what he wanted to do. He doesn't want to find himself too quickly, for that would spoil the game.[18]

Zen neither affirms nor negates. Lest we become too hasty to dismiss the "illusions" of our lives, note that, logically speaking, to say that "all is illusory" is the same as to say that "all is (equally) real." After all, if God is behind these dramas, what is the distinction between dream and reality? An eminent art critic and a devotee of Zen once remarked to R. H. Blyth that there is no Zen in Western art or literature since the word itself does not exist in any European language. Here is Blyth's reply:

> Eastern Zen art always portrays *satori*, enlightenment,... Western Zen art, on the contrary, very often shows us *mayoi* (maya), illusion, irresoluteness, the divided mind, the unsatisfiable desire, that of Faustus and Hamlet.... Should this, and other examples of mayoi, seem strange to Japanese "Zenists," let them remember the most difficult doctrine of Zen, that illusion *is* enlightenment, enlightenment *is* illusion.[19]

If the world is divine play, it seems that all is well. Indeed, this is precisely the conclusion reached by King Oedipus in his old age, despite the many trials and tribulations in his life.

So this is our mission in life: to be a good player, by accepting what is and living in the moment. If there is any recipe for happiness at all, this has to be it. After all, on a very deep level we are the author of our script and the setter of our stage.

— Seven —

Faith

The kingdom of God is within you.
—Jesus

Religion cannot be found in the temples and monasteries; it has to be found in people's hearts.... Perhaps one day we have to demolish the temples and monasteries in order to save religion.
—The Fourteenth Dalai Lama

Have you heard of the Temple of the Broken Gods? There is indeed such a temple in Taiwan. A compassionate Buddhist monk set it up to serve as a sanctuary for the "gods" people have abandoned. Many are images of Chinese folk gods; some are statues of the Buddhist bodhisattvas (enlightened sentient beings); others are the images of Taoist immortals. All of these "broken gods" met the same humbling fate of being thrown into the garbage pile. They are the live testimonies of how ugly "faith" can get when it becomes an expression of the ego.

As we mentioned earlier, the Chinese tend to be superstitious and materialistic. Religious sentiment, in the Western sense, has been lacking at the grassroots level. Many Chinese approach their "gods" for pragmatic reasons: to divine the future, to obtain blessings in worldly matters, to be cured, to get protection from evil spirits, etc. They do not so much worship their gods as they try to use them. Before a gambler visits the gambling place, for example, he may go to the temple to make a wish, which is effectively a deal, with his god. In exchange for his god's blessing, he promises to come back with big sacrifices if he wins. But if he loses, well.... The Temple of Broken

113

Gods gives you a good idea of what happens in that case: we have decapitated gods, gods missing an arm, and gods who are chopped in half by one angry stroke!

I grew up with this kind of cultural background in Hong Kong, so perhaps you can understand why I tend to be allergic to this whole "faith business." For a long time, "faith" meant only two things to me: *cosmeticized greed* or *cosmeticized fear.* The Chinese may be an extreme case, but it seems fair to say that there is always a trace of "spiritual materialism" in any religion — folk religions, Buddhism, Taoism, Islam, and Christianity. If there is any difference at all, it is only a matter of degree.

I was brought up as an Anglican. Though I was baptized as a child, I was never confirmed. My Christian friends are mostly Baptists with strong evangelical inclinations. When I am around them, I sense a dark element in their faith: fear. A Christian friend once said to me earnestly: "Ken, if you do not accept Jesus Christ as your personal savior, you are liable to hell-fire. You may find it highly doubtful that there is indeed a hell in the afterlife, but why take the risk? It doesn't cost you anything to believe in Jesus, you know."

I call this line of argument "the free insurance approach." It is clever, but it turns me off. Don't get me wrong; I really like my friend. He is a warm and good-hearted human being with great moral integrity. I am, in fact, moved by the sincerity with which he tries to share his religious experience. But I simply do not believe that God is a wishing well or a pusher of free insurance. Nor do I believe in a teddy-bear God, something that we cling to for comfort. Karl Marx once referred to religion as the "opium of the people." Unfortunately, his statement rings true because that is how many people use faith. We tend to go to our respective religions for comfort, for a vague notion of being blessed or protected, for a feeling of being taken care of.

But if this is what we understand faith to be, then Master Jesus has some news for us. For he told his disciples, "Do not think that I have come to bring peace on earth; I have not come to bring peace, but a sword" (Matt. 10:34). The Zen master Hakuin echoes: "Should you desire the great tranquillity, prepare to sweat white beads."

There is no "mellow" way to truth. Contrary to common understanding, true faith is more a challenge than a sanctuary. To have faith is not to be a sissy but a warrior. While faith has nothing to do with being a he-man with the associated aggressiveness, it does mean being courageous enough to face reality as it is, no matter how ugly it may look.

I renounced what I considered to be my Christian faith at around age seventeen, not without fear and trembling. I found the idea of using God as a crutch totally distasteful. I preferred to be on my own. In hindsight I now see that my apparent abandonment of "faith" has actually paved the way for real faith. Sometimes, it is necessary to tear down the old so that the new can be built.

> And no one puts a piece of unshrunk cloth on an old garment, for the patch tears away from the garment, and a worse tear is made. Neither is new wine put into old wineskins; if it is, the skins burst, and the wine is spilled, and the skins are destroyed; but new wine is put into fresh wineskins, and so both are preserved. (Matt. 9:16–17)

What has to go is the religion of fear and hope. Real faith and the cult of insecurity simply cannot coexist. The "faith" that I have been taught ever since childhood — the Santa Claus God, the teddy-bear God, the God of fire and brimstone — is fundamentally wrong. It has to be thrown out the window because it cannot serve as a foundation for a faith based on love. Of course, the demolition phase is always painful. After all, we are talking about parting with things that we have always cherished as children. But such is the price of growing up. Simone Weil made the following observation:

> Religion in so far as it is a source of consolation is a hindrance to true faith: in this sense atheism is a purification. I have to be atheistic with the part of myself which is not made for God. Among those men in whom the superficial part has not awakened, the atheist is right and the believer wrong.[1]

Weaning ourselves from the false God is painful enough, but it is nothing compared to the agony of coming to terms with the shadow side of God. I read the book of Job when I was in my mid-teens, and I was totally appalled by the way God treated Job in his wager with the devil. Job's protests thundered in my mind: Why do innocent people have to suffer? Why do some evil people go unpunished? Is Satan just another face (or mask) of God? I remembered very clearly a lucid dream that pictured the army of goodness and the army of evil confronting each other. The two forces appear to be at war, yet they are fully integrated with each other: evil is the ground of goodness, and goodness is the ground of evil.

It was not until much later that I resolved this issue about the amorality of God. It took me years and years of training in Zen and

Taoism before I could really see the beauty in this creative tension, how the *yin* and the *yang*, goodness and evil, the force of life and the force of death are intimate enemies who simultaneously fight and cooperate, how their apparent war enables our spiritual growth. No real faith is possible unless we squarely confront these thorny issues instead of trying to sweep them under the carpet. Real faith requires both courage and the insight to see into the nature of things.

What is *faith?* To me, faith is like Zen; it evades definition. But we can indicate a few of its characteristics. It is a matter of the heart and not a matter of the head. It is a right-brain phenomenon and not a left-brain one. As such, faith has nothing to do with beliefs, dogmas, creeds, or theology. Faith is *existential* and not intellectual; it has to do with openness, receptivity, trust, and love and not with arguments and proofs. It contains many Zen elements, the most prominent being gentleness, freedom, "ordinary magic," and courage. Tillich likes to use the term "the courage to be." This is the essence of faith: it has to do with the will to affirm life and its goodness despite all doubts, difficulties, and suffering.

This may not be obvious, but the Lord's Prayer tells us much about what faith is. So let us revisit it with a beginner's mind:

> Our Father who art in heaven,
> Hallowed be thy name,
> Thy kingdom come,
> Thy will be done,
> On earth as it is in heaven.
> Give us this day our daily bread;
> And forgive us our debts,
> As we also have forgiven our debtors;
> And lead us not into temptation,
> But deliver us from evil.

(Matt. 6:9–13)

Note how Jesus always used the word "our" instead of the word "my." Faith has nothing to do with the ego. Yes, there are petitions made in the Lord's Prayer too, but let us pay attention to their order. The first three petitions have no direct relevance to individual needs at all; they pertain to God, God's kingdom, and God's will. Actually the third petition captures the entire essence of Jesus' faith: Thy will be done!

The message is clear. Faith is a matter of *surrender* and not a matter of making demands. God is not a servant of ours who stands ever ready to grant our wishes. Neither is God a protector in any ordinary sense. The Lord's Prayer is a good illustration of the principle Jesus taught at the end of the Nature Sermon: "But seek first his kingdom and his righteousness, and all these things shall be yours as well" (Matt. 6:33). To put it more simply, to have faith is to put God above our ego. Jesus told the religious groupies: "Not everyone who says to me, 'Lord, Lord,' shall enter the kingdom of heaven, but he who does the will of my Father who is in heaven" (Matt. 7:21). The million-dollar question is: How do we know what is God's will and what is not? Any suggestions?

I used to lose sleep over this question; now I don't. The matter is not complicated at all. To do God's will is simply to surrender our ego and accept what is. It is to develop a *nonviolent* approach to life: to recognize and accept our weaknesses and limitations, to be friendly with the universe instead of fighting against it, to accept that there are things that we simply cannot control or predict.

While faith is not a matter of egotistic pursuit, neither is it a matter of blind obedience. Robots cannot have faith; only human beings can. Faith is possible only if the freedom to disobey is present. Traditionally, we portray the relationship between God and human beings as one between a king and his subjects, but it is actually much more "democratic" than that. A better metaphor for the God-humankind relationship is that of *erotic love* — the love between a man and a woman. The surrender that is required for faith is a tender and voluntary one. Thomas Merton says:

> But this element of submission in faith must not be so overemphasized that it seems to constitute the whole essence of faith: as if a mere unloving, unenlightened, dogged submission of the will to authority were enough to make a "man of faith." If this element of will is overemphasized then the difference between faith in the intellect and simple obedience in the will becomes obscured. In certain cases this can be very unhealthy, because actually if there is no *light* of faith, no interior illumination of the mind by grace by which one accepts the proposed truth *from* God and thereby attains to it, so to speak, in this divine assurance, then inevitably the mind lacks the true peace, the supernatural support which is due to it. In that event there is not real faith. The positive element of light is lacking. There is a forced suppression of doubt rather than the opening of the eye of the heart by deep belief.[2]

Perhaps we can understand faith better by drawing an analogy with sex: Jesus spoke of the brides and the bridegroom. In his Parable of the Ten Maidens, there are ten maidens but only one bridegroom. For every human soul is a maiden in the eye of God. A little girl, Anna, who had a very special friendship with God and an amazing gift of articulating deep spiritual truth in first-grade language, revealed this "fact of life" to us in her conversation with Fynn, the teenager who adopted her:

> "Fynn, is church sex?"
> I was awake, very much so!
> "What do you mean, is church sex?"
> "It puts seeds in your heart and makes new things come."
> "Oh!"
> "That's why it's Mister God and not Missis God."
> "Oh, is it?"
> "Well, it might be. It might be." She went on, "I think lessons is sex too."
> "You'd better not tell Miss Haynes that."
> "Why not? Lessons put things in your head and some new things come."[3]

This is the spiritual sexology of Anna. The bottom line is that we are all feminine in our relationship to God. Being *yin* (female), we can find happiness only in yielding to God. After all, God is Reality. We cannot fight Reality without incurring suffering for ourselves. And our yielding to God has to be done with love, enlightenment, and enthusiasm. For a bitter surrender is not real acceptance and will not lead to happiness. True lovers give themselves to each other in joy. As Erich Fromm has pointed out, "the active character of love is primarily giving, not receiving."[4]

When I was in middle school, my Bible teacher told me that our sole purpose in life is to glorify God. I could not understand it then. Why should our relationship to God always be such a one-way street? Why is God such a despot? It was only much later that I could understand that there is no "conflict of interest" between God and us: *to serve God is to bring happiness to oneself.* On the other hand, serving the ego can only be self-defeating. For the ego can never be satisfied, and desire is a bottomless pit. True happiness is not possible until we recognize this basic fact.

A parallel can be found in our contemporary mentality. One learns to view life as a zero-sum game: the loss of others is my gain, and my loss is other people's gain. This odd idea gets carried over even to one's intimate relationships, to the pillow politics between husbands and wives. In the me-generation, "giving" always sounds like a self-sacrifice. But the basic teaching of all spirituality is that this zero-sum vision of life is a fatal illusion. Using again the imagery of erotic love, no pleasure is possible unless the lovers willingly give their bodies and souls to each other in a sexual union. The more generous and enthusiastic the giving is, the greater the joy.

Giving is equally important in other expressions of love: between friends, between parent and child, between strangers. We are always enriched by our giving, provided that it is sincere. For it gives us an opportunity to exert our beings, utilize our creative power, and affirm our humanity. In giving, we become more alive, more human, more productive, and more confident of our own ability. As Zen master Seisetsu put it, "The giver should be thankful."

A dogged submission to God will not lead to genuine spirituality. Real faith is a function of *enlightened* surrender, which involves "the opening of the eye of the heart." When that happens, God fertilizes the human soul with the Holy Spirit. In Chinese, the character for the word "spirit" is the same as the one for "semen." The appropriateness of the sexual language and imageries is confirmed by the fact that historically some gnostic branches of Christianity have referred to the Spirit as the Holy Sperm.

Besides surrender, faith also contains the elements of mutual trust and intimacy. This is beautifully illustrated in Jesus' soulful expression: "I and the Father are one." Our trusting the universe can make a big difference in determining how happy we are. If we view our relationship with All There Is as antagonistic, then depression and existential anxiety are the natural results. On the other hand, if we view our relationship with All There Is as one of complete trust and openness, then there is a potential for joy and peace. As the great Zen master Dogen said: "To be enlightened is to be intimate with all things."

Above all, faith is a spontaneous expression of our soul's ability to love. The maturity of our faith depends on the maturity of our love. As Erich Fromm has pointed out, immature love says: "I love you because I need you." In contrast, mature love is not driven by needs; it is more an overflow of one's inner richness and joy. Mature faith, just like mature love, tends to be *unconditional.* When Jesus bid us not to be troubled about our life, our food, and our clothing, he was talking about mature faith. John A. Sanford, a Jungian analyst and an Episcopal priest, captures Jesus' understanding of faith as follows:

When Jesus speaks of faith, he is speaking of a certain capacity of a person to affirm life in spite of what life may bring, and even in the face of doubt....It has little to do with one's formal, intellectual beliefs, which may actually stand in the way of a living faith. It has a good deal to do with the relationship to one's soul, for the soul, with her capacity for love, is in touch with the fundamental meaningfulness of life and so can inspire faith.[5]

The Zen equivalent to faith is *gentleness*. As you recall from chapter 2 above, true gentleness is not a sign of weakness but an indication of inner strength. Zen master Yuen Mun once used the expression "Every day is a good day" to describe the state of enlightenment. "Every day is a good day" does not mean hitting the jackpot everyday. Nor does it mean getting a promise from God or Buddha. Rather, it refers to the blissful state in which one can accept reality totally and unconditionally.

The beauty of Zen gentleness is well illustrated in this poem by Zen master Mumon:

> The flower blossom in spring; the bright moon in autumn;
> The cool breeze in summer; the white snow in winter —
> When the mind is not obstructed by anything,
> Every season is a good season.

Gentleness is an expression of a nonattached mind. William Blake taught the joy of letting go in his poem "Eternity":

> He who bends to himself a Joy,
> Does the winged life destroy;
> But he who kisses the Joy as it flies,
> Lives in Eternity's sunrise.

The Christian equivalent to the *unobstructed mind* is the *pure heart*. Jesus said in the Beatitudes: "Blessed are the pure in heart, for they shall see God" (Matt. 5:8). Evidently, God can be seen only in the state of emptiness, when our hearts are no longer obstructed by all kinds of material, sensual, psychological, intellectual, and spiritual attachments. Here we see great harmony between Jesus' and Zen's teachings.

It is now evident that faith has a *feminine* character. Actually, the word "faith" is often used to name a girl. But while true faith has to do with letting go of one's attachments, many "religious" people have made a travesty of it by making faith their biggest attachment of all! By clutching to various doctrines, codes of conduct, and scriptural interpretations, they have effectively clothed faith in armor.

A sure sign of false faith is its militant stance. While true faith is marked by its gentleness to all aspects of life, false faith can be easily identified by its stubbornness, inflexibility, paranoia, and a desperate need to be "right."

Because false faith is basically paranoia in disguise, it has a strong tendency to turn violent. Many religious fanatics have a deep sense of insecurity. Consciously or subconsciously, they feel a need to hold on to some power symbol for their peace of mind. This symbol can be anything: a historical person, a set of sacred writings, religious doctrines, creeds, a sacred object. Having a symbol is not a problem in itself; the problem is that they have turned their religious symbol into a fetish. Because the fetish means so much to them, they will attack whatever or whoever seems to undermine it. The pathologies of a false faith are well-known: it is imprisoning rather than liberating, barricading instead of uncluttering, indoctrinating rather than enlightening. Fynn made the following diagnosis:

> The hoarding down the Broadway displayed in large red lettering: DO YOU WANT TO BE SAVED? I wondered just how many people would say yes to that. Had it read "Do you want to be safe?" millions of people would have said "Yes, yes, yes, we want to be safe," and another barricade would have gone up. The soul is imprisoned, protected, nothing can get in to hurt it, but then it can't get out either. Being saved is nothing to do with being safe. Being saved is seeing yourself clearly — no "bits a colored glass," no protection, no hiding — simply seeing yourself.[6]

Real faith does not mean living the fortified life of a hermit crab; we know that a faith is poisoned if the *yin* of gentleness and humility is replaced by the *yang* of rigidity, arrogance, cruelty, and hatred. Faith, once a beauty, has become a beast!

The world is terrorized by people whose "faith" has gone astray. We only need to take a brief look at history to find out how much human misery, suffering, and bloodshed have been caused by this monster. Nowadays, thanks to the separation between church and state in most parts of the world, the destructive power of perverted faith is held somewhat in check. Still, religious wars continue and religious follies are rampant. Several years ago, I watched with interest the textbook war between the creationists and the evolutionists in California and Texas. What exactly does faith have to do with whether human beings have evolved from apes or not? While the incident seems to be relatively harmless, it reminds us that the beast is definitely not yet dead and can raise its ugly head again any time. The recent shootings of abortion clinic doctors by the so-called pro-life religious groups are chilling reminders of this fact.

This being said, we must never demonize those who practice religious fanaticism, oppression, bigotry, and other forms of religious intolerance. For they too are victims, the victims of their own ignorance and illusions. Take, for example, the "religious" people during Jesus' time, the scribes and the Pharisees. They dedicated their whole lives to their religion. Although they might have been instrumental in putting Jesus on the cross, they were not evil people. Rather, they were people who pursued their faith with desperate earnestness. The Pharisees, in particular, were dedicated legalists who tried to observe every single detail of the law. While they were long on effort and devotion, they were short on wisdom. They could not see that spirituality has nothing to do with a dogged adherence to form.

The danger of perverted faith lies in the fact that it is self-justifying. Chances are that the scribes and the Pharisees who persecuted Jesus *sincerely* believed that they were serving God by stamping out the "heresies" of Jesus and that they were the defenders of the true faith. It is precisely this self-righteousness, disguised as strong faith, that is most devious and destructive. For it allows the religious fanatics to do what they want to do without any feeling of shame or guilt. It is heartbreaking to see people who are so devoted to truth end up doing something that is the exact opposite of it. But what happened to Jesus is still happening now. And it will continue to happen as long as there is still the illusion that truth is something that can be possessed, monopolized, or attached to.

Within this context we can understand why the Buddha was never too "serious" about truth. He had taught and preached for a full forty-nine years and yet he said that he had not spoken one word of truth. We can also understand why the Zen masters love to joke about the Buddha and other sacred objects. One famous Zen joke is to say that you should rinse your mouth out every time you say the word "Buddha." If this sounds irreverent, take a fresh look at the third commandment: "You shall not take the name of the Lord your God in vain" (Exod. 20:7).

No mortal can be absolutely certain that he or she knows the truth. Think about *how* we go about verifying our "truths." These are the relevant questions: What is the benchmark? Who is the verifier? Who has the ultimate authority? The empiricists among us may try to do their verification through empirical data. But so-called empirical data are a product of our own senses, which are not fool-proof. In the end, we can experience the world only through our subjective mind, and we have no way to tell how much distortion, filtering, and "selective listening" have taken place in this perception process. The basic problem is that we have no way to jump outside our system (our mind) to see what is really going on. Just like an eye cannot see itself or observe the process of seeing, we have no way to tell how much of what we consider reality is shaped by our genetics, upbringing, culture, and prior experiences. We are slaves to our subjective minds.

The world is terrorized by people who hold many "truths." I never doubt their sincerity regarding what they believe in; I only worry about their lack of self-knowledge. Buddha considers ignorance as the root of all evil. Dom Aelred Graham made this observation:

> The earnest seeker after truth has usually decided in advance what kind of truth he is looking for. He is apt to discover, at the end of his searches, "what I had always thought." ... It is the same predisposition of mind which leads us to read the books and newspapers which reinforce rather than challenge our views; the same that prompts us to seek counsel not from an impartial critic, but from a like-minded friend.[7]

This is not to say that there are no truths. Newton's laws of motion, Einstein's laws of relativity, the laws of thermodynamics are all *relative* truths; they are relative to our perception system, relative to our current scientific understanding, and relative to our subjective mind. Whether they will be overturned in the future when our understanding of the universe and of our own mind improves is not a question we can answer now. The computer right in front of me looks real and solid enough, but where will it be if there is no human being to perceive it? Isn't the form in which it appears to me dependent on the way my nervous system is built and the way my mind organizes sensory data? If so, what is objective reality?

As far as "absolute truths" are concerned, to say "I know" is an act of arrogance and ignorance. In the end, all we can assert with some sense of certainty is that we do not know (absolute) truth. The third patriarch of Zen, Seng-t'san, offered us the following advice:

> There is no need to seek after the truth,
> It is enough simply to stop holding on to opinions.

Only Don't Know is the name of a book published by contemporary Zen master Seung Sahn and represents the heart of his teachings. While a "don't-know mind" is alive and full of possibilities, a mind that claims to know is a closed and stagnant one. Master Seung Sung elaborates on his "don't-know" motto:

> Don't-know mind cuts through thinking. It is before thinking. Before thinking, there is no doctor, no patient; also no God, no Buddha, no "I," no words — nothing at all. Then you and the universe become one. We call this nothing-mind, or primary point. Some people say it is God, or universal energy, or bliss, or extinction. But these are only teaching words. Nothing-mind is before words.[8]

This "don't-know" mind may sound too radical and un-Christian, but Jesus had his own Zen buzzword: the "baby-mind." Jesus declared that God shows secrets to babes but not to the wise and understanding (Matt. 11:25). For babes are the real "don't-know" masters. When have you seen an opinionated baby?

The "baby-mind" of Jesus appears to be simply a continuation of a long legacy of anti-idolatry in the Judeo-Christian tradition. The opposite of faith is not atheism or agnosticism; it is idolatry. The admonition against idolatry is the second of the Ten Commandments, which states: "You shall not make for yourself a graven image, or any likeness of anything that is in heaven above, or that is in the earth beneath; you shall not bow down to them or serve them" (Exod. 20:4–5). By all standards, idolatry is a very serious offense.

The key question then is this: Why is God so uptight about people creating an image? Is God the kind who does not like having his picture taken? Actually, the answer is quite simple — no one has ever seen God. God cannot be seen because God is the Subject and not an object, Spirit and not a thing. Thus, to make an image of God is to make a claim for knowledge that one does not have, i.e., to lie. If one makes a lie an object of worship and attachment, suffering is obviously inevitable. The Judeo-Christian teaching of nonidolatry turns out to be an equivalent of the Buddhist teaching of nonattachment. In Zen language, idolatry is to "take the finger pointing to the moon as the moon itself."

This explains why Jesus, who was so gentle and mild-mannered in most circumstances, was so severe with the scribes and the Pharisees. They were the target of Jesus' seven woes. Jesus criticized them, not because they were hypocrites nor because they refused to accept him as their Messiah, but because of their idolatry. Effectively, the scribes idolized the scriptures and the Pharisees idolized the law. Jesus was teaching Zen when he said to them: "Woe to you, scribes and Pharisees, hypocrites! for you build the tombs of the prophets and adorn the monuments of the righteous" (Matt. 23:29). Tombs and adornments have limited spiritual value: the former can be used only to hold dead bodies and the latter can create only superficial beauty.

What Jesus points to is a *living truth,* i.e., a message of tremendous import and meaning to the person involved, at a particular moment in time. As such, truth is by nature instantaneous and situational; it cannot be frozen in words, thoughts, and concepts. We cannot grasp it or attach ourselves to it. *We must live it* (i.e., directly experience it) in the eternal now through the exercise of mindfulness. We have to learn from the babes.

In any case, spiritual truth is a living experience that cannot be repeated. "You can learn only through making mistakes," for example, is a great truth for someone who is devastated by a failure that is not due to a lack of effort. But when my son used the statement as a shield for my rebuke of his habitual sloppiness in his work, I felt really angry — for I saw a truth abused.

People with a Western education tend to think of truth as something that can be indefinitely generalized over time, culture, people, and events. But the Zen notion of truth is very different. The litmus test for Zen truth is its *context-dependency:* a truth, if it is going to have any spiritual impact on the person involved, has to be person-specific, time-specific, and situation-specific. Generalization, when applied to spiritual truth, is an open invitation to abuse. A general, repeatable truth is useless! Truth is in the moment and it takes an alert mind to catch it.

The early Christians were just as creative as the Asian Zen masters in teaching nonattachment. While Master Seung Sahn talked about the "don't-know mind," St. Paul talked about the "don't-know God." He told the Greeks in Athens, "What therefore you worship as unknown, this I proclaim to you. The God who made the world and everything in it, being Lord of heaven and earth, does not live in shrines made by man" (Acts 17:23–24). For the same reason, Jesus told the Samaritan woman at the well that "God is spirit, and those who worship him must worship in spirit and truth" (John 4:24).

What is a spirit like? Should we even venture to answer this, we will find ourselves grasping the wind. For "spirit" is Jesus' version of the unknown God. Unfortunately, these repeated messages have gone

largely unnoticed, and humankind continues to make idols. Bishop
John Shelby Spong told us that one of the biggest idols in history
turns out to be the frozen image of Christ:

> Christ is indeed the "hero of a thousand faces." He was the divine
> judge and the helpless infant. He was the life-denying monastic and
> the political revolutionary. He was the soft Jesus who sat on a hill-
> side and invited the children to come to him and the liberationist and
> radical organizer who drove money changers from the temple. Christ
> has been and still is many things to many people. All of them are
> Christ and none of them is Christ. Freeze any image and idolatry is
> the sure result. Allow no concrete images to emerge and the Christ
> will disappear from our consciousness.[9]

Faith is not the pursuit of security; it is the acceptance of insecurity. The faith of Jesus is that of the tiny seed, which is not afraid to
die in order to generate new life. As Alan Watts has pointed out, belief in a definite and frozen Christ to be leaned against is the antithesis
of faith. It is an attitude of rigidity rather than of trust. It reflects a
basic misunderstanding of the inverse laws that are the heart of Jesus'
teachings. An attachment to Jesus as one's savior is, therefore, the ultimate mockery of all that he represents and a pathetic betrayal of
true faith. Alan Watts elaborates:

> The Crucifixion gives eternal life because it is the giving up of God as
> an object to be possessed, known, and held to for one's own safety,
> "for he that would save his soul shall lose it." To cling to Jesus is
> therefore to worship a Christ uncrucified, an idol instead of the living
> God.[10]

It is within the context of the inverse laws that we can understand
Christian hope. Hope and faith are like twin sisters. The importance
of hope in Christianity is established by Paul's statement: "For in this
hope we were saved." (Rom. 8:24) But while Christians emphasize
hope, Buddhists emphasize hopelessness. The mystery is that while
the two religions are apparently so divergent on this subject, true
Christians and true Buddhists have both managed to live their lives
in joy and peace. How can we make sense of this?

Jesus never talked about hope. But much about Christian hope
can be learned through an understanding of the beatitudes, which
is a treasury of Jesus' inverse laws. In them, we can find the entire secret of Christian hope. This secret lies in a subtle point: the
beatitudes, expressed originally in Greek, contain no verb! The statement "Blessed are the poor in spirit," for example, can be translated

as "the exquisite joy of being poor in spirit!" Bible scholar William Barclay has this to say about this peculiar grammatical structure:

> That is most important, for it means that the beatitudes are not pious hopes of what shall be; they are not glowing, but nebulous prophesies of some future bliss; they are congratulations on what is. The blessedness which belongs to the Christian is not a blessedness which is postponed to some future world of glory; it is blessedness which exists here-and-now. It is not something into which the Christian will enter; it is something into which he has entered.[11]

Christian hopes are not hopes in the ordinary sense, which always imply some kind of expectation about future events and an element of uncertainty. St. Paul said that "hope does not disappoint us" (Rom. 5:5). This is possible only if the "hope" refers not to a future possibility but to a *present* reality.

In the aftermath of a recent natural disaster in which many lives were lost and property damages were rampant, a local evangelist led a public prayer regarding the event. What is notable is that she did not pray for a reversal of the damages that had been done. Neither did she pray for the nonoccurrence of similar tragedies. What she did pray for, however, was that all those involved in the incident would understand God's will. She prayed for illumination regarding the *meaning* of such an incident. This is the essence of Christian hope: it has nothing to do with ego gratification or getting God to do what we want done; it has to do with finding meaning in what is.

This interpretation of hope is confirmed by looking at the Greek word for "blessed": *makarios.* According to William Barclay, this term "describes that joy which has its secret within itself, that joy which is serene, untouchable and self-contained, that joy which is completely independent of all the chances and the changes of life." We conclude, therefore, that Christian hope refers to an existing, *but yet to be discovered,* reality. Hope hints at a new way to look at the world.

The beatitudes begin with a stark statement: "Blessed are the poor in spirit." It is as shocking as to say to a prisoner: "How wonderful it is to be in jail!" Again, we can gain some insight by taking a close look at the Greek language used. The Greek word for "poor" here is *ptochos,* which means absolute and abject poverty. Thus, the statement carries a ring of absurdity: how on earth can extreme poverty be a blessing?

In fact, none of the beatitudes makes sense unless we interpret them within the framework of the inverse laws. All inverse laws are based on this key psychological insight: our existential anxiety originates not from the objective state of reality but from our inflated expectations. The main problem is the discrepancy between our belief that we can handle everything by ourselves and the fact that, as mortals, we have severe limitations. Unaware of this, we try to do the impossible: to control the uncontrollable, to predict the unpredictable, to hold on to the impermanent, and to secure the unsecurable. This illusion of omnipotence becomes our torture.

But the solution can be found in the problem itself. The Zen way of liberation is not to obtain supernatural power so that we can become gods but to see through this illusion. When we actually come to see that in certain areas there is absolutely nothing that we can do, we will paradoxically attain inner freedom. For why double our suffering by worrying about things that we cannot control?

This sounds totally simple, but it is very difficult to do in practice. It is extremely difficult for us to see our own limitations and weaknesses, especially when everything seems to be going well for us. As a matter of fact, most people will not recognize their own limitations until they are virtually at their rope's end. This is precisely why a hopeless situation is a blessing in disguise, for the agony that we experience from the situation serves to wake us up to reality. Ironically, frustrations, disappointments, and hopelessness can be very good for one's spiritual health. Chögyam Trungpa, Tibetan meditation master, scholar, and artist, elaborates on this point:

> As long as we follow a spiritual approach promising salvation, miracles, liberation, then we are bound by the "golden chain of spirituality." Such a chain might be beautiful to wear, with its inlaid jewels and intricate carvings, but nevertheless, it imprisons us. People think they can wear the golden chain for decoration without being imprisoned by it, but they are deceiving themselves. As long as one's approach to spirituality is based on enriching ego, then it is spiritual materialism, a suicidal process rather than a creative one.
>
> All the promises we have heard are pure seduction. We expect the teachings to solve all our problems; we expect to be provided with magical means to deal with our depressions, our aggressions, our sexual hang-ups. But to our surprise we begin to realize that this is not going to happen. It is very disappointing to realize that we must work on ourselves and our suffering rather than depend on a savior or the magical power of yogic techniques. It is disappointing to realize that

we have to give up our expectations rather than build on the basis of our preconceptions.

We must allow ourselves to be disappointed, which means the surrendering of me-ness, my achievement.[12]

This is the inverse law of hope: *to have hope, give up hope.* Disappointment is the fast track to enlightenment because it accelerates our coming to terms with reality. This is also why Jesus said that the destitute are blessed. In Christian terminology, the more hopeless the situation is, the more likely it is for us to realize the futility of our own efforts and the more we will be drawn to God.

Therefore, "hope" in Christianity is the equivalent of "hopelessness" in Buddhism. They look like complete opposites but they are not, because they refer to different things. Ordinary hopes are hopes in *things:* hope about the future, hope for improvement, hope for change, hope to see results from one's effort. Since they are all future-oriented, they always run the risk of being frustrated. As such, future-oriented hopes are a potential source of suffering. That is why Buddhism teaches hopelessness.

Hope in Christianity, however, means hope in *God,* which is the negation of hope in *things.* It has nothing to do with expectations, wishful thinking, or superstition. It arises only when our worldly hopes are frustrated and the basic helplessness of the human situation is clearly seen. It is only then that we will surrender to God wholeheartedly. Rather than looking for a change in the external world, Christian hope aims at uncovering the divine meaning in what is.

Theologian Paul Tillich said that "Providence means that there is a creative and saving possibility implied in every situation, which cannot be destroyed by any event."[13] Even so, one will surely miss it if one is not paying attention. The practice of Christian hope and the practice of Buddhist hopelessness are one and the same: to live joyously in the moment and focus on the present. For it is in the present that we find God's kingdom.

To summarize, faith is the acceptance of insecurity and hope is an inner search for meaning. Both require a mind that is alive, open, and gentle.

It is often said that we are a godless generation. After being oppressed for centuries by our idols, scribes, and Pharisees, we have decided to wipe them all out. What we have gone through in the modern era is a period of weaning and purification. Although it has been a painful process, it is nevertheless critical for our continued growth. The idols have to be put back in their places. Contrary to what many people may think, I see the so-called spiritual crisis of the modern age as largely positive.

But Zen favors neither idolatry nor nihilism. After the work of demolition, there has to be rebuilding too. A culture that knows only how to tear down but not how to build up is pathetic. With our idols gone, we now have the right climate for rebuilding a gentle and enlightened faith that is based on love and not fear or need. The opportunity is historic. So this is where we are left: at the Temple of the Broken Gods.

— Eight —

My Yoke Is Easy

With man this is impossible,
but with God all things are possible.
— JESUS

If you know the sound of two hands clapping,
what is the sound of one hand clapping?
— ZEN KOAN

A River Runs through It, directed by Robert Redford, is one of the finest movies about Zen and spirituality. It tells a beautiful story about Norman Maclean, who lived with his minister father in frontier Montana. Maclean's ability to weave Zen spirituality into a rich American tradition is absolutely stunning. Mind you, Maclean has not professed any knowledge of Zen. In fact, the word "Zen" is never used in the movie. But it is definitely there, just as it is in the simple beauty of a tea ceremony. It is a beauty embedded in the ordinary, a song hidden in silence, a spirituality muted yet powerful. And all is accomplished with such austerity! It opens with one deceivingly plain statement: "In our family, there was no clear line between religion and fly fishing."

Can you see how religion and fly fishing are related? Most people cannot even see any connection between religion and everyday life. We are conditioned into thinking that religion has to be a very special and serious matter, not to be mixed up with everyday joy and fun. Webster's dictionary defines the word "sacred" as "dedicated or set apart for the service or worship of a deity." When something is "set apart" for worship, it is difficult to imagine how it can be integrated into mundane activities such as washing dishes, caring for children, gardening, or making love. The awe-generating air of formalized religions does not help much either. Alan Watts, a university chaplain turned Zen guru, related this childhood experience:

> When I was a schoolboy, we were dragooned into attending the services at Canterbury Cathedral, the Mecca of the Anglican Church. As we knelt, bowed, or stood in the courtly and austere ceremonies of this ancient fane, we had to take the utmost care never to laugh or smile — an offense punishable with ruthless floggings, and very difficult to avoid.[1]

I am one hundred percent sure that the aversion of many modern men and women to formal religions has something to do with experiences like this. Given the choice between attending the kind of church service described by Watts and fly fishing, I don't think that we need to bother taking the vote. Spirituality has much more to do with daily life than with things "set apart" and more to do with the ordinary than with the special.

Zen is everyday spirituality. As you may recall from chapter 3 above, when Chao Chou asked Nan Chuan what the Tao is, Nan Chuan answered that it is the *ordinary* mind. This is one of the most important Zen teachings. C. S. Lewis knew about the *spirituality of ordinariness*. When asked by someone whether he believed that the Holy Spirit could speak to the world through Christian writers today, he answered:

> I prefer to make no judgement concerning a writer's direct "illumination" by the Holy Spirit. I have no way of knowing whether what is written is from heaven or not. I do believe that God is the Father of lights — natural lights as well as spiritual lights (James 1:17). That is, God is not interested only in Christian writers as such. He is concerned with all kinds of writings. In the same way a sacred calling is not limited to ecclesiastical functions. The man who is weeding a field of turnips is also serving God.[2]

Elsewhere he was even more explicit. In a satirized conversation between a senior devil and a junior one, he emphasized the importance of seeing the extraordinary in the ordinary:

> You begin to see the point? Thanks to processes which we set at work in them centuries ago, they find it all but impossible to believe in the unfamiliar while the familiar is before their eyes. Keep pressing home on him the *ordinariness* of things...don't let him get away from that invaluable "real life."[3]

The Tao is in the ordinary. Norman Maclean experienced it while fly fishing. C. S. Lewis observed it in secular writings and in weeding. Real religion is ordinary and not special. If it cannot be integrated into our everyday activities, it is not a *living* religion. Jesus taught the importance of being ordinary in his conversation with a Samaritan woman who confused tradition with holiness. He said to her: "Woman, believe me, the hour is coming when neither on this mountain nor in Jerusalem will you worship the Father." (John 4:21). For we can worship God in any of our activities anywhere.

I came across what I consider the best definition of spirituality in a leaflet distributed by the Christophers: Spirituality is harmony with self, harmony with others, harmony with the world, harmony with God."[4] Spirituality has nothing to do with separation; it has to do with harmony. We should also note the order here. Harmony has to be developed first with ourselves, second with others, third with the world, and finally with God. In other words, it starts with the ordinary and the familiar.

If we associate religious life with too many "special" things — rituals, ceremonies, dogmas — we'll have difficulty seeing the spirituality of weeding, of everyday living. But if we cut through all the peripheral phenomena and get to the core, we will find that in the end there is only one thing that matters — *beauty.* True religion is, first and foremost, the pursuit of beauty. It starts with one basic question: how can I live beautifully? Norman Maclean made the same observation about his good father, who was a Scot and a Presbyterian minister:

> As for my father, I never knew whether he believed God was a mathematician but he certainly believed God could count and that only by picking up God's rhythm were we able to regain power and beauty. Unlike many Presbyterians, he often used the word "beautiful."[5]

When was the last time you noticed the beauty of a cool breeze or the wonder of a starry sky or the vibrancy of a wild flower on the roadside? I used to have the ability to instantly appreciate the beauty of all these when I was a child, but by the time I was twenty it was almost lost. (It took a lot of Zen practice for me to regain it.) The world has not changed that much; there are still summer breezes, night skies, and wild flowers. But where has the perception gone?

Although it is rarely noticed, Jesus did talk about the secret of beauty. We have already discussed at length how he taught beauty by relating to the birds of the air and the lilies of the fields. He also taught beauty in a dialogue with a successful young man who was rich and powerful (Luke identified him as a ruler). This is Matthew's account of it:

> And behold, one came up to him, saying, "Teacher, what good deed must I do, to have eternal life?" And he said to him, "Why do you ask me about what is good? One there is who is good. If you would enter life, keep the commandments." He said to him, "Which?" And Jesus said, "You shall not kill, You shall not commit adultery, You shall not steal, You shall not bear false witness, Honor your father and mother, and, You shall love your neighbor as yourself."
>
> The young man said to him, "All these I have observed; what do I still lack?" Jesus said to him, "If you would be perfect, go, sell what you possess and give to the poor, and you will have treasure in heaven; and come, follow me." When the young man heard this he went away sorrowful; for he had great possessions.
>
> And Jesus said to his disciples, "Truly, I say to you, it will be hard for a rich man to enter the kingdom of heaven. Again I tell you, it is easier for a camel to go through the eye of a needle than for a rich man to enter the kingdom of God."
>
> When the disciples heard this they were greatly astonished, saying, "Who then can be saved?" But Jesus looked at them and said to them, "With men this is impossible, but with God all things are possible." (Matt. 19:16–26)

The young man had approached Jesus with a great sense of urgency. In Mark's version, it was said that he *ran* up to Jesus and knelt before him. This is amazing, for the man was young and rich and powerful. He had all the things that the majority of the world seek after. But apparently he felt that there was something missing in his life, something which is very important. He inquired about eternal life. Again, we should note that the adjective "eternal" does not mean everlasting. The original text used the word *aiōnios,* which means "as befits God." But to live like a god is to live beautifully. It is the same whether we call it eternal life, Beauty, or Quality. The ultimate question is how to find happiness.

A Zen teacher is always demanding. He often sounds harsh or mean. And Jesus' answer to the young man is equally demanding: "Sell what you possess and give to the poor." The fact of life is that the appreciation of true beauty cannot start without total renunciation. We are talking about approaching the tip of the pyramid here. Have you ever heard of a mountaineer who carries a lot of baggage when hiking the Himalayas? For the same reason, Jesus told the young man that the door to the kingdom is like the eye of a needle: to pass through one has to drop all baggage!

Jesus was not a militant communist who had something against private property and material possessions. But to live beautifully, one needs an unfettered mind, a mind that is not clogged up with all kinds of attachments, opinions, or fossilized ways of looking at things. There is no need to get rid of anything as long as we can sever our attachments to it. Jesus is dramatizing what he had already said in the beatitudes: "Blessed are the pure in heart, for they shall see God" (Matt. 5:8). To experience beauty, we need an inner state of emptiness.

Talking about total self-renunciation and emptiness may sound intimidating. It may appear that the experience of true beauty is very difficult to achieve. This is definitely not true. In fact, the experience of beauty often arises naturally and unexpectedly. Several weeks ago, I went kiting with my children. It was a fine day. I have not flown a kite for a long time, and I am very glad that I did it again. For I discovered the beauty of kiting that day. To see the kite take off in the wind, to let it soar into the heights, to feel the tightness of the string in my hand and to run around laughing and screaming like a child — all these add up to an exhilarating experience. It was such a tremendous feeling of liberation. For a while, it looked as if the world was just one big kite, soaring into the blue sky. There was a lot of action in the sport, but I felt a genuine sense of stillness and harmony at the same time. I was one with the game. I was doing dynamic meditation.

This is self-abandonment: to live in the moment, not feeling the pressure to achieve something, not thinking about winning or losing, not worrying about acting foolish, breaking away from the neurosis of restraint or defense, enjoying the beauty of the moment yet not holding on to it, letting go without thinking about the need to let go, feeling the happiness without hoping for the happiness to continue, having no ego or attachment to anything. It is not work but pure play. It is not a matter of striving but *wu-wei*. It is not something planned for but a spontaneous event.

When we were children, we used to be enchanted by the most ordinary things. I still remember the joy I had when I got my first box of colored pencils and the thrill I created for myself making "rainbows" with a water spray. Equally unforgettable is the enchantment I had with my first sampler of leaves, how I just loved the different colors, shapes, and forms of nature's handiwork. It used to be a world of magic because we simply took things as they were. But alas, our world has grown as dull as our ego has grown big. Now King Ego sits on its throne and barks out its mantra at everything in sight: "What is there in it for Me?" With this, all wonder is lost. Everything becomes a means, an instrument, and a slave for the gratification of Ego. Beauty becomes a casualty to ugly utilitarianism.

Real beauty is not an object of desire. It is an inner ability: *the ability to abandon the ego and see the world without the me.* As J. Krishnamurti has pointed out, it is a state of inner freedom "when the mind is no longer thinking of the 'more,' in terms of having or becoming something through time." It is living in the moment.

The problem is that the abandonment of ego sounds too much like suicide and renunciation sounds too much like pulling teeth. The young man in Jesus' story walked away from him in sorrow. Even his disciples were greatly disturbed. "Who then can be saved?" they asked. But all they got from Jesus was a mystical answer: "With men this is impossible, but with God all things are possible."

Perhaps the best way to understand the practice of religion is to compare it to the practice of an art, any art. In a sense, all we ever need to know about the subject is already summarized in Norman Maclean's succinct statement about the philosophy of his father: "To him, all good things — trout as well as eternal salvation — come by grace and grace comes by art and art does not come easy." This is one of the most beautiful Zen statements I have come across. All good things are the result of *grace, art,* and *work.*

Art never comes easy. We learn how hard it can be in the fifth chapter of Matthew (5:20–47). What a jolt it is to read these passages! Listen to Jesus: "Anyone who ever looks at a woman with lust in his eyes has already committed adultery with her in his heart." Not only is touching not allowed; it is sinful even to look! Jesus was equally strict on the expression of anger: "If you curse [anyone], you are in danger of hell fire." If this were literally true, I know that I would not be lonely in hell. And what about the command to "love our enemy"? How many of us do that? "Art does not come easy."

Now compare these teachings with those of a typical Zen master. Among all the different schools and systems within Buddhism, the Zen school is commonly called "the lazy man's path to truth." (That's one reason I like it.) A Zen master made the following observation about the Zen way of life:

> Renouncing knowledge and doing nothing is the way of the leisurely
> Tao-man;
> He does not rid himself of illusions and he does not chase after truth.

What a contrast! On the surface, there is nothing that Jesus taught about religious life that even remotely resembles Zen teachings. As you may recall from chapter 1 above, one of the key elements of Zen is *wu-wei*, which means no striving and no effort. The way of the Tao is easy and leisurely (free from stress). But what Jesus was teaching here seems to be the exact opposite of *wu-wei*. There are other differences: Zen teaching appears amoral (it is supposed to transcend morality), but Jesus' teaching carries an extremely moralistic tone. Zen teaching is usually brief and to the point; Jesus' teaching here is wordy and painstaking. What sense can we make of it?

If this is not confusing enough, let us listen to what he said on another occasion:

> Come to me, all who labor and are heavy laden,
> And I will give you rest.
> Take my yoke upon you, and learn from me;
> For I am gentle and lowly in heart,
> And you will find rest for your souls.
> For my yoke is easy, and my burden is light. (Matt. 11:28–30)

Was Jesus contradicting himself? If so, he might be a Zen teacher after all, for self-contradiction is a sign of Zen. On the one hand, he was saying that "my yoke is easy"; on the other hand, he was saying that "with men this is impossible." How can we resolve this mystery? Is the spiritual path easy, or is it difficult? What is the secret of Jesus' yoke? Here is a hint in the form of another question: How can you hear the sound of one hand clapping?

Before we discuss the answers, let me share with you this Zen joke: "How many Zen Buddhists does it take to change a light bulb?" The answer is two: one to change the light bulb and another one not to change it. Paradox is the way of Zen.

To respond to the question of whether spiritual practice is easy or hard, we must answer in the same yes-and-no manner. Alternatively, we can also say that it is neither easy nor difficult. Precisely this answer has been given before by Seng-t'san, the third patriarch of Zen, who said, "The Grand Way is very broad; it is neither easy nor difficult." To understand this paradox, the following parable of the great Sufi and poet Rumi may help:

Once upon a time, there were three blind men who met an elephant for the first time. The first man touched one of the elephant's legs, and he said, "It is like a pillar." The second man touched one of the elephant's ears, and he said, "It is like a great fan." The third man got hold of the elephant's trunk, and he said, "It is like a snake." Each person holding on to his own opinion, they argued until the sun went down.

In one sense, each blind man was right. In another sense, they were all wrong. Similarly, we can view the spiritual path as easy or as difficult. They are not contradictory, but complementary to each other, just like "head" and "tail" are alternative ways to look at the same coin.

Jesus did have a tendency to emphasize the difficult side of religious practice instead of the easy side. Apparently, he was trying to make what was already burdensome even more unbearable. With regard to the law and the prophets, Jesus said, "I have come not to abolish them but to fulfil them. . . . Unless your righteousness exceeds that of the scribes and the Pharisees, you will never enter the kingdom of heaven" (Matt. 5:17–20). And to "fulfil the law," he transformed an *action-based* moral code to a *thought-based* one. While Mosaic law forbids physical adultery, the new ethics of Jesus makes even lustful thoughts an offense. Similarly, the old "thou shalt not kill" is replaced by "every one who is angry with his brother shall be liable to judgement; whoever insults his brother shall be liable to the council, and whoever says, 'You fool!' shall be liable to the hell of fire" (Matt 5:22).

Now it is obvious that laws like these are *impractical*. We do not even have complete control of all our actions, not to mention the complete control of our thoughts. Take, for example, the forbiddance of lustful thoughts. Sexual desire is a basic instinct. The Chinese have a saying that all men are like cats; there is no cat that does not have a craving for fish. Thus, to condemn sexual desire, which is a natural impulse, is ridiculous. Some theologians and Bible scholars seek to soften Jesus' demand by saying that he was not condemning all sexual desires but just lust. Now, I am not sure that I can distinguish between the two. Where shall we draw the line?

In any case, they miss the entire point: Jesus *was* trying to be ridiculous and unreasonable! He was *deliberately* making his ethics so demanding that it is impossible to keep. This is the secret: his moral standard is never meant to be achieved in the first place! If you are not sure about this, just try to find a person who will never get angry or someone who actually loves his or her enemy.

To clarify the role of moral code in a person's spiritual life, the following insight from St. Paul is critical:

> Law came in, to increase the trespass; but where sin increased, grace abounded all the more, so that, as sin reigned in death, grace also might reign through righteousness to eternal life through Jesus Christ our Lord. (Rom. 5:20)

A "reasonable" moral code is *useless* as far as spiritual life is concerned. According to Paul, the spiritual mission of any moral code is to demonstrate human weakness and to show the grace of God. It is meant to *increase,* not decrease, the trespass. Thus, a moral code that stands a chance of being workable would be self-defeating! As we mentioned in chapter 7, disappointment is the high road to enlightenment and salvation lies in our recognition of our own helplessness. Jesus said, "with man it is impossible; but with God, everything is possible." This is his unique way of saying that the secret of salvation lies not in human effort but in *letting go.* Spiritual practice can be either easy or hard, depending on whether one realizes the basic hopelessness of the situation. Prior to that realization, it is very hard; afterward, it is easy.

This is the only way to make sense of Jesus' new ethics: it is a smokescreen set up to induce our enlightenment. Jesus set the standard deliberately high to help us realize that it is simply impossible to earn salvation through human effort.

This sounds like a very roundabout way to teach, but it makes tremendous sense from the perspective of human psychology. For human beings are odd creatures; we have a secret masochistic tendency to love difficult things. If you tell us directly the plain truth— that salvation is a grace from God (i.e., it is not a matter of effort)— chances are that we will simply ignore it. On the other hand, if you tell us that salvation has to be earned through the observance of an excruciating code of ethics, which includes suppressing the craving for the opposite sex, controlling the anger that is boiling inside, etc., then there will be many takers. For everyone loves to be a hero and is willing to pay a high price for the honor of being one.

In Chinese military art, there is a strategy called "using a retreat as an advance." This is precisely what Jesus was doing. He built a maze, complete with mirrors and hidden passages, to *seduce* us into salvation. Jesus could have told us plainly that salvation is a matter of grace and not a matter of effort, but he did not want to go against human nature. Why fight something if you can use it to your advantage? So Jesus set a bogus high price for salvation, even though it is "free." In doing so, he was using ego to fight ego. He flowed with the Tao. This is the *wu-wei* of Jesus, and in it there is much wisdom and gentleness. And what efficiency!

Incidentally, this teaching method of Jesus is analogous with that of the Rinzi school of Zen. The Zen tradition has two major schools: Szoto and Rinzi. While Szoto Zen emphasizes sitting meditation, Rinzi Zen emphasizes the use of koans. We have already introduced several koans in the previous chapters. What is important to note is that most koans do not have any solution at all. Rather, they are meant to reflect the basic helplessness of the human situation. Alan Watts, for example, defines a koan as "a problem which admits no intellectual solution; the answer has no logical connection with the question, and the question is of such a kind as to baffle the intellect altogether."[6]

This may sound harsh, but the entire purpose of a koan is to induce frustrations. A student may work on a koan for several days or even weeks without getting anywhere. The point is to get him so tired and frustrated that he finally comes to the realization that effort will get him nowhere. When that happens, he will finally let go and be liberated. In Zen terminology, this is called "letting go of one's hold at the top of a cliff; finding life in the midst of death." It is an essential step for enlightenment.

The Great Way is neither easy nor hard. Easiness and hardship are simply different phases of the same path. Just like most artists cannot become "good" without spending thousands of hours practicing, most of us will not come to the easy part of the spiritual path until we have experienced the difficult part. The impossibility of a koan is usually obvious. But, paradoxically, the obvious often turns out to be the most difficult to see.

The Koan of One Hand Clapping is a case in point. It is obviously a nonsensical situation. For how can a hand clap itself? You think and think and think of an answer. The point is not to think! But you would be amazed at the number of Zen students who spend hours, days, even weeks working on it, looking at the problem from different angles, coming up with imaginative solutions. Alas, we are often too smart for our own good! Similarly, why does it take so long for us to realize that to try to end all lustful thoughts or to eliminate our anger is virtually impossible? The only explanation I can come up with is that we are a victim of our own seriousness. Being tense, we fail to grasp Jesus' humor.

That "all good things...come by grace and grace comes by art and art does not come easy" is a beautiful summary of what practice is all about. It is also a paradoxical expression. The logical mind asks: if all is grace, then why is art necessary? Maclean's statement seems to be just a poetic way of rephrasing the age-old controversy of "faith versus works" in the Christian tradition.

To solve this mystery, think about what it means to say that a pianist plays gracefully. Grace implies a certain ease or suppleness of movement, does it not? This is what grace means: the absence of effort, conflict, thought, and struggle. Grace is the state of perfection. Grace is *wu-wei*.

However, for most people who are addicted to the "work ethic" and all those who believe in the doctrine of "no free lunch," effort is the first response when we are encountered with a problem. So, as a rule of thumb, practice (works) is the prerequisite of grace. It takes effort to become effortless. In the case of spirituality, it takes effort for one to realize the vanity of effort.

To see why grace and works are not incompatible with each other, we must understand the mechanism through which practice makes perfect in the cultivation of any art. As a simple example, let us consider the art of walking. Much can be learned by watching a child learning how to walk. Walking is actually one of our earliest spiritual experiences. Do you realize what a miracle walking is? To do it well requires a whole set of physical skills and mental coordinations. What is amazing is that children start by just doing it. They do not need to know which muscle to use or which tendon to pull. In fact, no theory, knowledge, or thought about walking is ever needed; it is not a matter of the left-brain. All a child needs to do is to allow nature to do its work. Practice is really a matter of learning not to stand in nature's way by worrying or being intimidated by failures. It is a matter of developing trust!

It is the same with the practice of other arts. Artists have to learn to abandon themselves. The secret of peak performance lies in total relaxation and not thinking about success and failures. The sign of mastery is the loss of self-consciousness. When the performance becomes "graceful," the performer is no longer a doer but just a vehicle; there is no "work." Thus, ultimately, all practice is a matter of learning to trust and letting go. As long as there is even a trace of struggle or worry, we know that we are not there yet. Excellence is achieved when there is no longer any thought about achievement. It happens at play!

Zen is the art of excellence. The job of the Zen practitioner is mainly to forget — about the need to perform, to conquer, to worry, to be better than anybody....For all these are just self-defeating. Practice is learning not to think. Lao Tzu has the following advice for all artists:

> The practice of the Tao is not a matter of seeking gain or accumulation;
> It is a matter of forgetting and letting go.

To live beautifully is to live without struggle. To live without struggle is to have an ordinary mind. One of Master Seung Sahn's students spent a day with his family at the beach. He noticed a man sitting in formal Zen-like posture at the edge of the water, right in the middle of the beach crowd. Then, the man got up and plunged into the icy-cold water of the ocean for about fifteen minutes. The student wrote to ask the master, "Was that true emptiness — being able to walk into the icy-cold water, apparently feeling nothing?" Here is Seung Sahn's answer:

> Zen is clear mind, always clear mind. Clear mind means that everyday mind is truth. If somebody thinks, "I want to experience difficult practicing," then O.K. But if they always keep a difficult practice, that is making something. If you make something, if you are attached to something, then that thing hinders you, and you cannot get complete freedom. Maybe you will get freedom from some things, but not perfectly complete freedom. Then, what is perfectly complete? Don't hold I-my-me. Then you see, then you hear — everything is perfectly complete, not special.[7]

As Master Seung Sahn pointed out, the opposite to the ordinary mind is the *hero-mind*. Jesus knew it very well; it is also called the Pharisaic mind or the I-my-me mind. The Pharisees, ancient ones as well as modern ones, are masters of the I-my-me game. They always want to stand out against the crowd. The Pharisees during Jesus' time practiced an asceticism called "obeying the one thousand and one rules and regulations." Their main problem is that they wanted to be moral supermen. But to become a superman, one needs to pay a steep price. In fact, the very name "Pharisees" is revealing. It means "the separate ones." The asceticism of the Pharisees was so burdensome that they had to withdraw from ordinary life to practice it.

Pharisaism is not a thing of the past. We need only to look at the popularity of movies like *Superman* to see that the hero-mind is very much alive. One of the reasons why we are so unhappy in this affluent society is that most of us are slaves to this superman culture. Ambition, meaning the drive for money, power, and fame, is widely revered as the fuel for "progress" in modern capitalist society; its drawback of creating a dog-eat-dog world that destroys civility is largely ignored. The "virtue" of ambition is programmed into our brains from kindergarten or even earlier. Rare are the parents who do not hope that their children will grow up "to be somebody." Equally few are those who realize that our educational system has evolved into a cruel machine for the cramming of endless information into our children's little brains just to satisfy our greed for "success." Given the way things are going now, I won't be surprised if they soon start to teach children calculus in first grade.

While ambition may or may not be good for business, it is definitely detrimental to our spiritual health. An interviewer once asked C. S. Lewis whether it was wrong for a Christian to be ambitious and strive for personal success. He answered as follows:

> Ambition! We must be careful what we mean by it. If it means the desire to get ahead of other people — which is what I think it does mean — then it is bad. If it means simply wanting to do a thing well, then it is good.[8]

In a sense, Zen is the antithesis of ambition; it is everyday mind. The practice of Zen starts with doing away with all kinds of preferences or distinctions between saints and ordinary people. For it is precisely this type of discriminatory thinking that is the root of the problem. Hui Neng, the sixth patriarch of Zen, gives this advice in the Platform Sutra:

> When one's mind is ordinary, why worry about adhering to precepts? For the one who acts straight, where is the need for sitting (meditation)?

This is humorous. Master Hui Neng, perhaps the best-known and most respected man in the entire history of Zen, was denying the usefulness of sitting, which is the traditional way of practicing Zen. In fact, he went so far as to deny the existence of enlightenment, which is the Holy Grail in the Zen tradition. Elsewhere in the sutra, Hui

Neng said that "in the end, there is not even enlightenment to talk about, not to mention the need for sitting."

But this is the most logical conclusion of a spirituality that renounces the special and treasures the ordinary. For it is only when even the ultimate good (enlightenment) is denied that the "ordinary mind" can appear. As Lao Tzu said, "unless all saints have died, there is no stopping of the Big Thief." For striving for holiness is still an expression of the ego. Similarly, Master Jesus taught the virtue of ordinariness:

> But you are not to be called rabbi, for you have one teacher, and you are all brethren. And call no one your father on earth, for you have one Father, who is in heaven. Neither be called masters, for you have one master, the Christ. He who is greatest among you shall be your servant; whoever exalts himself will be humbled, and whoever humbles himself will be exalted. (Matt. 23:8–12)

Even today, there are many people who would humble themselves in order to be great. What else is new? Isn't it the same old egotism camouflaged as "goodness"? Alas, waking up is never easy!

Jesus has an "ordinary" statement: "Come to me, all who labor and are heavy laden, and I will give you rest." That remark is golden. As Tillich observed, "He [Jesus] frees us from religion. They all make new religious laws; He overcomes the religious law."[9]

The ultimate goal of religion is the abolition of itself.

— Nine —

What Defiles a Man

Hear and understand: Not what goes into the mouth defiles a man, but what comes out of the mouth.

—JESUS

Those who talk do not know; those who know do not talk.

—LAO TZU

I wonder what it is like to be a deaf-mute. Imagine a world without speech, words, or symbols. A world of total silence. If we really want to understand the Holy, we may wish to start here.

Although I am not a deaf-mute, I do know that I occasionally behave like one: when people talk, I am not listening; when I talk, I am not communicating. And I know that I am not alone in this. After all, we are a nation more interested in talking than in listening. We are a people handicapped by self-obsession, fettered by words that have long ago lost their meaning, and paralyzed by ever-chattering thoughts.

A meditation center in my vicinity occasionally holds one-week meditation retreats in which participants are forbidden to talk. My wife participated in one of them. (I was not brave enough to go. One week of Zazen seemed a sure way to get a sore behind!) Seven days of austere silence, no newspapers, no TV, no phone calls, no talking — what appears to be a complete cut-off from civilization. For a modern man or woman, a week like this has to be a total shock, since our mainstream culture is so extremely verbal. But I wondered — after the initial resistance and adjustment — whether the participant would experience something totally unusual. Something that may be called *beauty*. Perhaps this is exactly what we need to do every once in a while. Perhaps we have to experience deafness in order to learn how to listen, experience muteness in order to learn how to express ourselves.

What exactly is this thing called *listening?* Is it simply hearing — the passive reception of audio stimuli, the mechanical vibration of the eardrums, its conversion into electrical signals and the subsequent registration of mental data in the brain? Granted, this is a wonder by itself. Such intricacies! But is that all? If so, why do we have so many problems communicating with our spouses, our children, our colleagues, and our customers? If listening is an innate ability, why is there so much talk about communication skills?

Perhaps we can get a little help from someone who became an artist in listening after she lost her hearing. "To listen means to be aware, to watch, to wait patiently for the next communication clue," says Hannah Merker, an author with a hearing disability. "Listening is not always auditory communication." She shares with us her insight into the Zen of listening:

> How then do we define the word "listening" to include all the interacting phenomena that occur when a deaf or hearing impaired person is talking to a friend, walking alone on a beach.... The ear for such a one misses much. The wonder that is the human body seems willing to soar over the gap. When earth's auditory energy is received as a whisper, or perhaps not at all, other senses become sharpened, grasping communicative clues we have forgotten, in the rush of life, are there. Listening becomes visual, tactile, intuitive.
> Listening...perhaps...is just a mind aware.[1]

Listening has to do with awareness. I have always believed that God has a good sense of humor. As it turns out, people who have hearing disabilities are often better listeners than those who don't. This is the wonder of compensation. The hearing-disabled learn the importance of paying attention, and they sharpen the other senses to make up for their loss. They learn to "listen" with their sight, with their intuition, with their mind, and with their entire being. They are empowered by their weakness.

Hearing is easy; listening is difficult. Few of us recognize this, but listening is an ability and not an instinct. As such, it is an art that has to be learned. To listen is to be sensitive to reality. Good listeners live in the moment and pay attention to what is going on in the here-and-now. As Percy C. Buck observed, "Listening is the application of the mind to sounds which the ear...may or may not hear." This is what Zen is all about: a listening that is *beyond* words.

The inability to listen is not a modern problem. Jesus often complained about the listening disability of first-century people: "Do you not yet perceive or understand? Are your hearts hardened? Having eyes do you not see, and having ears do you not hear?" (Mark 8:17–18). The relationship between listening and holiness is well established by this message from Isaiah, in which God commanded the prophet:

> Go, and say to this people:
> "Hear and hear, but do not understand;
> See and see, but do not perceive."
> Make the heart of this people fat,
>   and their ears heavy,
>   and shut their eyes;
> Lest they see with their eyes,
>   and hear with their ears,
>   and understand with their hearts,
>   and turn and be healed. (Isa. 6:9–10)

The last clause is most interesting. We often associate the term "holy" with being different or separate. Actually, this is a complete violation of its original meaning. When we go back to the root of the word, we find that holiness originates from the word "whole" (*holos* in Greek). It is closely related to the words "heal" and "save." In the King James Version of the Bible, the expression "make whole" is often used in place of the term "heal." *Holiness is the state of being whole.* The last clause of this quotation implies that holiness is related to our ability to see with our eyes, hear with our ears, and feel with our hearts, although the reason is not spelled out here. In any case, we should note that seeing, listening, and feeling are all right-brain activities.

Unfortunately, our culture tends to underappreciate the value of listening. I know many people who question why psychotherapists should be paid substantial fees for "doing nothing but just listening." It never occurs to them that listening can be a big part of healing. It is true that psychotherapy sessions often involve nothing more than the patient talking and the therapist listening. But let us remember that in many ancient civilizations storytelling was considered a sacred art, for, indeed, it is a form of meaning-giving and an integration of life experience. The listening of the therapist serves at least two holistic functions. First, it creates a nurturing environment for the patient's storytelling. Second, it expresses care and symbolizes the overcoming of interpersonal alienation. Certainly, the value of listening is universal and not restricted to the psychotherapeutic setting. One of the reviewers of this book is a registered nurse who is working on her master's thesis. She communicated this to me after reading my draft:

> In my thesis work, I am finding that the nurses' ability to truly listen to the patient and the family enables them to not only enhance the intimacy between all parties, but often predict the date of death. From this perspective, I don't believe many nursing skills exceed listening in importance. Listening with a full presence provides authenticity and trust.

While holiness seems to be related to the eyes and ears, defilement seems to be related to the mouth. Jesus told us about the origin of defilement in one of his mystical teachings: "Hear and understand: Not what goes into the mouth defiles a man, but what comes out of the mouth" (Matt. 15:10). When his disciples asked him to elaborate, Jesus added:

> Do you not see that whatever goes into the mouth passes into the stomach, and so passes on? But what comes out of the mouth proceeds from the heart, and this defiles a man. For out of the heart come evil thoughts, murder, adultery, fornication, theft, false witness, slander. These are what defile a man. (Matt. 15:17–20)

Herein lies a bridge between the Judeo-Christian tradition and Eastern mysticism. The experience of the Holy is closely related to the *spirituality of silence*. Jesus' association of the mouth with defilement has a precedent in the book of Isaiah. The prophet Isaiah described his experience of the Holy as follows:

> In the year that King Uzziah died I saw the Lord sitting upon a throne, high and lifted up; and his train filled the temple. Above him stood the seraphim; each has six wings; with two he covered his face, and with two he covered his feet, and with two he flew. And one called to another and said:
>
>> "Holy, holy, holy is the Lord of hosts;
>> The whole world is full of his glory."
>
> And the foundations of the thresholds shook at the voice of him who called, and the house was filled with smoke. And I said: "Woe is me! For I am lost; for I am a man of unclean lips, and I dwell in the midst of a people of unclean lips; for my eyes have seen the King, the Lord of hosts!"

Then flew one of the seraphim to me, having in his hand a burning coal which he had taken with tongs from the altar. And he touched my mouth, and said: "Behold, this has touched your lips; your guilt is taken away, and your sin forgiven." (Isa. 6:1–7)

Mark this: a burning coal touched the prophet Isaiah's lips and his guilt and sin were instantly erased. What does this symbolize? Why is there so much emphasis on the mouth and lips? And how is it related to holiness? What can we make out of this koan of Isaiah and how is it related to Jesus' teaching on defilement? Perhaps we can find help in this little Mahayanist tale in the Vimalakirti Sutra:

Once, a group of bodhisattvas (enlightened beings with great power) assembled to discuss the dharma (truth). Vimalakirti, the wisest of all Buddhist laypeople, said to the others, "Virtuous ones, could each of you please say something about the non-dual Dharma (i.e., Absolute Truth) as you understand it?" Thereupon, the bodhisattvas took turns to express their views on the subject. When all had finished, the bodhisattva Manjusri asked Vimalakirti about his own understanding of it. *Vimalakirti kept silent.*

At that, Manjusri exclaimed, "Excellent, excellent! Can there be true initiation into the non-dual Dharma until words and speech are no longer written or spoken?"

This incident is widely celebrated by Zen people as "the Thunderous Silence of Vimalakirti." Now, we can see better the deep insight of Jesus into the nature of defilement and the secret of Isaiah's koan. What defiles a person is what comes out of the mouth, and what comes out of the mouth are words, words, and still more words! Words are the problem. We are defiled by our words, words that are reflections of our thought.

What is wrong with words? Why are they the origin of defilement? Before we get into the questions, let us take a brief look at the world's legends about the creation of words and their import. According to Chinese mythology, when words were invented by human beings, the heavens shook and the spiritual world wept; it was indeed important! Words are considered as equally pivotal in the Judeo-Christian tradition. In Genesis, we are told that humanity was divided due to a confusion in language during an incident at the Tower of Babel (Gen. 11:1–9). The Gospel of John begins with this message:

In the beginning was the Word, and the Word was with God, and the Word was God. He was in the beginning with God; all things were made through him, and without him was not anything made that was made. In him was life, and the life was the light of men. (John 1:1–4)

To find out about the Holy, we must start with the understanding of words, and from there the whole process of thinking.

What is in a word? Isn't it a crystallization of thought? What underlies a word are thoughts, and what underlies thoughts are concepts. In the basement of the whole structure of language we have concepts, which are the Lego chips of the mind. They are the smallest building blocks. The first thing to note is that a word is never quite the same as the reality that it tries to represent. It is a metaphor at best. When we say "flower," flowers do not spring out of our mouth. As Alfred Korzbyski recognized, "The map is not the territory."

A concept is necessarily an abstraction, and an abstraction is necessarily a simplification. Being simplifications, concepts can never capture the full detail, richness, fluidity, and integrity (wholeness, undivided nature) of life. Nietzsche had this to say about words:

> The "thing in itself" (for that is what pure truth, without consequence, would be) is quite incomprehensible to the creators of language and not at all worth aiming for.... Every concept originates through our equating what is unequal. No leaf ever wholly equals another, and the concept "leaf" is formed through an arbitrary abstraction from these individual differences, through forgetting the distinctions; and now it gives rise to the idea that in nature there might be something besides the leaves which would be "leaf" — some kind of original form after which all leaves have been woven, marked, copied, colored, curled, and painted, but by unskilled hands, so that no copy turned out to be a correct, reliable, and faithful image of the original form.[2]

Let us take the word "cup" to illustrate what fluidity means. We look up the word in the dictionary and read: "a small, open container used for drinking." But can the concept of a cup really grasp all the details of an object that we call a cup? I can use the same "cup" as a paperweight, as a musical instrument (it sounds good too), as a weapon (I can whack people with it), as a compass (I can trace circles with it). I can also use it as a chamber pot if there is such an emergency.

Now let us talk about *integrity*. Take the word "rice." To a Westerner whose staple food is not rice, the word may not mean very much. To a Chinese person brought up in a traditional family like I was, however, the word "rice" is very rich in meaning. When I was a small boy, my grandmother told me that I should consider every single grain of rice in my bowl to be a treasure and a product of sweat and toil. (In the old days, farming was very hard labor.) When we eat our rice, we are supposed to think about the farmers who labor to make the rice available to us. By the same token, we should also think about our father, who works so hard to bring food to our table, and his customers and his employer. Then our thought may go back to Mother Nature, who brings us the sun, the clouds, and the rain, without which a harvest would not have been possible.

Thus, the Chinese's meditation on their rice is the equivalent to a Westerner's saying grace before meal. Both are beautiful customs and rituals. In these rituals of thanksgiving, we remind ourselves of our interconnectedness with everyone and everything in the universe. We see the meaning in the timeless words of William Blake: "to see the world in a grain of sand [rice?].... " This is how holiness begins: to be aware of the wholeness of life, to see our interdependency, to celebrate our oneness.

Unfortunately, this integrity is never captured in the word "rice" (or "bread"). Much is lost in the process of abstraction. In the letters *r, i, c,* and *e,* we cannot see the toil of the farmer or re-create the feeling of thankfulness or rejoice in our interconnectedness. As Friedrich Nietzsche observed, "compared with music all communication by word is shameless; words dilute and brutalize; words depersonalize; words make the uncommon common." Indeed, words desecrate and defile! Thich Nhat Hahn gives us another illustration of the problem of abstraction, this time with adjectives, in a short chapter titled "Flowers and Garbage":

> Defiled or immaculate. Dirty or pure. These are concepts we form in our mind. A beautiful rose we have just cut and placed in our vase is pure. It smells so good, so fresh. A garbage can is the opposite. It smells horrible, and it is filled with rotten things.
>
> But that is only when we look on the surface. If we look more deeply we will see that in just five or six days, the rose will become part of the garbage. We do not need to wait five days to see it. If we just look at the rose, and we look deeply, we can see it now. And if we look into the garbage can, we see that in a few months its contents can be transformed into lovely vegetables, and even a rose. If you are a good organic gardener, looking at a rose you can see the garbage, and looking at the garbage you can see a rose. Roses and garbage inter-are. Without a rose, we cannot have garbage; and without garbage,

we cannot have a rose. They need each other very much. The rose
and the garbage are equal. The garbage is just as precious as the rose.
If we look deeply at the concepts of defilement and immaculateness,
we return to the notion of interbeing.[3]

Adjectives are dangerous; they create an impression of indepen-
dence when there is none. Where is good without bad? Where is pure
without defiled? Where is rich without poor? Where is light without
dark? These so-called opposites rely on each other for their existence,
do they not? When I showed the first draft of this chapter to a friend
of mine who is a schoolteacher, he told me that he has started teaching his children antonyms as complements. (Complements are pairs
of objects that need each other for completion.) What a good way to
teach wholeness to young people!

What happens when we attack, criticize, or condemn a phenomenon? What happens when we single out a human being and call him
or her a jerk, a piece of garbage, or something even worse? We act as
if that person had an isolated and independent existence, do we not?
Just like Pontius Pilate, we wash our hands and declare to the world:
"I have nothing to do with it!" But are we really not responsible in
any way? When there is a crime, when there is someone starving in
the world, when there is an abandoned child, when someone has to
make a living as a prostitute, can we really wash our hands?

In weather forecasting, there is a phenomenon called the Butterfly
Effect. It has to do with the notion that a little butterfly flapping its
wings today in Peking can transform the storm systems next month
in New York. It is a vivid way of saying that even tiny changes to
the inputs to a large system can have an overwhelming effect on
the system's output. Perhaps we should consider ourselves as little
butterflies.

The ancient Jews had a notion that when they sinned, they sinned
as a nation. The Buddhists have always had a notion of *participatory karma* (a kind of communal karma jointly created by all sentient
beings). The Buddha taught the truth of *dependent co-origination*,
meaning that everything in the world depends on others to exist and
that nothing has an independent existence. Similarly, when I asked
my Muslim friend what the most important teaching in Islam is, she
did not hesitate to reply that "God is One." Oneness is a cornerstone
of all religions, although our words have often failed to reflect this
basic reality.

If you are a Christian who is unfamiliar with this idea of oneness, the following passage from St. Matthew may help:

When the Son of man comes in his glory, and all the angels with him, then he will sit on his glorious throne. Before him will be gathered all the nations, and he will separate them one from another as a shepherd separates the sheep from the goats. And he will place the sheep at his right hand, but the goats at the left. Then the King will say to those at his right hand. "Come, blessed of my Father, inherit the kingdom prepared for you from the foundation of the world; for I was hungry and you gave me food, I was thirsty and you gave me drink, I was a stranger and you welcomed me, I was naked and you clothed me, I was sick and you visited me, I was in prison and you came to me." Then the righteous will answer him, "Lord, when did we see you hungry and feed you, or thirsty and give you drink? And when did we see you a stranger and welcome you, or naked and clothe you? And when did we see you sick or in prison and visit you?" And the King will answer them, *"Truly I say to you, as you did it to one of the least of these my brethren, you did it to me."* (Matt. 25:31–40)

Do you know what it means to be holy? Are you interested in finding out how holy you are? Here is a very simple test: Do you honestly see the holiness in everybody? And I do mean *everybody*. It is not enough just to see the holiness in your priest, in your guru, in your teacher, and in your parents. This is what Jesus meant: Christ is in the bum down the street who is asking you for money, Christ is in all those suffering from AIDS, Christ is in all the criminals who fill our prisons.... What do you do when you see one of them? One of the basic practices in Tibetan Buddhism is to see everyone as Buddha. Just think about it. It is difficult enough to see every person as not guilty, filthy, or malicious. But to see each person as Buddha or Christ, even though society may have already labeled the person as a criminal, a terrorist, a whore, to really see that *inner holiness* in such a person despite all.... To be holy is to see the oneness that unites us all.

Jesus said that we are defiled by our words and our thoughts. To really understand defilement, we have to first understand the way our mind (left-brain) functions. Words are generated by thought and thought is generated by the mind. What exactly is thinking? What happens when we formulate concepts of clean and unclean, purity and defilement, goodness and evil, self and others? We are separating, isolating, fragmenting, and setting up artificial boundaries, are we not? We are effectively saying that the clean has nothing to do with the unclean, that purity is unrelated to defilement, that the good is independent of the evil. We are ignoring the basic oneness that ties us together. In doing so, we are straying from reality and violating the wholeness of life. The fact is that all distinctions are arbitrary in an interdependent world. As Meister Eckhart has observed, "All distinctions are lost in God."

Now we can have a better understanding of why the angel touched Isaiah's lips with a piece of burning coal and why Jesus asked us to watch what comes out of our mouths. These metaphors point to the underlying process of thought. As St. Paul remarked, "I know and am persuaded in the Lord Jesus that nothing is unclean in itself, but is unclean for any one who thinks it unclean." (Rom. 14:14) The bottom line is that defilements are inventions of the mind. They are the result of thinking, which is always fragmentary and unholistic due to the process of conceptualization involved. The following *mondo* (questions and answers in Zen) makes the point:

STUDENT: Teacher, doesn't the sutra say that everything is illusion? If so, why should we bother with practicing?

TEACHER: That's right. Do not bother with practicing; just do not defile.

STUDENT: Could you please tell me what defilement is?

TEACHER: You are defiling again!

How do things like sin, defilement, and guilt arise? This deep question is answered most beautifully by Italian director Federico Fellini in his movie *8½*. In a memorable scene a group of young boys went to a beach outing with a priest. When the priest was away, a prostitute passed by. Never having seen a prostitute before, the boys were fascinated. They greeted her and asked what she did for a living. "I am a prostitute," she answered. The children did not have much idea of what this meant. But an older boy suggested to his peers that a prostitute is someone who would do interesting things for money. The boys talked among themselves and decided that they wanted to be entertained. They pooled their money and gave it to the prostitute. The prostitute too thought that this might be fun, so she took off her clothes and started dancing. The boys were thrilled. They clapped their hands and danced along. Everything was going fine until the priest came back and started yelling. Fellini added his Zen note: "At that moment, the children were spoiled; until then they were innocent, beautiful."

Do not be deceived by the apparent light-heartedness of the movie; it is nothing less than the cosmic drama of Genesis replayed! In the Genesis story, the fall of man is a result of Adam and Eve's eating from the Tree of Good and Evil, which caused the opening of their eyes. What a wonderful metaphor for the emergence of consciousness! With "the opening of the eyes," we can come to know the world and make all kinds of differentiation, comparisons, and selections. We become fully human.

But like many things in life, consciousness is a double-edged sword. While consciousness increases our chance of survival and makes civilization possible, it is also the source of all suffering. With the emergence of intellect comes fear, shame, and guilt. Whether we like it or not, anxiety is the price we pay for the benefit of consciousness. That the situation is really not as bad as it may seem is only gingerly hinted at by the question of the Lord: "Who told you that you are naked?" It was not until much later that the same question was rephrased in a more enlightening way and raised again by a compassionate Zen teacher, Jesus, who asked: "Who condemns you?" (John 8:10).

While Vimalakirti gave a thunderous answer of silence, God asked a thunderous question: "Who told you that you are naked?" This is the koan of God. The best commentary I have seen on this is provided by Joel Goldsmith, America's home-grown mystic:

> In that query is summed up the whole essence of human life. All of us are in that same predicament in which Adam found himself. As long as we entertain a belief of good and evil, we are the Adam who is hiding, the Adam who is outside the Garden of Eden, and because of that we are all covering up our "nakedness."
> ...Who told him that it is more moral to cover up the body than to expose it? Who told him that there is sin? Who made this condition? From his very question, God certainly implies that He did not. God did not say there was anything wrong about a naked body, nor did He say that there was anything wrong on the face of the earth.[4]

Amen. And the first book of the Bible also has this observation: "And God saw everything that he had made, and behold it was very good" (Gen. 1:31). So sin turns out to be an act of self-deception and self-condemnation. This seems to be the universal understanding of the mystics. A Zen mondo makes the same point:

Once a Zen student came to a master to seek the way of liberation. The master asked him, "Who binds you?" The student was taken aback, but then answered, "No one binds me." Upon this the master asked, "Then why seek liberation?"

Indeed this sheds new light on another beautiful passage from the Gospels, which many people find hard to understand. This is where Jesus made the remark on the "unforgivable sin," which sounds so awful on the surface:

> But when the Pharisees heard it they said, "It is only by Beelzebul, the prince of demons, that this man [Jesus] casts out demons." Knowing their thoughts, he said to them, "Every kingdom divided against itself is laid waste, and no city or house divided against itself will stand; and if Satan casts out Satan, he is divided against himself; how then will his kingdom stand? And if I cast out demons by Beelzebul, by whom do your sons cast them out? Therefore, they shall be your judges. But if it is by the Spirit of God that I cast out demons, then the kingdom of God has come upon you. Or how can one enter a strong man's house and plunder his goods, unless he first binds the strong man? Then, indeed he may plunder his house. He who is not with me is against me, and he who does not gather with me scatters. *Therefore I tell you, every sin and blasphemy will be forgiven men, but the blasphemy against the Spirit will not be forgiven.* And whoever says a word against the Son of man will be forgiven; but whoever speaks against the Holy Spirit will not be forgiven, either in this age or the age to come." (Matt. 12:24–32)

I have always wondered why there can be a sin that is not forgivable, given that God is all-loving. Why is the "blasphemy against the Spirit" so special that it leads to eternal condemnation? This continued to intrigue me until I realized that Spirit is not an external reality at all. Jesus revealed this when he taught us how to pray:

> But when you pray, go into your room and shut the door and pray to your Father who is in secret; and your Father who sees in secret will reward you. And in praying do not heap up empty phrases as the Gentiles do; for they think that they will be heard for their many words. Do not be like them, for your Father knows what you need before you ask him. (Matt. 6:6–8)

This is the big secret: the Spirit is our True Self and the center of our being. Who can redeem us if we keep condemning or speaking ill of our innermost being? That would be like having an inner war. Jesus used the imagery of "a kingdom divided against itself"; it is beyond all help. Thus, the first step is to make peace within.

God knows not sin. The guilt-ridden Prodigal Son said to his father: "Father, I have sinned against heaven and before you; I am no
longer worthy to be called your son" (Luke 15:21). But his father
ignored him. He simply said to his servant: "Bring quickly the best
robe, and put a ring on his hand." If sin is an estrangement from
God, it is an imaginary one. It is an illusion produced by the mind,
whose function is to make distinctions, to create preferences, and to
label things as good and bad. It is a natural result of the evolution
of human consciousness and a part of growing up. Rabbi Lawrence
Kushner calls the scene at the Garden of Eden a setup:

> What Adam and Eve did in the garden of Eden was not a sin; it is
> what was supposed to happen. Indeed, it has happened in every gener-
> ation since. Children disobey their parents and, in so doing, complete
> their own creation. Adam and Eve are duped, not by the snake, but
> by God....
>
> The price of autonomy, individuation, is the trauma of separation
> from parents. At the core of every psyche lies a deep pain. We are not
> guilty because of Adam and Eve's sin, as in orthodox Christianity's
> doctrine of original sin....The issue is not sin, guilt, or even disobe-
> dience. The necessary price for becoming an autonomous adult is the
> unending pain of separation.[5]

So what is the solution? How can we reenter the Garden? If the
problem starts with the emergence of consciousness and intelligence,
does it mean that we have to abandon our words, our thoughts, and
our civilization in order to regain our peace?

One thing is certain: thinking, due to its fragmentary nature, will
not solve our spiritual problem. We cannot access truth through the
mind since the Holy cannot be conceptualized. To modern men and
women, the mind appears to be omnipotent. It has put us on the
moon. It drives our scientific research and our technological break-
throughs. It may eventually find a cure for AIDS. But alas, the mind
is utterly powerless in certain matters: it cannot bring us happiness;
it cannot stop our wars, either within or without; it cannot make
us whole.

What then is the way? How can we break our addiction to thinking? How can we heal the world's wound? Here is a suggestion from
St. John of the Cross: "If a man wishes to be sure of the road he
treads on, he must close his eyes and walk in the dark."

Very helpful advice, St. John: to close the eyes and walk in the
dark! But perhaps it is not supposed to be taken literally. After all,

if the fall of humankind is due to our ancestors' eating from the Tree of Knowledge and "having their eyes opened," then it seems not so far-fetched that the healing can be activated by reversing the process. If suffering is a result of our intellection and conceptualization, then perhaps we should return to what is concrete. "Zen," says R. H. Blyth, "is the unsymbolization of the world." But the question is how.

Philosopher Ludwig Wittgenstein has this suggestion: "Don't think: Look!" The Holy can be experienced only directly, without the intermediation of words and thoughts. Perhaps this is what St. John of the Cross means by "walking in the dark." D. T. Suzuki notes that "when Zen wants you to taste the sweetness of sugar, it will put the required article right into your mouth and no further words are said." In this sense, Zen is direct and not intermediated, concrete and not abstract, practical and not theoretical, sensual and not intellectual, down-to-earth and not otherworldly. He elaborates further:

> I raise my hand; I take a book from the other side of this desk; I hear the boys playing ball outside my window: — in all these I am practicing Zen, I am living Zen. No wordy discussion is necessary, nor any explanation.[6]

But in order to look, one has to start with a beginner's mind, a mind that carries no preconceptions or presumptions. The beginner's mind looks to find out what is new; it does not look to confirm. To look, we have to be ready to enter into the unknown. We have to be willing to throw away our armor of beliefs, knowledge, tradition, or whatever we cling to for comfort. We have to open up ourselves and be vulnerable.

Thich Nhat Hahn teaches the art of looking through concrete examples. He shows us how to discover the subtle relationships between the flowers and the garbage, the noble and the lowly, the rich and the poor, despite their apparent incongruities. He teaches us how to be an explorer and turn to the underside of the embroidery of life — to see the hidden needlework, to appreciate the beauty of the paradoxes, to surrender to the fluidity and fuzziness of what is. Only then can we break through our intellectual prisons and overcome the isolation and the fragmentations. Only then can the healing begin.

But all these are just other ways to listen, to pay attention to the reality that is. Has it ever occurred to you that it is impossible to talk and listen at the same time? Perhaps this is precisely our problem. We are a generation that talks too much, either overtly through our mouths or covertly through our mind. But Jesus said, "What comes out of the mouth proceeds from the heart, and this defiles a man." Defilements originate from thoughts.

If we are constantly talking, how can we pay attention to the people around us and relate to them. If our inner chattering does not stop, how can we appreciate the beauty of the moment? To really listen, the mind has to be very quiet and very relaxed, free of attachments and worries. For true listening is the ending of thought, which, in turn, means the forgetting of the ego. Dr. Harvey J. Gordon, director of the Huntington Hearing and Speech Center, describes the essence of listening as follows:

> ...a state when one does not know one is listening...one is spontaneous, no longer conscious of self...it is a form of ego loss where there is no barrier between you and someone else.[7]

True listening happens when we are totally absorbed in what is, when we are free from fear and greed, when the mind is no longer thinking about the need to perform or to impress. Only then is the experience of the Holy possible. Let us conclude with another Zen tale:

> One morning, a Zen master was about to give his disciples a sermon. Just when he was getting on the podium, a little bird came and sat on the windowsill. It began to sing. Its song was so beautiful that everyone present was totally enchanted. Afterward, the bird flew away. The master told his disciples, "Today's sermon is over."

When the meaning is grasped, why worry about the words?

Ten

Resist Not Evil

Love your enemies and pray for those who persecute you.
—JESUS

Passions are bodhi [Wisdom].
—HUI NENG

You need not fear the demon hosts around you;
it is most important to tame your mind within.
—THE HUNDRED THOUSAND SONGS OF MILAREPA

One of the most terrifying serial killers in history was scheduled to be executed on December 31, 1993. The execution was never carried out. A stay was put on the death sentence, even without any petition for clemency from the accused. The reason: the killer might provide extremely valuable information for finding a cure for AIDS. The killer's name: smallpox.

This story was reported in the August 21, 1994, issue of the *New York Times Magazine* in an eye-catching article titled "Saving Smallpox." The postponement of the death sentence had to do with the fact that scientists have recently discovered that a protein from smallpox may provide the clue for how a cell will shut itself down when invaded by a virus. It is ironical that we can often learn more from our enemies than from our friends — if we learn to respect them, that is.

The history of Western civilization may be summarized as a series of battles — with nature, with others, and with oneself. We tend to take a hostile or adversarial attitude toward life. Perhaps we are born fighters. We fight for our survival. We fight for our rights. We fight for our freedom. We fight for everything. It is not surprising, therefore, that we are one of the most litigious societies of the world.

Recently, a medical team from China was visiting the New York University Medical School, and the university asked a friend of mine to be the interpreter. My friend was very enthusiastic about combining American medical technology with the Chinese art of healing. But after talking with members of the visiting team, he found that the chance for such collaboration is remote. Basically, Chinese researchers and American researchers have gone on two very different paths. The American team focuses on finding ways to eradicate the AIDS virus while the Chinese team focuses on finding ways to build antibodies, assuming the continued existence of the AIDS virus. In a way, this highlights the difference between Eastern and Western thinking.

Being a fighter is not necessarily bad. It would be a pity, however, to be so busy fighting our enemies that we fail to learn from them. If our attitude to our enemies is that of hatred, anger, or fear and we typically react to them by either fighting or fleeing, then chances are that we will fail to pay them due attention. This can be a fatal mistake. To Christian soldiers who take pride in their militancy, this passage from the Sermon on the Mount may help:

> You have heard that it was said, "You should love your neighbor and hate your enemy." But I say to you, Love your enemy and pray for those who persecute you, so that you may be sons of your Father who is in heaven; for he makes his sun rise on the evil and on the good, and sends rain on the just and on the unjust. (Matt. 5:43–45)

Have you ever met anyone who actually loves her enemies and prays for her persecutors? It is difficult enough just to talk about it without sounding hypocritical. To love our enemy sounds like an admirable thing to do, but the important question is, *How?* Is there any way to love our enemy without requiring us to become moral superheros? I have not found any Bible commentary that provides any practical advice on this. But perhaps the following insight from Nietzsche will help:

> Another triumph is our spiritualization of hostility. It consists in a profound appreciation of the value of having enemies: in short, it means acting and thinking in the opposite way from which has been the rule.... In the political realm too, hostility has now become more spiritual — much more sensible, much more thoughtful, much more

considerate. Almost every party understands how it is in the interest of its own self-preservation that the opposite should not lose all
strength.[1]

Apparently, religious people can learn something from the politi-
cians. After all, loving our enemies is not so difficult as long as we
can see their value — their value as enemies and not as friends. What
is needed is a radical change in the way we view the world. We need
to see holistically if we do not want to continue to live our lives as
a series of battles.

While valuing external enemies is difficult enough, valuing internal
enemies is even harder. Traditional morality teaches that we should
be tough with our vices, that we should fight our greed, lust, fear,
sloth, and addictions, just to name a few. But even these inner enemies can be angels in disguise. John A. Martin, a Catholic priest who
works as a consultant to drug rehabilitation centers, has this to say
about addictions:

> And thank God that there are addictions! For it is through the ex-
> perience of addiction that one can become aware of the call of life.
> Through addiction, one is given the opportunity to wake up, to ma-
> ture, to respond to that call in a positive and creative way. One can
> finally say a conscious yes to one's destiny and become one with
> oneself, one's world and one's God.[2]

If even smallpox can be valuable to us, why not addiction? The
spiritual value of an addiction experience is that it can draw our
attention to our powerlessness. As you may know, Alcoholics Anonymous (AA) offers a highly effective Twelve Step program for drug
rehabilitation that is based on the *power of powerlessness*. We might
think that the most important thing for a drug addict is to build self-
confidence and will power, but Step One of this program begins with
this startling statement: "We admitted we were powerless over alcohol — that our lives had become unmanageable." A co-founder of
AA elaborates:

> No other kind of bankruptcy is like this one. Alcohol, now become
> the rapacious creditor, bleeds us of all self-sufficiency and all will to
> resist its demands. Once this stark fact is accepted, our bankruptcy as
> going human concerns is complete.
> But upon entering A.A. we soon take quite another view of this
> absolute humiliation. We perceive that only through utter defeat are
> we able to take our first steps toward liberation and strength. Our ad-

mission of personal powerlessness finally turns out to be firm bedrock upon which happy and purposeful lives may be built.

We know that little good can come to any alcoholic who joins A.A. unless he has first accepted his devastating weakness and all its consequences. Until he so humbles himself, his sobriety — if any — will be precarious.[3]

John Martin sees alcoholism as a gift from God. If this sounds like an excessively liberal way of looking at the world, it should be noted that the belief in the power of weakness is very deeply entrenched in the Christian and Taoist traditions. St. Paul, for example, confided with us that three times he besought the Lord to remove his "thorn in the flesh," only to find this reply: "My grace is sufficient for you, for my power is made perfect in weakness" (2 Cor. 12:7–9). It is not too farfetched to think, therefore, that even thorns are a part of God's grace. As Catholic mystic Thomas Merton observed, "Everything that is, is holy." To see the truth of this statement is the beginning of an abundant life.

In this chapter, we are going to explore some nasty little things in life: enemies, poisons, illness, and demons. Before we begin, it is important to realize that our traditional way of thinking about them can be detrimental to our health — physical, psychological, and spiritual. Let us start with demons. A demon is either an evil spirit or an undesirable emotional state. The Western attitude to demons was well caricatured in the movie *The Exorcist,* which shows a life-or-death confrontation between good and evil. There are many violent scenes in the movie: the attack of the "green stuff" from the mouth of the demoniac, chairs and chests dashing across the room, people crashing through windows, a priest clutching a crucifix in hand, yelling in exasperation: "The name of the Lord impound you!" There is no dialogue whatsoever, no room for any negotiation. It is similar to the American attitude to AIDS: eradication of the enemy is the objective. Jesus' attitude to the demons is much different:

> They came to the other side of the sea, to the country of the Gerasenes. And when he had come out of the boat, there met him out of the tombs a man with an unclean spirit, who lived among the tombs; and no one could bind him anymore, even with a chain; for he had often been bound with fetters and chains, but the chains he wrenched apart, and the fetters he broke in pieces; and no one had the strength to subdue him. Night and day among the tombs and on the mountains he was always crying out, and bruising himself with

stones. And when he saw Jesus from afar, he ran and worshipped him; and crying out with a loud voice, he said, "What have you to do with me, Jesus, Son of the Most High God? I adjure you by God, do not torment me." For he had said to him, "Come out of the man, you unclean spirit!" And Jesus asked him, "What is your name?" He replied, "My name is Legion; for we are many." And he begged him eagerly not to send them out of the country. Now a great herd of swine was feeding there on the hillside; and they begged him, "Send us to the swine, let us enter them." So he gave them leave. And the unclean spirits came out, and entered the swine; and the herd, numbering about two thousand, rushed down the steep bank into the sea, and were drowned in the sea. (Mark 5:1–13)

It is easy to miss the deep meaning of this passage. In fact, we may miss the whole point if we regard Jesus as a special divinity who had much more power over evil than we do. For then the exorcism would be just an isolated, nonrecurring event with no educational value whatsoever. This story becomes relevant to us only if we regard Jesus as an ordinary human being who was showing us the right way to deal with our own demons through a life case.

A few things are remarkable. First, note that neither the demon nor Jesus were militant. Mark reported that the demoniac ran to Jesus and worshiped him, pleading: "I adjure you by God, do not torment me." Doesn't it strike you as a little strange that the demon should make such a request? It seems that Mr. Demon was not the aggressor but the *victim!* Has it ever occurred to you that the demons of our mind could be asking for our acceptance and that they need our love and understanding too? Jesus says, "Love your enemies...."

Second, note that Jesus did not come with a cross and a stake in hand. Unlike the exorcists we have seen on television, Jesus was ready for a dialogue with the demon. He asked the demon: "What is your name?" This question is very significant, for it shows that Jesus was familiar with the ancient art of shamanism. Shamanism teaches the importance of *naming* the demon. Shamans know that the naming of what we fear is a direct and practical way to gain power over it. Could it be that the reason we are often ineffective in dealing with our inner demons is that we are fighting a battle in the dark, that we have not paid enough attention to what we are fighting against? The fourth step in the Alcoholics Anonymous recovery program is to take an honest and exhaustive inventory of our inner demons. What exactly are our problems? Hatred? Fear? Greed? Sloth? Restlessness? The identification of problems is critical.

Third, Mr. Demon had a petition: he did not want to be deported. The last time we saw the usage of this "out of the country" metaphor was in the Parable of the Prodigal Son. There it was said that the prodigal son took his share of the family property and went to "a far country." To be "in a far country" is to be out of sight and out of mind. Could it be that the demon is actually a metaphor for the "prodigal son," who is banished to the netherworld of our consciousness by our judgmental and moralizing ego?

The conclusion of this story is bizarre. It ends with two thousand pigs rushing into the sea to be drowned. This has left many Bible scholars and theologians dumbfounded. What could be the lesson? William Barclay, for example, observed that "many have found it strange and...heartless that Jesus should destroy a herd of animals just like this."[4]

Poor pigs! What have they done to deserve this? Those who read this passage without feeling a sense of gross inequity are not paying attention. And what about the herdsmen who owned the pigs? We are talking about the loss of two thousand pigs here! A loss of this magnitude would be enough to ruin anyone's livelihood. Unless there is another story beneath the surface, this has to be one of the most wanton acts ever recorded in the Bible. We have to look deeper.

No matter how we look at it, the drowning of two thousand pigs as an act of exorcism still seems absurd. But this is precisely the point Jesus would like to get across. Zen masters have a habit of going to extremes to make a statement. The lesson here is that scapegoating (or "scapepigging") does not solve any problems and it is grossly unjust. Matthew's account of the incident ends in a negative tone: "And behold, all the city came out to meet Jesus; and they begged him to leave their neighborhood" (Matt. 8:34).

Not only did the incident not make Jesus a hero; it actually made him an unwelcome personality. What is also notable is that unlike the other miracle stories, there is no mention here of any euphoria whatsoever over the departure of the demons. In fact, there is not even any indication that the demoniac was healed! All we know is that the incident generated a lot of bad karma, and many people were left unhappy. But what can we expect out of scapegoating?

Pointing the finger is easy. Take the problem of pollution. When we see an oil spill or when we smell chemicals, our natural tendency is to react in disgust and accuse someone. Immediately, a new public enemy is created for us to vent our anger. What we refuse to do is to look deeper. Surely, an oil spill may be due to someone's oversight. But the fact is that when we keep transporting so much petroleum back and forth from one place to another, accidents are bound to happen. We simply refuse to come to terms with reality and recognize that the oil slick and the foul air are as much a result of our industrial development and our energy consumption pattern as a result of someone's carelessness or heartlessness. We single out an individual or a group and project on them the entire blame. We *externalize* the enemy because it is too painful to work with ourselves.

Incredible as it may seem, the drowning of the pigs was one of Jesus' Zen teachings. The pigs are not the problem. Mr. Demon is not the problem either. *We are!* The real enemy is us, and the problem is not going to disappear unless we are willing to work on ourselves rather than finding scapegoats. Jesus made his point even clearer in the following parable about the danger of exorcism:

> When the unclean spirit has gone out of a man, he passes through waterless places seeking rest; and finding none he says, "I will return to my house from which I came." And when he comes he finds it swept and put in order. Then he goes and brings seven other spirits more evil than himself, and they enter and dwell there; and the last state of that man becomes worse than the first. (Luke 11:24–26)

One can never cure a disease by eliminating the symptoms alone. If the root of the problem is not treated, then all that is going to happen is the substitution of one symptom by another. The mystic poet Kabir illustrates this beautifully:

> ...I pull back my sexual longings,
> And now I discover that I'm angry a lot.
> I gave up rage, and now I notice
> that I am greedy all day.
> I worked hard at dissolving the greed,
> And now I am proud of myself.
> When the mind wants to break its link with the world,
> It still holds on to one thing.[5]

The tendency to find scapegoats and to demonize things that are intrinsically neutral is universal. It is a defense mechanism of our ego, intended to frustrate our search for truth and inner knowledge. Sigmund Freud refers to this trick of the ego as "projection," which is a psychological term for the externalization of blame, guilt, or responsibility as a defense against anxiety.

Puritans are masters of the game of projection. They are the people who see celibacy and physical poverty as *intrinsically* pure and sensual pleasure and money as *intrinsically* impure. If there is anything that is certain, it is that Jesus was no Puritan. His confrontation with the morally impeccable Pharisees and his teaching on what defiles a person made this very clear. In essence, Puritanism is a form of scapegoating and the result of a superficial view of the world. Within the ever-young heart of every Zen master, there is always a child who loves to play pranks with this type of mind-set. Here is an example:

> You have heard that it was said, "You shall not commit adultery." But I say to you that every one who looks at a woman lustfully has already committed adultery with her in his heart. If your right eye causes you to sin, pluck it out and throw it away; it is better that you lose one of your members than that your whole body be thrown into hell. And if your right hand causes you to sin, cut it off and throw it away; it is better that you lose one of your members than that your whole body go into hell. (Matt. 5:27–30)

I refer to this as the "amputational approach" to purity. Since when has an eye or an arm ever caused a person to sin? The real problem lies in our mind, and we cannot amputate our mind without committing suicide. It seems that these severe statements are simply Jesus' dramatic way to draw people's attention to the source of the problem.

Although the barbarism of the amputational approach to purity is obvious, you will be surprised by the number of people who still practice it in one way or another. The practice is not restricted to Christians either. During Buddha's time, there was a monk who was obsessed with sex and tortured by his own desires. In an attempt to put an end to all these, the monk cut off his own genitals. But he received serious rebuke from the Buddha for this action, for the root of his illness lay in his mind and not in that physical part of his body. Scapegoating is not the way to truth; wisdom and clarity are. One of the early Christian fathers, Origen, did exactly what the foolish monk had done: he castrated himself. He was never canonized as a result. These cases of folly show that not only are we quick to transfer blame to others; we are also inclined to do the same to different parts of ourselves through some kind of internal scapegoating. Such spiritual violence! The basic problem is the lack of holistic vision.

If purity cannot be attained via amputation, neither can it be attained via the suppression of our "negative" emotions — greed, lust, anger, fear, etc. Who is the entity that is going to suppress the negative emotions anyway? One thing is obvious: a desire can be suppressed only by an even greater desire. It is all part of the ego's game. The situation is not unlike bringing in a tiger to chase away a wolf. Substitution may take place, but the problem remains. In fact, an antagonistic approach may bring more harm than good. If defilement is an illusion, then an effort to erase a defilement will only make it look more real. As Jesus commented in his parable of exorcism, "The last state of that man became worse than the first" (Luke 11:26).

Amputation does not work. Suppression does not work. So what then is the solution? Not to fight. We have to drop our gladiatorial approach to life. Jesus offered his Zen advice: resist not evil! Resistance will only lend more strength to the opposition. Purity is not a matter of fighting or suppression. It is a matter of *insight*. When we actually see that we are like a little puppy chasing its own tail, that we are getting nowhere with our petty fighting, the craziness will stop and the mind will become very quiet. Awareness purifies.

Healing begins with the adoption of a gentle approach to life. According to Thomas Moore, author of the bestseller *Care of the Soul,* the critical step is to learn to "honor the symptoms as a Voice of the Soul." Even greed, lust, hatred, and fear can be our teachers, and they can lead us to inner truth if we learn to respect them. Moore elaborates on the art of listening:

> The basic intention in any caring, physical or psychological, is to alleviate suffering. But in relation to the symptom itself, observance means first of all listening and looking carefully at what is being revealed in the suffering. An intent to heal can get in the way of seeing. By doing less, more is accomplished. Observance is homeopathic in its workings rather than allopathic, in the paradoxical way that it befriends a problem rather than making an enemy of it.[6]

Demons constantly come back to haunt us. They keep knocking on our door because they have important messages to tell us, and yet we are not listening. Renowned meditation teacher Jack Kornfield recommends that we make the demons part of our spiritual path:

> Choose one of the most frequent and difficult demons that arises in your practice, such as irritation, fear, boredom, lust, doubt, or restlessness. For one week in your daily meditation, be particularly aware each time this state arises. Carefully name it. Notice how it begins and

what precedes it. Notice if there is any particular thought or image that triggers this state. Notice how long it lasts and when it ends. Notice what state usually follows it. Observe whether it ever arises very slightly or softly. See how loud and strong it gets. Soften and receive even the resistance. Finally, sit and be aware of your breath, watching and waiting for this demon, allowing it to come and go, greeting it like an old friend.[7]

Do not fight with your inner demons. Learn to absorb them into your being with compassion — for they are part of you! Remember what Jesus says: love your enemies. To love means to respect, to attend to, to be ready to respond to, and to understand. The most difficult part of spiritual practice is to open up our hearts to our enemies. This may sound like surrendering. However, it is a crucial step. Perhaps we should learn to think of our inner demons as smallpox; they are horrifying beings, but they do have much to teach us.

On the surface, the Buddhist attitude toward inner enemies is far from holistic. According to Buddhist teaching, greed, anger, and ignorance are considered the Three Poisons. But Buddhism also teaches that even poisons can be used as medicine. The sixth patriarch of Zen, Hui Neng, said that passions are *bodhi* (Wisdom). There is no need to be apprehensive about passions; we have to learn to *use* them.

Resist not evil! This is one of Jesus' greatest Zen teachings, albeit an underappreciated one. It has seldom been understood or accepted by the general public because it runs against our common sense and our traditional notion of morality. The mind is a fighter. It asks, "If it is evil, why not fight it?" Not long ago, I was in a Bible study session with a group of Christians. We were studying a verse from Ecclesiastes: "Be not righteous overmuch, and do not make yourself overwise" (Eccles. 7:16). No one knew what it meant. Yet these are the great Zen sayings from the Bible.

"Resist not evil" is a profound teaching. On a psychological level, it means the genuine acceptance of all our negative emotions, no matter how vicious or poisonous they may look on the surface. It is extremely difficult to do, for it requires a high level of spiritual maturity. One does not develop a genuine acceptance of these poisons until one really understands the nature of the ego and will no longer be fooled by the games it plays.

There are two alternative paths of spiritual practice: the *fighter's path* and the *Tantric path*. The former is the path of the ascetic.

It is the path embraced by most religions. Fighters are forever obsessed with "purity." Consciously or subconsciously, they seek to be heros by pursuing complete control. Because control is their objective, they are hostile to whatever may jeopardize their effort. They condemn desires. They condemn anger. They condemn sensual pleasure. They condemn all of humanity's basic instincts and, in doing so, they condemn life itself. But the path is doomed to fail because life is uncontrollable after all. The only way that the fighter's path can "work" is to induce failures and frustrations. For discovering what is wrong means heading toward what is right, albeit in a very slow manner.

In sharp contrast is the Tantric path, which is the path of *love.* Unfortunately, "Tantra," is a much-abused word, both here and in Asia. In the U.S. in particular, there is a lot of misplaced enthusiasm about using Tantric techniques to attain sexual fulfillment. One of the reviewers of this book told me that she recently received a catalogue of "Buddhist supplies" and found many sexual toys labeled as aids for Tantric practice. The misunderstanding is indeed serious.

Actually, Tantra has to do with the spirituality of gentleness and the acceptance of what is. According to Tibetan master Chögyam Trungpa:

> Tantric wisdom brings nirvana into samsara. This may sound rather shocking. Before reaching the level of Tantra, you try to abandon samsara and strive to achieve nirvana. But eventually you must realize the futility of striving and then become completely one with nirvana. In order to really capture the energy of nirvana and become one with it you need a partnership with the ordinary world.... One cannot reject the physical existence of the world as being something bad and associated with samsara. You can only understand the essence of nirvana by looking into the essence of samsara.[8]

The Tantric path takes an affirmative and friendly approach toward life and does not condemn anything. It recognizes our limitations and weaknesses as part of being human and is willing to accept them just as they are. The Tantric approach sees the kingdom of God in the here-and-now rather than in some distant, uncertain future. Tantric practitioners do not struggle to achieve or control. The way of Tantra is complete self-abandonment. There is nothing for them to do because love, being unconditional acceptance, does not make any demand. Tantric practitioners simply live in the moment. There is nothing to fight, suppress, condemn, or reject, for everything is seen as holy. Tantra means nonduality, which means no goal, no striving, no conflict, and no thinking. Tantra is the practice of Zen.

Historically, the practice of Tantra has been very controversial because it goes against virtually everything that the traditional religions and morality teach. While the traditional religions teach the suppression of passions, Tantra teaches the gentle art of using sex and anger as vehicles for enlightenment. Tantra puts a heavy emphasis on sex because it is indeed one of the most important primal energies. Traditional religions say, "Stay away, it is poison!" But Tantra says, "Have no fear. Relax and observe!" Although passions are powerful, they are *neutral* by themselves. The gentle path is also the path of *efficiency*. Instead of fighting our passions, we conserve our energy and learn to harness their power for our self-discovery. The practice of Tantra is the art of turning enemies into friends. Needless to say, it requires a complete revision of the way we look at our world. Lama Yeshe makes this observation:

> The tantric solution to this problem is extremely radical; it involves a complete transformation of our ordinary vision. This is the central point of the tantric approach. The same desirous energy that ordinarily propels us from one unsatisfactory situation to another is transmuted, through the alchemy of tantra, into a transcendental experience of bliss and wisdom. The practitioner focuses the penetrating brilliance of this blissful wisdom so that it cuts like a laser beam through all false projections of this and that and pierces the very heart of reality.[9]

It is not surprising that Tantra has received so much criticism and opposition from "religious" people, for the practice of Tantra means the death of ego. The nature of ego is to control, to dominate, and to strive for achievement. But Tantra says that the kingdom is *now!* Samsara is equated with nirvana. Why strive for something you already have? The ego refuses to accept this truth because it takes away its right of existence. To survive, the ego has to delude. It is not an accident that in Christianity the devil is called the Father of Lies.

It is critical to understand that the ego has to continue to confuse and deceive in order to sustain its life. So it tells us to control, without revealing the identity of the one who is trying to control. Similarly, it says, "Cleanse your defilements!" but gives us no clue about how defilements arise. It also tells us to hold on to our shame and guilt while hiding from us the fact that these are precisely what are preventing us from seeing reality and correcting our mistakes. This is the function of the ego: to imprison us by its lies.

Tantra is the *gentle* path. Many people tend to confuse spiritual gentleness with indulgence or some kind of moral laxity. A literary agent who reviewed my manuscript commented that I should add a section on "tough love." He did not realize that there is toughness (uncompromising determination) in real gentleness.

In fact, Tantric practitioners often consider themselves as *warriors,* i.e., people who are skilled in the art of war. A warrior is fundamentally different from a fighter. Fighters are pugnacious individuals who are attached to the idea of fighting and winning. Typically, they adopt a dualistic and antagonistic attitude toward life. Tantric warriors, on the other hand, are holistic in their vision. They do not see the world as a gigantic fighting arena and are not addicted to combat. They are warriors by virtue of their *courage* and not their belligerence; they are determined to accept reality as it is, no matter how ugly or unpalatable things may seem. They have an uncompromising commitment to truth, and their actions reflect this commitment. To be true warriors requires both great discipline (the discipline of living in the moment) and great courage (the courage to *be).*

Thus, gentleness and toughness are two sides of the same coin. Tantric warriors are *gentle* in the sense that they are able to accept, yield to, and adapt to reality. Gentle warriors are willing to admit their personal limitations and do not try to do the impossible or fight the inevitable. Far from being a sign of weakness, this gentleness is a sign of strength. In fact, it is almost a form of asceticism, albeit without the associated ambition, ego, or will to win. Tantric warriors are *tough* in terms of their unwavering commitment to what is. In this sense, we need to be gentle in order to be tough, and we need to be tough in order to be gentle. It is paradoxical.

Tantra appears to be amoral or even immoral because of its sincere affirmation of the human passions, which traditional religions reject. This fearless acceptance of the thorns and poisons of life is part of Tantric courage, the courage to embrace, instead of condemn, what *is.* Without such fearless acceptance, no transformation is possible. In the Mahayanist sutras, there are two legendary figures, Manjusri and Sudhana. Manjusri is a bodhisattva who is famous for his supreme wisdom. Sudhana is a Buddhist youth who has a strong zeal for truth. The following drama played by the two illustrates the Tantric spirit:

One day, Manjusri had a very special request for Sudhana. He told the youth, "Go out and collect for me some herbs which cannot be used as medicine."

Sudhana went out for a long time and came back empty-handed. He reported to Manjusri, "There is no herb which meets your requirement." Upon this, Manjusri said, "Well, then, just give me one which can be used as medicine."

Sudhana simply stayed where he was and grabbed something from under his feet.

Manjusri lifted up the herb and showed it to all those present. He declared, "Listen, everybody. This herb can be used as either poison or medicine. Truly, it can either heal or kill."

Tantra finds treasure in the shadow side of existence. As long as we keep rejecting the unpleasant aspects of life, we can never be made whole. Thomas Moore observes that an important part of soulful living is to develop "a taste for the perverse." His experience as a psychotherapist teaches him that one particularly effective "trick" for the care of the soul is to look with special attention and openness at what a patient condemns, rejects, belittles, or hides in the closet. He finds that much soul is lost in our arbitrary labeling of experiences as either "good" or "bad."

Moralists tend to consider Tantra's friendliness with the shadows of life as dangerous. It must be made clear that Tantra does not endorse a licentious lifestyle or an outlandish pursuit of perversions. Much of Tantric practice is simply an honest recognition of the libido elements *already present* in our lives. Bringing into the open these normally hidden and repressed elements makes healing possible.

It is important to recognize that Tantra is not just an esoteric spirituality practiced by only a handful of Tibetan people. In a sense, Tantra is the *only* viable spiritual path, for we are all sentient beings and we must come to terms with the reality of our passions. Greed, lust, anger, jealousy, etc. are basic facts of life, and we cannot simply shove them under the carpet. Avoidance is an expression of fear more than of courage. Asceticism says, "Avoid pleasure and guard your senses." But Tantra says, "Celebrate pleasure and open up your senses to the joys of the world."

Buddha had tried the path of asceticism. He practiced asceticism for six years, only to find that it did not work. In fact, his enlightenment came shortly after this shocking discovery. The practice of asceticism is to mortify the body, deaden the senses, and close one's doors to the world. By condemning the pleasures of life, it is hostile to life itself. But the practice of true spirituality is to become more alive. It is not the rejection of the world but the transcendence of the world through the total acceptance of what is, including sensual pleasures, psychic poisons, and human follies. Asceticism does not work because it is a form of escapism. Tantra is not about escape; it is a fearless entry into life, taking its pain along with its joy, accepting its poisons as well as its nectar.

We conclude, therefore, that the practice of Tantra is not an option; it is a *necessary* step for spiritual growth. As Lama Yeshe points out, "If the only way we know how to deal with desirous objects is to avoid them, there will be a severe limit as to how far our spiritual practice can take us."

Although our ego may wish us to think so, the practice of Tantra does not mean indulgence, and the love of sensual pleasures does not mean to become an addict to them. If this were true, we would all be Tantric masters by now. Jesus says, "Resist not evil." He told us to be gentle with evil, but he did not encourage us to seek evil. One of most critical steps for the practice of spirituality is to learn to listen and read carefully.

Like avoidance, indulgence is also a form of escape. The objects of indulgence, be they drugs, alcohol, or sex, are simply used as painkillers. Experienced healers know that the real problem often does not lie in the drug or whatever object an addict is addicted to. For most addicts, the problem existed long before they started taking their drug of choice. Experienced healers also realize that getting rid of the drug does not get rid of the problem. In fact, it is critical to address the real problem at the time the drug is removed. More often than not, the drug-taking behavior is a symptom for a deep-seated unwillingness to face life as it is, i.e., a lack of gentleness. Thus, forced abstinence, without treating the root of the problem, may do more harm than good.

Jesus, the Tantric master, says: "Love your enemy and pray for those who persecute you." To love our enemies does not mean to indulge or to be enslaved by them. The practice of love (which is the practice of Tantra) means to respect, to attend to, to understand, and to respond to. The Buddhist equivalent of the Christian notion of love is *metta,* a term whose root is the Pali term for friend. Respect, attention, understanding, and the ability to respond to a friend's needs are all key ingredients in true friendship.

To illustrate with a concrete example, let us say that our problem is lust. The first step is to learn to *respect* it. Yes, we have to learn to respect lust, the emotion that we are often embarrassed about. To do this, we have to relinquish our value judgment and treat everything with equanimity (i.e., with equal respect). It requires giving up our old habit of labeling, scapegoating, fighting, and denial. We have to learn to relate to lust without shame, guilt, or embarrassment. Instead of treating it as an inferior instinct unworthy of us, we have to learn to respect it as a teacher and a friend. Only then can the spiritual journey begin.

Attention is a natural result of respect, for we listen only to things we consider important. Most people have little understanding of their negative emotions because they constantly repress them, treating them like second-class citizens or "prodigal sons." But once we learn to accept lust as our teacher and open our heart to it, it will guide us through the labyrinth of our psyche.

To pay attention to lust does not mean to watch it as if it were a criminal. It is more a matter of developing a relaxed awareness of its existence in our everyday lives — as we are walking in the street, as we are interacting with others, as we are by ourselves, as we are engaged in sex. True practice is a moment-to-moment, day-to-day thing. As our awareness of lust develops, we will gradually get to know its habits. How and when does it normally arise? How and when does it normally subside? How long does it stay when it pays us a visit? Does it usually come along with other emotions such as sadness, boredom, or anxiety? We have to get to know lust as an old friend.

Besides developing an overall familiarity with the emotion, simultaneously we have to cultivate the depth of our experience. Most of us do not really experience our negative emotions, although we think we do. We either repress them because we regard them as undesirable, or we simply act them out under impulse. Neither mode allows for the depth of experience that is necessary for the healing quality of these "poisons" to come out. Instead of glossing them over, we have to embrace these emotions with a refined sense of awareness. As the Tibetan master Chögyam Trungpa observed, "If one actually feels the living quality, the texture of the emotions as they are in their naked state, then this experience also contains ultimate truth."

Attention leads to *understanding*. As we continue to open our hearts to lust, for instance, we will discover more and more things about ourselves that are normally buried in the netherworld of our awareness. Our friend Lust is a guide in this inward journey. It is an expert in opening doors and uncovering secret passageways within our inner castle. Eventually, we will reach a point at which our friend Lust feels comfortable enough to reveal to us its humble origin. It will take us down memory lane, back to the early days of our childhood, to take a good look at its birthplace. To our dismay, we will find that it is not the offspring of malice or vulgarity. We will witness how Lust is born out of a sea of loneliness, in the heart of a child who is frightened and helpless, desperate to make connections and find consolation within an isolated existence.

Finally, when Lust is convinced that we can be totally trusted, it will bring us back to the present and show us how abusive we have been in our dealing with it in our adulthood. Unfeelingly, we drag it out to do a dirty job: to act as a filler for the love that is missing in our lives, to blank out our pain, our boredom, and our frustrations in adulthood, to provide a momentary relief. For all that Lust has done for us, we remain totally ungrateful. In the midst of our heartlessness, we call it all kinds of bad names and attack it with a myriad of abuses.

Miracles do happen in these inward journeys. Sooner or later, we will find Lust transfigured; it sheds its monster-like mask. It now appears to us as innocent as a snowflake. The original ugliness dissolves in a sense of tragic beauty. Fear exits and compassion enters, experienced as a healing warmth. We do not know where this compassion comes from or to whom it is directed. Is it directed toward Lust, our much misunderstood friend? Or is it directed toward the little child in us, who is hurting and helpless. Is Lust our enemy, our servant, or just an alienated part of our self? But perhaps it does not matter. For true healing has begun.

Such is the way of Tantra. It is the path of heart. The key is to open our heart to what we fear and touch it with our deep and authentic feelings. It is never a matter of fighting; it is a matter of doing the necessary *soul work* — observing, tending, touching, and understanding. Only then can we start making the appropriate *response*, which is the fourth element of love. Response does not have to be a physical one. It can be simply a quiet acknowledgement, a stir in the heart, or a change in our attitude. In the end of this journey, Lust is transformed, through the miracle of mindfulness, into love and compassion.

When we find the dark side of life too much to take, when we feel an urge to fight or escape from it all, perhaps we should visualize a lotus flower, the timeless Buddhist symbol for purity. While the lotus flower itself is clean and beautiful, it is nevertheless rooted in dirty, stinking mud. Unsightly as the mud may be, it provides the necessary nutrients for the lotus flower. Should the flower be disconnected from the mud, it cannot continue to live. Perhaps we should think of our greed, anger, and lust in the same way: they provide the necessary food for our soul.

— Eleven —

Love

For he makes his sun rise on the evil and on the good,
and sends rain on the just and on the unjust.
–JESUS

To see into self-nature is merit;
to treat all things as equal is virtue.
–HUI NENG

That Christianity emphasizes love is common knowledge. Yet "love"
is a term that is virtually unknown in Zen sayings, although Buddhism does consider the development of love-kindness (*metta*) and
compassion (*karuna*) as critical to one's spiritual path. The question
naturally arises as to whether Zen masters are afraid of love. Hui
Neng, the sixth patriarch of Zen, put the emphasis on "no-mind."
On the surface, love and no-mind look like direct opposites. Is the
gulf between Christianity and Zen really so wide in the matter of
love? What is the true meaning of love? Is love an emotion or an
attachment? How can love be practiced? What is the relationship between love, freedom, and goodness? Let's look again at the Sermon
on the Mount:

> You have heard that it was said, "You shall love your neighbor and
> hate your enemy." But I say to you: Love your enemy and pray for
> those who persecute you, so that you may be sons of your Father who
> is in heaven; *for he makes his sun rise on the evil and on the good, and
> sends rain on the just and on the unjust.* For if you love only those
> who love you, what reward have you? Do not even the tax collectors
> do the same? And if you salute only your brothers, what more are
> you doing than others? Do not even the Gentiles do the same? *You,*

therefore, must be perfect, as your heavenly Father is perfect. (Matt. 5:43–48)

Apparently, the love that Jesus talked about is very different from ordinary human love, for it makes no distinctions. As Jesus observes, God "makes his sun rise on the evil and on the good." He says that love is the highest virtue: to love is to be like God.

Most people are not aware of any connection between Confucianism and Zen. But interestingly, the closest Chinese equivalent for the English word "love" is the Confucian term *jen*. No other Chinese word for virtue carries the same mystical and elusive character. The great sinologist Arthur Waley noted that *jen* denotes a "transcendental perfection attained to by legendary heroes such as Po I, but not by any living or historical person."[1] Confucius remarked that the quality is so rare and peculiar that we "cannot but be chary in speaking of it" (Analects 12:3). He was hesitant in attributing the quality to anybody, and his disciples also noted that "the Master rarely discoursed upon *jen*" (Analects 9:1).

Waley notes that *jen* is a mystical entity not only analogous to but practically identical with the Tao. He made the following insightful remark about the translation of the term:

> It seems to me that "good" is the only possible translation of the term *jen* as it occurs in the Analects. No other word is sufficiently general to cover the whole range of meaning; indeed terms such as "humane," "altruistic," "benevolent," are in almost every instance inappropriate, often ludicrously so. But there is another word, *shan,* which though it wholly lacks the mystical and transcendental implications of *jen,* cannot conveniently be translated by any other word but "good." For that reason I shall translate *jen* by Good (Goodness, etc.) with a capital; and *shan* by good with a small g.[2]

Confucius's reservation and Waley's care in the use of words related to goodness are understandable. In fact, Jesus would not even let others call him "good." This is documented in the Gospel of Mark in the story about the young ruler who inquired about eternal life. He addressed Jesus as "good teacher." But Jesus immediately corrected him: "Why do you call me good? No one is good but God alone" (Mark 10:17–22).

These quotations from the Analects and from the Bible help to drive home some key points: Confucian *jen* is to Christian love as the Tao is to God. *Jen* is the way of the Tao and love is the way of God.

According to Master Jesus, to love is to be perfect and to be God-like. He denied this quality to any mortal. It helps also to remember John's remark that God is Love (1 John 4:8).

In the Sermon on the Mount, Jesus asked us to turn to nature as our teacher. Nature does not make any distinction in its treatment of the good and the evil, nor does it discriminate between the just and the unjust. To treat all things and all people as equal is the way of nature. Jesus said that our love of others should also be like that. True love is *indiscriminate*. In this light, the instruction to "love your enemies" and to "pray for those who persecute you" is more a reflection of this nondiscriminatory mentality than an intention to go overboard. Here we should note that this nondiscriminatory attitude to life is much emphasized in Buddhism. In fact, the wisdom of the Buddha is called the *Wisdom of Non-discrimination*, hinting that nondiscrimination is a key to spiritual development.

This is Jesus' main message: to love indiscriminately is to be perfect like the Father. The equivalence between love and goodness is thus established. Love is goodness, and goodness is love. But, of course, to love indiscriminately is quite impossible for humans. We may be able to do so occasionally but certainly not all the time. That is why Jesus told the young ruler that "no one is good but God alone." Nevertheless, to learn to love and to approach perfection is the mission of life.

Christian love is often associated with self-renunciation. But we must understand renunciation correctly. It is common for religious people to confuse asceticism with spirituality. The renunciation of material possessions, in particular, is often considered as an expression of spirituality. Even social and family relationships are viewed as obstacles. For Jesus said:

> If you love your father and mother more than you love me, you are not worthy of being mine; or if you love your son or daughter more than me, you are not worthy of being mine. If you refuse to take up the cross and follow me, you are not worthy of being mine. (Matt. 10:37–39)

But note that Jesus was not demanding that his disciples should love him more than anything else; he was simply cautioning them against *unevenness* of love. Real renunciation is not self-deprivation or asceticism. If it were, many masochists would qualify as spiritual people. True spirituality is an affirmation of life and not a negation of it. The main point is to have equal love for all. This is confirmed by Jesus' proclamation of the greatest commandments:

> One of them, a lawyer, spoke up: "Sir, which is the most important commandment in the laws of Moses?"
>
> Jesus replied, "Love the Lord your God with all your heart, soul and mind!" This is the greatest commandment. The second most important is similar: "Love your neighbor as much as yourself." All the other commandments and all the demands of the prophets stem from these two laws and are fulfilled if you obey them. *Keep only these and you will find that you are obeying all the others.* (Matt. 22:35–40)

Listen very carefully. We have the world's greatest moral teacher talking here. What Jesus accomplished in these few statements is nothing short of earth-shaking, especially when we take into account the historical context. People during Jesus' time were obsessed with the law and all kinds of external behaviors associated with it. The Pharisees, in particular, followed the scribal law to such a painstaking extent that they were not able to function as ordinary citizens in the society.

Given this background, what Jesus said was truly amazing, both in terms of its extraordinary beauty and in terms of its radicalism. It was simply Jesus at his best as both a moral teacher and a Zen master. It is beautiful because of its astounding simplicity. He was able to condense a huge and formidable moral code into just two requirements: love God and love others as oneself. It is radical in a sense that it was so completely out of the mainstream. While other people were trying to follow the law to the nth degree of detail, Jesus was effectively saying: "Drop all these shenanigans about dogged compliance. Love is the only test for morality."

Why should the love of God precede the love of others? Some insight can be gained from reading Mark's version of the Gospel. Mark reported that when Jesus was asked which one is the greatest commandment of all, he gave the following answer:

> The one that says, "Israel! *The Lord is one.* And you must love him with all your heart and soul and mind and strength." (Mark 12:29)

What does it mean to say that "the Lord is one"? The superficial interpretation is that there is only one true God to love. However, this will not explain the connection between the love of God and the love of humankind. A deeper interpretation is that "love of God" means remembering that all things in the universe are issued from

God (since God created them all from nothing) and are hence one integrated whole. To understand wholeness, think about the teeth in your mouth. Should we have to extract a bad tooth, it is important that we replace it with an artificial one (unless it is supposed to be regrown). If the gap is left unfilled, we will find that the other teeth will soon move in to take up the space. The different teeth only look separate. In reality they are all one.

Similarly, all beings in the universe are interdependent. Thus, the love of God means the love of All There Is. The one who loves God is the one who adopts a loving attitude to all things in life, for all are intimately connected and do not exist apart from one another. Therefore, the second greatest commandment is simply a *derivative* of the first one. Our love for others is due to our recognition that each one of them is also an integral part of God, inseparable from Ultimate Reality. The recognition that "I and the Father are one" forms the basis for neighborly love.

When the second commandment says "love your neighbor as yourself," it doesn't mean "to love your neighbor more than yourself," because you are also part of that Ultimate Reality and thus equally lovable and equally important. The self-denial that Jesus was asking for is not depriving oneself in favor of others. As explained before, the real key is indiscriminate love.

Ego (i.e., who we pretend to be) is the root of the problem, not material wealth, secular life, or social relationships. As long as there is a trace of ego left, as long as we are still seeking illusory gains and gratification, love is not possible.

Real love means the death of the ego, the false self. This is where Zen and Christian love meet. Love is possible only when one's mind is not attached to anything, which means the disappearance of ego. Nature is the best role model for learning about love. Chapter 5 of the *Tao Te Ching* makes the following observation:

> Heaven and earth are not kind;
> They treat all things as straw dogs.
> The saints are not kind;
> They treat all people as straw dogs.

Not only are heaven and earth not loving; they are not even kind. A "straw dog" is a dog-puppet made of straw. In the old days, it was one of the ceremonial objects for making sacrifices to heaven. After the performance of the ceremony, the straw dog is discarded without any feeling or attachment. Lao Tzu comments that heaven and earth treat us in the same way: we are all treated the same, with neither love nor hate. For "leaving things alone" is the way of the Tao. But it is precisely because heaven and earth have no special love for anything that they can love all things. They "love" by being indiscriminate. The key does not lie in being "loving" or not. It lies in being indiscriminate. Partiality is an expression of the ego; equality is an expression of love.

For most of us, this "equality" aspect of God's love is very difficult to comprehend. We find it hard to accept the fact that God will not give us any special favor. The first traumatic experience for many children is probably the death of a pet. Agonized by a sense of loss, they will ask, "Why doesn't God let Sparky live?" The implicit assumption is that if God is truly loving, he will not let our loved ones die. When God does not "behave" as we expect him to, we are taken aback. This is the first time we realize that we really do not understand God. This is the first test of faith.

As we grow older and as the problems we have to face in life increase, our dissatisfaction with God's "apathy" tends to increase. Like Job, we often complain about God's apparent hostility to us. Whenever an unhappy event happens, we tend to ask, "Why does it have to happen to me? Why doesn't God do something?" We act as if we were always victims of God, not understanding that nonfavoritism is the way of the Lord. Sometimes our dissatisfaction develops into moral outrage, and we interpret God's equality as injustice. We ask, with Job, "Why do the wicked live, reach old age, and grow mighty in power?" (Job 21:7).

Actually, it helps to have a sense of humor here. We crave for unconditional love. We want to receive unconditional love from our loved ones and from God. But when God does love unconditionally and blesses both the righteous and the evil, we complain. Poor God! What can God do to make us happy? How can the finite mind understand the Infinite? Unconditional love is simply *nonsense* to the rational mind. As left-brained people, we do everything for a reason. How can our love be an exception? It is only natural for us to love only when we think we can get a return from loving. Why love strangers and enemies? The ego is interested in only this: what is in it for me?

This is the difficulty: while we practically live in a world of "rational" (i.e., conditional) love, we nevertheless expect to get unconditional love from everybody. We do expect unconditional love from God, but only for ourselves and *not* for everybody else. Frankly, what we want is favoritism. The dilemma for God is that everyone is asking for the same thing: *self-centered unconditional love*. It seems that even God cannot please everybody.

Nondiscrimination is a keystone of spirituality. Jesus, using a positive language, proclaims the greatness of nonpartial love. Zen, using a negative language, talks about the importance of "no-mind" (*wu-hsin*). For Hui Neng, this practice of "no-mind" is the foundation of Zen. No-mind is the mind that is not attached to or obstructed by anything. True love cannot arise as long as there are still attachments, which are expressions of the ego. So love and freedom are intricately linked. J. Krishnamurti explains this relationship as follows:

> So freedom and love go together. Love is not reaction. If I love you because you love me, that is a mere trade, a thing to be bought in the market; it is not love. To love is not to ask for anything in return, not even to feel that you are giving something — and it is only such love that can know freedom.
>
> Now, you and I have to understand this whole problem of freedom. We must find out for ourselves what it means to love; because if we don't love we can never be thoughtful, attentive; we can never be considerate. Do you know what it means to be considerate? When you see a sharp stone on a path trodden by many bare feet, you remove it, not because you have been asked, but because you feel for another — it does not matter who he is, and you may never meet him. To plant a tree and cherish it, to look at the river and enjoy the fullness of the earth... — for all this there must be freedom; and to be free you must love.[3]

Freedom and love are two faces of the same reality. The "no-mind" of Hui Neng is a free mind not obstructed by desire, greed, anger, fear. True freedom is attained only with the death of the ego. Jesus gave an excellent illustration of "no-mind":

> Thus, when you give alms, sound no trumpet before you, as the hypocrites do in the synagogues and in the streets, that they may be praised by men. Truly, I say to you, they have their rewards. *But when you give alms, do not let your left hand know what your right hand is doing*. (Matt. 6:2–4)

"Not letting your left hand know what your right hand is doing" means not only that you are not showing off your good deeds to impress people, but you do not even value the action as a good deed yourself! It is to be *ordinary.* For all distinctions vanish in true love. If you do not even make the distinction between self and others, where is the "good deed"? This is the practice of "no-mind."

The interrelationship between "no-mind," love, and *wu-wei* is illustrated by the following Zen tale:

> A young monk was given a koan to meditate on. The koan was no-mind. He worked hard at it for a long time but was getting nowhere.
>
> One day, the monk was doing his regular alms rounds. As he was walking, the same old questions rang in his mind, "What does it mean to have no mind? If I have no mind, how can I walk? If I have no mind, how can I talk?" Just when he was passing by a house of pleasure, he overheard a girl saying to her customer, "Your mind is not with me today."
>
> The words struck the monk like a lightning. He was instantly enlightened and became a buddha.

When a person has been working on a koan for an extended period, it sometimes takes only a little push to trigger an enlightenment. The young monk in the story had been running into blind alleys, for he was fixated on the idea that having no-mind means blanking out all consciousness. But the remark of the girl gave him a fresh inspiration. In a sense, her customer had no mind. For he was not thinking about her that day. It then dawned on the monk that no-mind does not mean losing one's consciousness; it is just the *ordinary mind* that is not trying to make something special. Further, the monk realized that it was with no-mind that he had been walking and talking. He did not have to consciously think about how to move his muscles in order to walk, or about how to vibrate his vocal cords in order to talk. Nature did it all, without any effort. The no-mind is the *wu-wei* mind.

Nowadays it is common for psychologists to say that "love is not a feeling." The rational mind tends to jump from one extreme to another. "If love is not a matter of passion," the rational mind reasons, "it must be a matter of will power." Thus, we try to force ourselves to love, and we feel guilty when we are not able to do so. We have turned love into another game for the ego, another obsession, another symbol of achievement.

But can love be willed? Isn't will just another expression of the ego? It seems that we are often confused about what the ego can do and what it cannot. One thing that the ego definitely cannot do is to love. Unfortunately, we tend to overestimate the ego's ability. St. Paul told us that we do not even know how to pray without the help of the Spirit (Rom. 8:26). Jesus was even more humble. He told us that he could do nothing on his own authority (John 5:30). Could it be then that when we love, it is actually God loving through us? Perhaps we are just conduits of God.

If we follow Jesus' logic, we would have to conclude that love is not a matter of will but a matter of grace. As such, it cannot be cultivated or strived for. The best we can do is simply to open ourselves to it and clear away our inner obstacles so that it can flow through us. Learning to love is like learning to walk. There are no textbooks to read or classes to take. The main thing to "do" is to let go of our fear and have trust in the Tao. For love is another expression of *wu-wei*.

This sheds new light on the greatest commandment: "Love the Lord your God with all your heart, soul and mind!" To do something with one's heart, soul, and mind is to do it with one's entire being and with utmost sincerity. But sincerity is incompatible with fear or coercion. Thus, the "greatest commandment" turns out not to be a commandment after all!

Actually, we do not need to be commanded to love God. We simply need to see that there is no conflict between the love of self and the love of others. Erich Fromm states:

> Not only others, but ourselves are the "object" of our feelings and attitudes; the attitudes towards others and toward ourselves, far from being contradictory, are basically conjunctive....Love, in principle, is indivisible as far as the connection between "objects" and one's own self is concerned. Genuine love is an expression of productiveness and implies care, respect, responsibility and knowledge. It is not an "affect" in the sense of being affected by somebody, but an active striving for growth and happiness of the loved person, rooted in one's own capacity to love.[4]

Love is a *general* ability. Those who cannot love others cannot love themselves either. The converse is also true. For love is essentially an openness to life. In order to love, we have to open ourselves to both the beauties and the thorns of life. There seems to be some kind of built-in justice: people who cannot accept the imperfections in others cannot accept the imperfections in themselves either.

To learn about love, simply observe yourself in a detached manner and see under what kind of circumstances your impatience, anger, and animosity toward other people arise. I do this with myself all the time. Why do I curse the bus or train that has arrived late? Why do

I yell at my children when they do not perform as I expect them to. The underlying reason is always fear or some sense of insecurity. I fear that the delayed train will make me miss my important meeting. I fear that my underperforming child will become a bigger and bigger burden for me, a burden that I am not sure that I can deal with.

The inability to love also reflects a lack of creativity. Creative people tend to see life's problems as opportunities to exercise their creativity, to explore something new, to build character, to grow spiritually, and to develop self-knowledge; uncreative people tend to view problems as inconveniences and threats. Love, creativity, and gentleness are closely linked. People who are creative and open to life are more able to love others and themselves. Once we learn the art of turning problems into opportunities, there is no more distinction between self-love and love of others. Meister Eckhart made this observation:

> If you love yourself, you love everybody else as you do yourself. As long as you love another person less than you love yourself, you will not really succeed in loving yourself. But if you love all alike, including yourself, you will love them as one person and that person is both god and man. Thus, he is a just and righteous person who, loving himself, loves all others equally.[5]

Buddhism recognizes that all love begins with self-love. Obviously, it is extremely difficult and unlikely for those who are full of misery themselves to try to help others. As Walpola Piyananda Thera observes, "In Buddhism, apparent self-love is a crucial first step. It is a cleansing and purifying of one's mind to be able to love another, without which love just becomes raga (eros)."[6] In the Pali Canon, Buddha taught the art of loving others by loving ourselves:

> "I shall protect myself": with that thought the Foundations of Mindfulness should be cultivated. "I shall protect others": with that thought the Foundations of Mindfulness should be cultivated. By protecting oneself one protects others; by protecting others one protects oneself.
>
> And how does one, by protecting oneself, protect others? By repeated practice (of mindfulness), by its meditative development, and by frequent occupation with it.
>
> And how does one, by protecting others, protect oneself? By patience, by a non-violent life, by lovekindness and compassion.[7]

Similarly, Jesus taught the primacy of self-love when he said, "First take the log out of your own eye, and then you will see clearly to take the speck out of your brother's eye" (Matt. 7:5). In other words, love of others begins with our own enlightenment.

But if love is not a matter of effort or will power, how can it be practiced? Jesus illustrates the art of loving through the following story:

> As he was speaking, the Jewish leaders and Pharisees brought a woman caught in adultery and placed her out in front of the staring crowd.
>
> "Teacher," they said to Jesus, "this woman was caught in the very act of adultery. Moses' law says to kill her. What about it?" They were trying to trap him into saying something they could use against him, but Jesus stooped down and wrote in the dust with his finger. They kept demanding an answer, so he stood up and said:
>
> "All right, hurl the stones at her until she dies. But only he who never sinned may throw the first!"
>
> Then, he stooped down again and wrote some more in the dust. And the Jewish leaders slipped away one by one, beginning with the eldest, until only Jesus was left in front of the crowd with the woman. (John 8:3–8)

Jesus is teaching none other than Zen here. His main message is clear: seeing reality is the beginning of love. Unless we can look honestly into ourselves and see our own limitations, we can never learn to forgive. Similarly, unless we can see Christ in ourselves and in others, we can never learn to love. Love has more to do with seeing than with doing. Action follows seeing, not the other way around. Actually, action without seeing is dangerous and may lead to more confusion and misery. Jesus said, "Truth will make you free" (John 8:32). But first we have to see it for ourselves.

Love is not necessarily selling all one's possessions and giving to the poor. Love is not necessarily doing endless hours of community work. Rather, the practice of love starts with being sensitive to reality. In Buddhism, the way to liberation is called the Noble Eightfold Path. The first factor on this path is called "Right View." Certainly, without Right View, any action will just lead to more suffering. On the other hand, when one can see reality as it is, true love and compassion will automatically arise.

If love is a reflection of one's gentleness toward life and sensitivity to reality, what is compassion? Most people associate compassion with feelings and wisdom with the intellect. But then compassion and wisdom would be like water and oil; they could not mix. Buddha is supposed to have both great compassion and great wisdom. How could this be?

Vietnamese Zen master and poet Thich Nhat Hahn teaches us the true nature of compassion by relating to us the life stories of the young prostitutes working in the city of Manila, who are often forced into the skin trade due to extreme poverty and the immense income gap between the rich and the poor. These human beings, despised by society and ashamed of themselves, live a very wretched life. Nhat Hahn made the following observation:

> But if she [the prostitute] could look deeply at herself and at the whole situation, she would see that she is the way she is because other people are the way they are. How can a "good girl," belonging to a good family, be proud? Because the "good family's" way of life is the way it is, the prostitute has to live as a prostitute. No one among us has clean hands. No one of us can claim that it is not our responsibility. The girl in Manila is that way because of the way we are. Looking into the life of that young prostitute, we see the lives of all the "non-prostitutes." And looking at the non-prostitutes and the way we live, we see the prostitutes. Each thing helps to create the other.[8]

Our lack of compassion stems from our inability to see deeply into the nature of things. We tend to look down on street bums, prostitutes, and other "bad elements" of society because we cannot see all the intricate factors that cause them to be what they are. Prostitution is an excellent example. The true nature of prostitution becomes obvious when we look at the demand and supply flows. Where does the bulk of the supply of prostitutes come from? Poor countries and poor families within affluent countries. We may complain all we want about the vices of prostitution, but the fact remains that poverty is a primary factor in prostitution. Since when have we found rich girls in the business?

In a special report on the booming sex industry, *Time* magazine found that "poor women and children are commodities traded on the street, products bartered, haggled over, smuggled and sold as hedges against hunger or as cruel but quick routes to profit."[9] The industry is soaked with human despair. Not all pimps are gangsters. The same report finds that "often it is Father who sits in the backup car or Mother who negotiates the deal for her daughter. Little Brother may appear with a sponge and a pail of soapy water to wash a client's car for an extra $5."

In fact, the changing patterns of the sex trade in Asia read like the modern economic history of the region. While Japanese men flocked to Taiwan and South Korea on organized sex tours in the 1960s and 1970s, they now favor Thailand and the Philippines. The reason: Taiwan and South Korea have matured as economic powers and their people are now affluent. The point is very simple: prostitution is more a matter of macroeconomics and purchasing power than a matter of libido. As such, its fate is driven by income differentials, patterns of urban development, patterns of international trade, and the allocation of wealth across the different strata of society. In a very real sense, we all take part in it.

To dump the entire blame on a prostitute is, therefore, a gross act of injustice and another instance of scapegoating. Certainly, the prostitute is responsible for her situation, but no more so than we are. To drug our conscience, we have invented the myth that the prostitute is the way she is because of her laziness or moral corruption and that she has the wherewithal to get out of it if she wants to. This may be a good justification for making arrests, but it is far from truth. Isn't it because it is too painful for us to address the issues of unevenness in the distribution of wealth in the society and the resultant inequality of opportunities for our children that we prefer not to look at the facts? Jesus told the self-righteous people, "The tax collectors and the harlots go into the kingdom of God before you" (Matt. 21:31). Perhaps we can now understand why.

Compassion is not a matter of charity, pity, or sympathy. It is a result of seeing the interconnectedness of all things and recognizing that this is a participatory universe in which we are all one. Unless we come to see ourselves in the life of the prostitute and see the prostitute in our lives, we can never have true feelings for another human being. She will remain a stranger, a recipient of our abuse and a dump site for our guilt.

So what is compassion? Actually, the roots of the word offer us very good clues. For *com-* means "together," and *pati* means "to bear or suffer." Compassion is thus the sharing of suffering as one life, recognizing that we have no independent existence. Paradoxically, the sharing of suffering also brings in joy and elevation. As D. Brandon observes:

> Compassion has nothing to do with achievement at all. It is spacious and very generous. When a person develops real compassion, he is uncertain whether he is being generous to others or to himself because compassion is environmental generosity, without direction, without

"for me" and without "for them." It is filled with joy, spontaneously existing joy, constant joy in the sense of trust, in the sense that joy contains tremendous wealth, richness.

At this highest level, karuna (compassion) does not attach itself to the intricacies of suffering or to individual human situations. It is involved with the salvation of all living things. It spreads out the map of enlightenment for all who care to look.[10]

Jesus said, "I am the Resurrection and the Life" (John 11:25). He also said that "before Abraham was, I am" (John 8:58). These are not proclamations of a special and exclusive divinity, but a heartfelt recognition that we do, in a very deep and real sense, share one life and one destiny. They are not Jesus' attempt to distance himself from the rest of humanity, but his poetic way of affirming his common bond with the criminals, the harlots, the oppressed, and the wretched of the earth. Perhaps it is only in this "environmental generosity," this intermingled joy and sorrow that we can find our true liberation, not as individuals, but as the mystical, one-and-only Son of God.

The Beginning of a New Paradigm

Intelligibility or precision: to combine the two is impossible.
—BERTRAND RUSSELL

All sacred writings contain an outer and an inner meaning.
—MAURICE NICOLL

When I was in eighth grade, my teacher in Chinese literature told me something memorable: the reading of the classics is a dynamic and a life-long enterprise.

The reading of scriptures should be no different. Some people who reviewed the earlier manuscripts of this book indicated to me that they do not agree with the way I interpret certain passages of the Bible. Let me make this very clear: I never pretend that I have the last or even close to the best word on these matters in the first place. The presence of multiple interpretations is never a problem; it is simply a manifestation of the diversity of life. It is only when we try to enforce uniformity in interpretation that acts of violence, human suffering, and the deadening of the soul begin. I do change my interpretation of the scriptures from time to time, and I regard these changes with joy and not with apprehension. For growth is possible only through change.

Many people have completely missed out on the joy, humor, and profundity of Jesus' teachings because they keep holding on to the first interpretation they were taught back in Sunday school. In a way, they are like butterflies that are too afraid to come out of their cocoons or grown-ups who will not let go of their childhood clothes. By refusing to let their understanding grow with their personal experience, they are ensuring that the scriptures remain as a dull document progressively fading into oblivion rather than metamorphosing into the *living words* of God.

The problem has to do with the Western notion of truth. Close your eyes for a minute and think about "truth." What kinds of images come to mind? For most people, truth is closely associated with solidity, finality, permanence, universality, and security. But Jesus used the metaphor of "living water" for truth. This is another of his outrageous teachings. While we tend to visualize truth as some kind of sacred rock, Jesus visualized it as water: amorphous, adaptable, and incapable of being grasped. The adjective "living" should not be neglected either. For truth is a living thing that grows in us and with us.

Truth is like life in that we cannot freeze it without killing it. Spiritual growth means rediscovering truth anew every day. Buddha told a story about a traveler who made himself a raft to cross a river. Much impressed by the usefulness of the raft, he was reluctant to discard it although it had served its purpose. Carrying his raft on his back wherever he went, he became a laughingstock. "My teaching," Buddha says, "is like a raft—it is for crossing over, and not for holding on to."

Impermanence is the way of reality. The world changes. Situations change. We ourselves change. Change is the only truth. Therefore, to hold on to a fixed idea, concept, doctrine, or opinion is like committing spiritual suicide. Similarly, scientists are not supposed to be wedded to their theories but are supposed to use the current theories until better ones come along. Truth and security are therefore mutually incompatible. As Hans Küng observed: "The more banal a truth (truism, platitude, etc.), the greater the security. Conversely, the more significant a truth (as, for instance, aesthetic and a fortiori moral and religious truth, in comparison with mathematical truth), the weaker the security."[1]

This is why spiritual education is so different from other types of education. Unlike the study of academic subjects, spiritual education is not a matter of accumulation of knowledge. The Taoist master Lao Tzu once said, "In studying worldly matters, we accumulate; but in practising the Tao, we drop what we have." Zen practice is primarily a matter of unlearning, deprogramming, and letting go. This accounts for the undogmatic character of Zen. Zen prides itself as "a special transmission outside the scriptures" that has "no dependence on words and letters." This is the logical conclusion of not being attached to truth.

Ambiguity is another problem of biblical interpretation. A friend of mine complained to me more than once that he finds the Gospels very hard to read because their meanings are so often ambiguous. My friend is a veteran in the public communications field and was the president of a marketing firm before his retirement. It appears to him that Jesus is a poor communicator. As he has put it: "If this is truly what Jesus meant, why couldn't he say it more clearly and more directly? Why all this beating around the bush?"

I have a lot of sympathy for my friend. Exactly the same problem has been bothering me for a long time. Trained as a mathematician and a scientist, I used to share his aversion to imprecisions. Until quite recently, I did not have any real appreciation of the world's poetry and literature because I am never sure of what is the "right" way to interpret it. Thus, I had shut myself out of the rich literary heritage of humankind. I had been a fundamentalist when it comes to literature, until I discovered the beauty of ambiguity.

While most of us regard ambiguity as a shortcoming, it is indeed useful. One use of ambiguity is to allow for individualized lessons. The value of ambiguity does not become obvious until we realize that we are all at different levels of spiritual maturity and that the scriptures are not meant to serve the purpose of only one elite group of highly sophisticated people.

Bertrand Russell thinks that intelligibility and precision are not compatible. As poets know, meaning seems to thrive with ambiguity. Spiritual truth has more to do with meaning than with facticity, and meaning is a function of personal experience. If we reread the fairy tales that were told to us as children, it is very likely that we will discover a wealth of new meanings. But these meanings could not have been made available to us when we were children because we simply did not have the maturity then to understand them. In a sense, there is not just one Bible but millions of them. For each of us is effectively reading a personalized version of the Bible, even if we all try hard to be "objective" in our reading. Subjectivity in interpretation is built-in — *for we read what we are.*

Herein lies the beauty of ambiguity: it allows for a kind of automatic custom-tailoring so that the scriptures will always be speaking to us on our own level of understanding; the message will neither be above our heads nor so babyish as to insult our intelligence. The meaning grows as we grow. Another miracle of *wu-wei!*

Ambiguity also serves the purpose of concealing the higher spiritual meaning of the scriptures from those who are not ready to receive it. Maurice Nicoll observes that "all sacred writings contain an outer and inner meaning." The outer meaning is for mass consumption whereas the inner meaning is for a mature audience. To administer a dosage of high-powered spiritual teaching to an immature mind can be counterproductive. What impresses me about the Bible is its versatility; it can be used either to convey "classified" Tantric secrets or to serve as elementary Sunday school material.

Jesus did not hesitate to tell us that many of his higher teachings have restricted access and are encrypted in the form of parables. He told his disciples, "To you it has been given to know the secrets of the kingdom of God; but for others they are in parables, so that seeing they may not see, and hearing they may not understand" (Luke 8:9–10). Nicoll talks about the encoding process:

> So the meaning is veiled, because if it were expressed in literal form no one would believe it, and everyone would think it mere nonsense.... It is not a question of misleading people, but a question of preventing this higher meaning from falling in the wrong place, on lower meaning, and thereby having its finer significance destroyed.... The development of the understanding, the seeing of differences, is a long process.[2]

Before writing this book, I agreed with Thomas Jefferson that parts of the New Testament "have proceeded from an extraordinary man; and other parts are of the fabric of very inferior minds." For a long time, I have shared with many scholars and intellectuals the opinion that the words of Jesus have been tampered with and his central teachings distorted to serve the purpose of the religious establishment. But if the veiling of the higher meaning starts with Jesus himself, it seems that the suspicion of foul play has to be reconsidered.

The recognition of the simultaneous existence of outer and inner meanings holds a key to resolving the age-old conflict between the mystics and religious orthodoxy, between Jesus and the Pharisaic mind, between the intellectuals and the religious conformists, and between those guided by their inner light and the fundamentalists. For a long time religious orthodoxy has regarded the words of the mystics and the spiritually advanced as dangerous heresies and perversions of the "true faith." On the other hand, the spiritually advanced tend to regard the fundamentalists as adults in children's clothes, forever refusing to grow up. Indeed, this problem is universal and not unique to Christianity. The wide discrepancy in spiritual understanding accounts for the split between the Hinayanists and the Mahayanists in the history of Buddhism, the contempt of the Tantric practitioners by the mainstream Buddhists, and the difficulties the Sufi mystics encounter within the Islam tradition.

The tension between the fundamentalists and those guided by their inner light is not going to disappear soon. The lack of understanding of the scriptures' inner meaning is only one of the problems. An even deeper problem is the nature of our psyche. In a sense, we all have the fundamentalist instinct. For fundamentalism is a reflection of the soul's yearning for security, certainty, comfort, and ready-made answers. The fundamentalist attitude is similar to that of a drug addict in that both represent a reluctance to accept the challenges of life. Social psychologists Stanton Peal and Archie Brodsky make the following distinction between love and addiction:

> The [addicted] person does not see a new situation as an opportunity for exploration, satisfaction, or accomplishment. For him, it only holds out the threat of disgrace through the failure he believes as likely. A person with a high fear of failure avoids new things, is conservative, and seeks to return life to safe routines and rituals.
>
> The fundamental distinction [between love and addiction]...is the distinction between a desire to grow and experience and a desire to stagnate and remain untouched.[3]

To the extent that the need for security and attachment reflects a deep-seated reality of the soul, we cannot expect to eradicate it; we can only counterbalance it and heal it with love. For there is also a need of the soul to adventure, to plunge into the unknown, to explore life's richness, to let go of oneself, and to search for truth, beauty, and poetry. Herein lies the creative tension. Remember, Zen does not fight anything that is part of reality. Balance is the key.

The primary intent of this book is to introduce a holistic approach to life that sees value in tensions, finds treasure in shadows, creates opportunities out of difficulties, and cherishes human imperfection as a higher form of perfection (for it allows growth). This approach does not seek complete control over life for it recognizes that complete control is an illusion. It leaves room for paradoxes and mysteries and sees them as beautiful. While it promises neither comfort nor "salvation" (quick fixes), it does offer a way for us to grow through the path of self-discovery. This is the essence of Zen.

As the Zen people say, every ending is a new beginning. I hope that the ending of this book is also a new beginning for you: a new paradigm for reading the scriptures, a new appreciation of the depth of Jesus, a new vision of the unity of the world's spiritual traditions, and, above all, a fearless (i.e., loving) entry into life!

Notes

Prelude / Reading the Gospels, Zen Style

1. Cited in Dom Aelred Graham, *Zen Catholicism* (New York: Crossroad, 1994), 62.
2. Marianne Williamson, *A Return to Love* (New York: HarperCollins, 1992), 58.
3. Ellen M. Rosenberg, *Southern Baptists: A Subculture in Transition* (Knoxville: University of Tennessee Press, 1989), 134.
4. Harold Bloom, *The American Religion* (New York: Simon & Schuster, 1992), 221.

One / What Is Zen? (I): The Art of Living

1. Thomas Moore, *Care of the Soul* (New York: HarperCollins, 1992), 83.
2. Lin Yutang, *My Country and My People* (New York: John Day, 1935), 107.
3. R. H. Blyth, *Zen and Zen Classics* (Union City, Calif.: Heian, 1978), 116.
4. Thomas Merton, *The Way of Chuang Tzu* (New York: New Directions, 1969), 16.
5. Blyth, *Zen and Zen Classics*, 25.
6. Walpola Rahula, *What the Buddha Taught* (London: Gordon Fraser Gallery, 1978), 111.
7. John Welwood, *Ordinary Magic* (Boston: Shambhala, 1992), xiii.
8. Dorothea Brande, *On Becoming a Writer* (Los Angeles: Tarcher, 1981).
9. D. T. Suzuki, *Introduction to Zen Buddhism* (New York: Grove Weidenfeld, 1964), 45.
10. Albert Camus, *The Myth of Sisyphus and Other Stories* (New York: Vintage Books, 1955), 31.
11. Huston Smith, *The Religions of Man* (New York: Harper & Brothers, 1958), 204.

Two / What is Zen (II): The Heart of the Matter

1. Robert Fulghum, *All I Really Need to Know I Learned In Kindergarten* (New York: Random House, 1986), 6–7.

2. Alan Watts, *Cloud-Hidden* (New York: Random House, 1974), 112.

3. Ellen Kessner, "The Delights of Sexual Mystery," *Cosmopolitan,* September 1984, 258.

4. Thomas Moore, *Care of the Soul* (New York: HarperCollins, 1992), 286.

5. R. H. Blyth, *Zen in English Literature and Oriental Classics* (Tokyo: Hokuseido Press), 180.

6. B. Russell, "Vagueness," *Australian Journal of Philosophy* 1 (1925).

7. Shree Rajneesh, *Zen: The Special Transmission* (Rajneeshpuram, Ore.: Rajneesh Foundation International, 1984), 17–18.

8. Robert Linssen, *Living Zen* (New York: Grove Weidenfeld, 1978), 75.

9. Walpola Rahula, *What the Buddha Taught* (London: Gordon Fraser Gallery, 1978), 61–62.

Three / The Magic Kingdom

1. Lucy Oliver, "Clarity, Will-Power, Creativity," *Lotus* 2 (Spring 1993): 28.

2. Abraham Maslow, *The Farther Reaches of Human Nature* (New York: Penguin Group, 1972), 169.

3. Bhagwan Shree Rajneesh, *Zen: The Special Transmission* (Rajneeshpuram, Ore.: Rajneesh Foundation International, 1984), 2.

4. Bhagwan Shree Rajneesh, *The Mustard Seed* (Rajneeshpuram, Ore.: Rajneesh Foundation International, 1975), 301.

5. Peggie Noonan, *Forbes,* September 14, 1992, 58.

6. Erich Fromm, *To Have or to Be* (New York: Harper & Row, 1976), 6.

7. David Meyers, "Pursuing Happiness," *Psychology Today* (July/August 1993): 34.

8. Ibid.

Four / Zen: The Art of Seeing

1. Dale Carnegie, *How to Stop Worrying and Start Living* (New York: Pocket Books, 1985), 162.

2. Ibid., 163.

3. D. T. Suzuki, *Introduction to Zen Buddhism* (New York: Grove Weidenfeld, 1964), 95.

4. John Marsh, *Saint John* (New York: Viking Penguin, 1968), 178.

5. Edward Conze, *Buddhism: Its Essence and Development* (New York: Harper & Row, 1975), 39.

6. Walpola Rahula, *What the Buddha Taught* (London: Gordon Fraser Gallery, 1978), 40.

7. Albert Camus, *The Myth of Sisyphus and Other Stories* (New York: Vintage Books, 1955), 121.

8. Ibid., 122.

9. M. Scott Peck, *The Road Less Traveled* (New York: Simon & Schuster, 1978), 15.

10. Camus, *The Myth of Sisyphus,* 123.

11. Albert Einstein and Leopold Infeld, *The Evolution of Physics* (New York: Simon & Schuster, 1938).

12. Marsh, *Saint John,* 181.

Five / The Looking-Glass Universe

1. C. S. Lewis, *The Grand Miracle* (New York: Ballantine Books, 1970), 114.

2. G. B. Caird, *Saint Luke* (New York: Viking Penguin, 1963), 245–46.

3. C. S. Lewis, *Miracles* (New York: Collier, 1947), 109.

4. Albert Camus, *The Stranger* (New York: Vintage Books, 1942), 154.

5. Bill Moyers, *Healing and the Mind* (New York: Doubleday, 1993), 359–60.

6. Bernie S. Siegal, *Peace, Love and Healing* (New York: Harper & Row, 1989), 192.

7. Leonard Koren, *Wabi-Sabi* (Berkeley: Stone Bridge Press, 1994), 7.

8. Siegal, *Peace, Love and Healing,* 193.

9. Lewis, *Miracles,* 125.

10. Ibid., 130.

11. Alan Watts, *This Is It* (New York: Vintage Books), 18.

Six / The Usual Hell

1. Alan Watts, *Beyond Theology* (New York: Random House, 1973), 40.

2. C. S. Lewis, *The Screwtape Letters* (New York: Macmillan, 1982), ix.

3. C. S. Lewis, *The Problem of Pain* (New York: Macmillan, 1962), 127.

4. Ibid., 119.

5. M. Scott Peck, *Further Along the Road Less Traveled* (New York: Simon & Schuster, 1993), 171.

6. Paul Tillich, *Systematic Theology* (Chicago: University of Chicago Press, 1957), 1:284.

7. Lewis, *The Problem of Pain,* 127.

8. Lewis, *The Screwtape Letters*, 68–69.

9. Tillich, *Systematic Theology*, 1:284.

10. Paul Tillich, *The Shaking of the Foundations* (New York: Macmillan, 1948), 110.

11. Ibid.

12. Paul Tillich, *Systematic Theology* (Chicago: University of Chicago Press, 1957), 2:110.

13. Peck, *Further Along the Road Less Traveled*, 209–10.

14. Tillich *Systematic Theology*, 2:110.

15. Marianne Williamson, *A Return to Love* (New York: HarperCollins, 1992), 7.

16. Louis Sachar, *There Is a Boy in the Girls' Bathroom* (New York: Alfred A. Knopf, 1987), 88–89.

17. Ibid., 90.

18. Alan Watts, *The Book* (New York: Random House, 1972), 14.

19. R. H. Blyth, *Zen and Zen Classics* (Union City, Calif.: Heian International, 1978), 149–50.

Seven / Faith

1. Simone Weil, *Gravity and Grace* (London: ARK, 1987), 104.

2. Thomas Merton, *New Seeds of Contemplation* (New York: New Directions, 1972), 133.

3. Fynn, *Mister God, This Is Anna* (New York: Ballantine Books, 1974), 74–75.

4. Erich Fromm, *The Art of Loving* (New York: Harper & Row, 1974), 18.

5. John A. Sanford, *The Kingdom Within*, rev. ed. (New York: Harper-Collins, 1987), 123–24.

6. Fynn, *Mister God, This Is Anna*, 60.

7. Dom Aelred Graham, *Zen Catholicism* (New York: Crossroad, 1994), 47.

8. Seung Sahn, *Only Don't Know* (Cumberland, R.I.: Providence Zen Center, 1984), 5.

9. John Shelby Spong, *Rescuing the Bible from Fundamentalism* (New York: HarperCollins, 1991), 230.

10. Alan Watts, *Beyond Theology* (New York: Vintage Books, 1973), 109.

11. William Barclay, *The Gospel of Matthew* (Philadelphia: Westminster Press, 1975), 1:199.

12. Chögyam Trungpa, *The Myth of Freedom* (Boston: Shambhala, 1976), 5.

13. Paul Tillich, *The Shaking of the Foundations* (New York: Macmillan, 1948), 109.

Eight / My Yoke Is Easy

1. Alan Watts, *Beyond Theology* (New York: Vintage Books, 1973), 29.
2. C. S. Lewis, *The Grand Miracle* (New York: Ballantine Books, 1970), 157.
3. C. S. Lewis, *The Screwtape Letters* (New York: Macmillan, 1982), 10.
4. *Spirituality, Happiness and Health,* Christopher News Notes.
5. Norman Maclean, *A River Runs through It* (New York: Pocket Books, 1992), 2.
6. Alan Watts, *The Spirit of Zen* (Boston: Charles E. Tuttle, 1992), 70.
7. Seung Sahn, *Only Don't Know* (Cumberland, R.I.: Providence Zen Center, 1984), 27.
8. Lewis, *The Grand Miracle,* 30.
9. Paul Tillich, *The Shaking of the Foundations* (New York: Macmillan, 1948), 99.

Nine / What Defiles a Man

1. Hannah Merker, *Listening* (New York: HarperCollins, 1994), 17.
2. Walter Kaufmann, *The Portable Nietzsche* (New York: Viking Press, 1954), 45–46.
3. Thich Nhat Hahn, *Peace Is Every Step* (New York: Bantam Books, 1992), 96–97.
4. Joel S. Goldsmith, *The Thunder of Silence* (New York: Harper-Collins, 1961), 55.
5. Lawrence Kushner, *God Was In This Place and I, i Did Not Know* (Woodstock, Vt.: Jewish Lights, 1991), 75.
6. D. T. Suzuki, *Introduction to Zen Buddhism* (New York: Grove Weidenfeld, 1964), 74.
7. Merker, *Listening,* 25.

Ten / Resist Not Evil

1. Walter Kaufmann, *The Portable Nietzsche* (New York: Viking Press, 1954), 488.
2. John A. Martin, *Blessed Are the Addicts: The Spiritual Side of Alcoholism, Addictions and Recovery* (New York: HarperCollins, 1990), xv.
3. Alcoholics Anonymous, *Twelve Steps and Twelve Traditions* (New York: Alcoholics Anonymous Publishing, 1953), 21.
4. William Barclay, *The Gospel of Matthew* (Philadelphia: Westminster Press, 1975), 1:322.
5. Jack Kornfield, *A Path with Heart* (New York: Bantam Books, 1993), 103.

6. Thomas Moore, *Care of the Soul* (New York: HarperCollins, 1992), 10.

7. Kornfield, *A Path with Heart,* 100.

8. Chögyam Trungpa, *Cutting through Spiritual Materialism* (Boston: Shambhala Publications, 1973), 220.

9. Lama Yeshe, *Introduction to Tantra* (Boston: Wisdom Publications, 1987), 37.

Eleven / Love

1. Arthur Waley, *The Analects of Confucius* (New York: Random House, 1989), 28.

2. Ibid., 29.

3. J. Krishnamurti, *Think on These Things* (New York: Harper & Row, 1970), 19.

4. Erich Fromm, *The Art of Loving* (New York: Harper & Row, 1956), 50.

5. Raymond Blakney, *Meister Eckhart* (New York: Harper & Row, 1941), 204.

6. Walpola Piyananda Thera, *Love in Buddhism* (Los Angeles: Dharma Vijaya Buddhist Vihara, 1990), 12.

7. Nyanaponika Thera, *The Heart of Buddhist Meditation* (York Beach, Me.: Samuel Weiser, 1991), 77.

8. Thich Nhat Hahn, *Peace Is Every Step* (New York: Bantam Books, 1992), 98.

9. "Sex for Sale," *Time,* June 21, 1993.

10. Thera, *Love in Buddhism,* 10.

Epilogue / The Beginning of a New Paradigm

1. Hans Küng, "Theology for the Third Millennium" (New York: Doubleday, 1988), 218.

2. Maurice Nicoll, *The New Man* (Boston: Shambhala Publications, 1981), 2.

3. Stanton Peal and Archie Brodsky, *Love and Addictions* (New York: Penguin Group, 1976), 60.